MEGAN MCKENNA is an i[...] storyteller. On several occasions I have listened with rapt attention as she recounted her sensitively crafted tales. Always I have appreciated her frank observations and been impressed by her keen insights into current reality. Hers has frequently been heard as a prophetic voice.

The suggestions she makes take me back to the time of Vatican II Council. A variety of different voices, opinions, and experiences was found among the Council Fathers, including Popes John XXIII and Paul VI. Good Pope John drew the attention of the Council Fathers to the fact that what we have in common is more important than what separates us. Voices that had been silenced prior to the Council were invited back to contribute to the search for renewal of gospel values.

Later, when Pope Paul VI reconvened the Council, he drew attention to the necessity of dialogue. In his first major encyclical, "Ecclesiam Suam," he underscored the importance of achieving mutual understanding and insight by respecting our partners in the search for truth and wisdom. He stipulated that we should listen with the ears of our hearts and always recognize the positive intentions of others.

Reading Megan McKenna's book challenges us to listen to one another in search of other Good News. Our traditions both religious and social have advanced primarily through dialogue and respect.

I will never forget a statement made by the late Bishop Christopher Butler, himself an excellent biblical scholar. As a Council Father he spoke in defense of researchers who delve into arcane fields of thought or uncover facts not previously considered. He declared: "Why should we fear that truth might somehow tell against truth?"

I was deeply moved when, toward the end of Vatican II, Pope Paul invited a number of leading scholars to concelebrate Eucharist with him in Saint Peter's Basilica. He thereby testified to the world how necessary it is to consider and to benefit from the advice of researchers and forward-looking thinkers. I was aware that several of the concelebrants were eminent scholars who had been silenced before the Council.

Megan McKenna has used her gifts of insight to help us take a fresh look at the role of the gospels in contemporary church life. I found her observations very challenging. They called me to think "outside of the box," as the expression goes, and to look for truth in areas I had not considered previously. We have much to gain in pondering what she presents, even if we might find some of her reflections challenging or disturbing. Ours are times of great upheaval. We are called to revisit the very foundations of our faith as we scrutinize the signs of the times. I trust that many readers will find her reflections a fertile field to till in our search for further and richer truth.

—REMI J. DE ROO
Vatican II Council Father
retired (1999) Bishop of Victoria

LIKE A HAMMER
SHATTERING ROCK

LIKE A HAMMER
SHATTERING ROCK

Hearing the Gospels Today

MEGAN McKENNA

IMAGE

NEW YORK

Published in the United States by Doubleday Religion, an imprint of
Crown Publishing Group, a division of Random House, Inc., New York.
www.crownpublishing.com

IMAGE is a registered trademark, and the "I" colophon is a trademark of
Random House, Inc.

All quoted biblical passages are from the New Revised Standard Version
of the Bible, unless otherwise noted.

Library of Congress Cataloging-in-Publication Data
McKenna, Megan.
Like a hammer shattering rock : hearing the
Gospels today / Megan McKenna.
      p. cm.
1. Bible. N.T. Gospels—Criticism, interpretation, etc. I. Title.
BS2555.52.M36 2012
226'.06—dc23
2012030714

ISBN 978-0-385-50854-4
eISBN 978-0-7704-3784-8

Printed in the United States of America

Book design by Lauren Dong
Cover design by Rebecca Lown
Cover photograph copyright © Ryan McVay/Getty Images

10 9 8 7 6 5 4 3 2 1

For the people of God, the Church, the Body of Christ . . .
all of you who are the Good News of God in Jesus
in your corners of the world.

Keep dancing! Keep those hammers in your hands!
Keep being the Word of God in your flesh! Keep the faith!
Keep remembering: "I AM with you all days
even to the end of time."

And finally, for all those who are friends of God to me.

Contents

LIKE A HAMMER
SHATTERING ROCK

INTRODUCTION

Lord, who can comprehend even one of your words? We lose more of it than we grasp, like those who drink from a living spring.

EPHREM OF SYRIA (C. 306–373)

THIS BOOK AROSE FROM A NUMBER OF PEOPLE ASKING ME THE same question over and over again: if the gospels were written today would they be different from those we have now: Mark, Matthew, Luke, and John? I did a good deal of thinking on the subject and initially thought, yes, they'd have to be different. But when I thought about it again—and echoing many past writers like G. K. Chesterton and John Henry Cardinal Newman, as well as many preachers—I discovered we really haven't paid due attention to the ones we already have. In fact, upon further reflection I realized sadly that we have ignored whole segments of the gospels; picked and chose among those we would emphasize; twisted them to suit other agendas; contradicted them, even outright disobeyed them; used them to proof-text words that often contradict what they were originally proclaiming—generally speaking, we do not believe them or put them into any level of consistent practice. In fact, more often than not we have betrayed the words, the meaning, and the intent of the gospels while loudly acclaiming that we are believers in the Word Made Flesh dwelling among us: Jesus the Word of God.

In a sense we have grown so familiar with and accustomed to the gospels that we stopped listening and hearing them as the Word of God Made Flesh among us, calling us to conversion, and have often felt free to misuse them, quote them out of context, ignore

them, and alter them to our own fancy, or to use them so individually and pseudo-spiritually that they no longer have any impact on
our behaviors and ways of being in the world. Someone once said
that "familiarity breeds contempt"—perhaps all too true in regard
to the Words of Jesus. On the cover of this book—a mosaic from
Ravenna in the late third century—is a detail described as "the
closet keeping the Gospels." The closet is open, the books are on
the shelf for all to see, but there is the sense that they are stored
and taken out only on occasion, or for liturgy and prayer; they are
no longer dynamic and living in the community and in the mouths
of believers—alive with the breath, fire, and powerful force of the
Spirit. Already they are kept in a closet for reference and reading
rather than found first and strongest in the lives of those who are
the Good News of God in flesh on earth.

Let's begin with a story that will put these introductory remarks
and the book in perspective. It is a true story and was told to me by
the grandson of the preacher in the story.

Once upon a time, there was a traveling itinerant preacher who
was missioned to the mountains of West Virginia in the 1860s
and '70s. He was sent by a large church in Virginia and outfitted
with a horse, two donkeys to carry his bags, supplies, and what was
needed for services, and so he set off. It was rough territory, and
he would arrive in a small town in a holler in the backwoods and
set up camp. He'd stay a couple of weeks—with more and more
folks coming on Sunday to his sermons and talks. And he would
make the rounds, visiting and returning to the same places about
once or twice in a year. Periodically he'd get supplies and rest a bit
and then return to his circuit of towns. This had gone on for years,
and the people he visited finally told him that they loved Jesus's
stories, especially the parables and how he confronted people and
told the truth, and they wanted the stories to keep for themselves
during the long absences when the preacher was traveling and away
in other towns. They wanted Bibles.

And so on his next trip back he started arranging to have Bibles
printed—at least one or two and if possible more for the big families

in each of the towns he visited. It would take years to get them printed—the process was long and tedious, and he needed to arrange the money for the transaction, which would be substantial, too. But on his next trek around the towns, when he told the people that he was going to get them Bibles though it would take awhile, he was surprised to learn that there was another major problem—none of them could read! And so he started lessons on reading and writing so that when the Bibles finally arrived, there would be people in each town who could read the stories aloud to the rest of the folks who gathered on Sundays and for funerals and celebrations. This went on for years, too. And then it came closer to the time that the Bibles would be ready, and he went to the printer's to check on them.

Someone had given him money for gilt—so that the title could be pressed in gold on the spine of each book and across the front cover. He had also been given good leather so that the Bibles would be bound beautifully. But his first disappointment came from the printer: the money just wouldn't cover typesetting the contents of the Bible—not by a long shot. In fact, with the money he had, all he could print in a book was the books of the New Testament, specifically Matthew, Mark, Luke, and John. That was it. And so he had to settle for just those books—and he requested that the leather be used for the books and the gold be used for the title "The New Testament" on the spines and covers of the book. And to his delight he was told to return in a year and they would be ready for him to pick up around late fall. He could hardly wait: on his circuit to the towns, he was so tempted to tell them that they would all be getting a unique and marvelous Christmas gift the next year—but he wanted it to be a surprise and so he said nothing.

The day finally came when he went to the printer's to pick up the books. He was so excited: he had waited so long and prepared the people who could now read and write for these books—the New Testament, the words of Jesus that they already so loved and honored, and wanted more of for themselves. The printer had a number of the books opened on the table so that he could examine the type, the print, the texture of the paper—good and solid, long lasting. He was delighted. And he lifted the book to feel the leather—again, perfect. But as he went to close the book in his hands, the printer stopped him with the words, "Uh, I did make one mistake."

There was silence and the preacher said, "Oh, what mistake?"

"Well," said the printer, "I set the type for the title THE NEW TESTAMENT for the spine and the covers of the book and realized it was too big and wouldn't fit on the cover, or the spine. So I shortened it—that way I could use the gilt, and every book would have the shortened title on the cover in big letters and on the spine, too."

The preacher froze and asked, "What did you use for the title?" If the printer couldn't get THE NEW TESTAMENT on the cover and spine, he certainly wouldn't have been able to get Matthew, Mark, Luke, and John on, either.

The man answered, "Close the book and look at the cover and you'll see what I did."

And the preacher did and was shocked beyond words. He couldn't speak, and when he did he sputtered, "How could you do this? It's ruined! We can't have this."

For the title that the printer had carefully and beautifully lettered in gold on the cover and then again along the spine of the book in large letters was TNT!

The preacher finally found his voice and said, "That can't be the title—that's the abbreviation for dynamite!"

And then the printer looked at him straight in the face and said, "Sir, I never read this book before I started setting up the print to typeset, and I've been reading it now for the last couple of years as I work on it, and I don't know if you've noticed, but that's exactly what this book is—dynamite. It's loaded—if you actually believe this stuff and begin to make it part of your life, everything explodes—the way you live, your relationships, the way you look at other people and do your job and how you treat everybody, even your enemies and strangers. The title is perfect TNT, and it certainly tells the truth about what's inside the covers."

The preacher was stunned. Finally, he thanked the printer for all his work, collected and packed up his books, and went on his way.

He began his journey with some trepidation. The book was beautiful and the words of the gospels were all there—it was just the title on the cover that was "off" and not perfect like he'd planned. He wondered what the people would think when he gave each of the families their treasure and what all the people would think when they saw the book. But he needn't have worried. The people were delighted and pleased. In fact, they had no problem with the title TNT at all! They thought it was just perfect, because they had come to know the power and effect, what the consequences of hearing these words and trying to put them into practice had meant in their lives and towns—the Words of Jesus really were dynamite. They were that shocking and life altering. They all took their books and it was a marvelous gift. And as the preacher rode out of town—all of the towns as it turned out—he began to wonder and question himself. Why didn't he think of the Words of Jesus as dynamite, as TNT, as so shocking and revelatory and life changing? Had he gotten so used to them that the power was diluted and they were washing over him like water off a duck's back? Or did he need to hear them with others, not just preach them, so that they could continually shock him and shake up his life? His grandson, who told me the story, said it was the beginning of a whole new way of believing for his grandfather. And then he showed me his book—a worn copy of the four gospels. The gilt had long ago rubbed off but the letters TNT were still etched deeply in the cover and the spine of his treasured possession, one of the few copies of his grandfather's gift to so many. When he told me the story I was reminded of a line by the monk Thomas Merton: "Make it ready for the Christ whose smile—lightning—sets free the song of everlasting glory that now sleeps in your paper flesh—like dynamite."

And so, with others, I began to look closely at the gospels to discern core truths, sayings, and practices at the heart of the texts to see what we and other believers had decided we were not going to obey—or worse, bend to our own advantage politically, economically, culturally, and religiously, both as individuals and as community and church. What we discovered was, in a word, appalling. We talked about what the contemporaries of Jesus would have found radical, disorienting, and shocking to their sensitivities, practices, and traditions when they heard it proclaimed—and then asked ourselves, Why aren't we shocked like them to hear the words again and again preached in our midst? The words of Jesus in the gospels haven't affected us like TNT, not that we remember. On one level, and perhaps the most obvious level, is that we are human beings and sinners and often fail to live up to our words in practice—we are simply not what we proclaim ourselves to be and believe. But in some ways that is too glib and easy to use as an excuse. Our perversity in misappropriating and bending the gospels is too far ranging and insidious to dismiss it as personal failure.

History, of course, played a huge role in using the gospels, the words of Jesus, to validate what the Church became by the middle of the third century: the "holy" Roman Empire. The structures and powers that once persecuted the Christians became themselves those who persecuted and demanded, even forcing all to become Christians, and Christianity began quickly to lose the core practices found in its foundational precepts: clear prohibitions against war, murder, or any harm of others, alongside the command not to use power, as those dominant in society enforced their rule; forgiveness and its extension of inclusivity and reconciliation; care for the poor as a primary characteristic of the community; justice that developed into compassion for all—not only one's kin and friends, but beginning with one's enemies and strangers, and all in need of help; as well as equality among all members as the beloved children of God. These values disappeared rapidly in favor of the spread of the Roman Empire that became medieval Europe. (We limited our reflections to Western Christianity, though we were well aware that many of these realities developed in common ways in Eastern Christianity's rise to power, as well.) The overarching words of Jesus from John's gospel, "Love one another as I have loved you," that permeated the early Christian communities faded and were recognizable only in patches and pockets of the Church and Western history since the end of the third century.

As I traveled throughout Asia especially but also in South and Central America, it was shocking, even disconcerting to hear non-believers reading the Sermon on the Plain in Luke and the words of Jesus in the gospels applied to individual Christians' lives as experienced by those who were not Christian (or Catholic) and hear the questioning and cynicism leveled at the institutions, practices, decisions, and historical realities of the Church by those who had never known any connection between the Words of the gospels and the presence of Christians. Even among those conquered by Christian nations who brought the Cross along with the sword, colonialism, slavery, disease, and mandatory forced conversions, the gap between the experience of meeting Christians and meeting the words of Jesus were brutal at times. In being privileged to work with Native Peoples across North and South America—most of whom are now Catholic/Christian—they would be clear in singling out their association to the Crucified Jesus and not necessarily bound with equal devotion to the structures that brought the religion of Jesus to them. In the sixties and seventies of this past millennium many of those conquered began to read the Scriptures in small groups (just prior to, during, and since the second Vatican Council—1964 onward) and were radically converted to the actual teachings and following of Jesus, minus the add-ons of the last sixteen or seventeen hundred years by others in the Church. And from these struggling groups of Christians (many millions of them, many poor, indigenous peoples, those seeking justice and their lands and dignity) came a renewed and Spirit-driven sense of what it means to be a follower of Jesus in a community that held them accountable in listening to the gospels and putting them into practice each in his or her own life and together as a community that reached out to others in thanksgiving to share what they had—not only in faith but in actual economics and presence. They read the gospels for conversion, for hope, for solidarity, and for an alternative way of living within and in opposition to the dominant cultures and religious practices that culturally, economically, politically, and religiously had grown like barnacles onto the original sayings and practice of those who were called the Followers of the Way—the way of the Cross, the way of peace and justice, the way of the poor, and the way of Jesus, to the Father in the power of the Spirit. They reclaimed for themselves the power of the Word of God in their presence, dwelling with them, struggling, living and dying with them as the first Christians knew in their flesh and blood as well as their hearts and minds.

A note: this is not to utterly disclaim or ignore many of the contributions of the Church and believers, individually and in small communities and groups, over the past generations—or even more so to discredit the belief and lived practice of faith among the many millions of the last thousands of years. They all struggled within the contexts of their societies, histories, limited educations, the great inequalities of rich and poor, racism, colonialism, nationalism, and the blurred boundaries of church/state/economics/society to live faithfully as believers—often with very little access to the Scriptures, the sacraments, or any sense of communities of support as known in the early Church, or among those that are now members of small base communities. These groups of Christians live in opposition to all injustice, violence, and war; they live in solidarity with the poor and they read the Word of God for conversion of life; they practice with others and are often persecuted for doing so— both by society and sometimes by groups within the Church that see them as threats to their own power and control, and use that power to call into question their integrity and belief while not experiencing what they know of life and spirituality. Sometimes these people and structures are quick to declare that the Spirit of God works in them primarily and first, and not in the Body of Christ, in 1.2 billion people of God.

But the structures of the institution of the Church, geographically, universally, nationally, and on diocesan and parish levels, as well as much of the leadership of the existing Church along with many Christians, do not in fact put into practice or even teach the words of Jesus that are in the four gospels and were the bedrock of the first three hundred years of Christianity as it surged across the known world. This is the reality we find ourselves mired in at the moment. We have been and still are resistant to the Word of God in the gospels and have become adept at using the gospels to subvert Jesus's revelation of God among us and what is demanded of those who follow in Jesus's footsteps and practice as believers and disciples. So much has accrued over the generations that has become more important than Jesus's teachings and obscures Jesus's core demands. This shouldn't surprise us, but we must look at it squarely and honestly if we are to live with integrity and grace in this twenty-first century and call it the year of the Lord, "Anno Domini," with any honesty. Hence the title of this book: *Like a Hammer Shattering Rock: Hearing the Gospels Today*. It comes from a section of the book of the prophet Jeremiah that rails against false prophets who "dream" and use their dreams and words to teach, ignoring and contradicting the Word of God that calls the people to faithfulness, to the covenant and to justice, to care of the poor, and to true worship of God and lasting peace upon the earth. All those who follow the false prophets, the religious leaders, and the political and economic leaders are "like rocks" in need of hammering and breaking up by the true Word of God. This is the context of the saying:

> *Am I a God near by, says the Lord, and not a God far off? Who can hide in secret places so that I cannot see them? says the Lord. Do I not fill heaven and earth? says the Lord. I have heard what the prophets have said who prophesy lies in my name, saying, "I have dreamed, I have dreamed!" How long? Will the hearts of the prophets ever turn back—those who prophesy lies, and who prophesy the deceit of their own heart? They plan to make my people forget my name by their dreams that they tell one another, just as their ancestors forgot my name for Ba'al. Let the prophet who has a dream tell the dream, but let the one who has my word speak my word faithfully.*

What has straw in common with wheat? says the Lord. Is not my word like
fire, says the Lord, and like a hammer that breaks a rock in pieces? (Jer
23:23–29)

It is a shocking and powerful image—a hammer breaking a rock
into pieces and shattering it to bits. But it is used by the prophet
Jeremiah, speaking in the first person as the Lord against those
who mix their own dreams and words with the Word of the Lord
and lead the people astray. The text goes on to say that these prophets, leaders, and people are "the burden of the Lord"—because they
use their own words and pervert the words of the living God. It is
blunt—descriptive and a warning.

Thus shall you say to one another among yourselves, "What has the Lord
answered?" or "What has the Lord spoken?" But "the burden of the Lord"
you shall mention no more, for the burden is everyone's own word, and so
you pervert the words of the living God, our God, the Lord of hosts, our
God. . . . [T]herefore, I will surely lift you up and cast you away from my
presence, you and the city that I gave to you and your ancestors. And I will
bring upon you everlasting disgrace and perpetual shame, which shall not
be forgotten. (Jer 23:35–40)

These are the words of a prophet hundreds of years prior to the
time of Jesus, but Jesus himself echoed many like them. As Jesus
says, anyone who "hears these words of mine and acts on them will
be like a wise one who built their house on rock . . . but . . . everyone
who hears these words of mine and does not act on them will be
like a fool who builds their house on sand . . . and it will fall—and
great will be its fall" (Mt 7:24–28). In the paragraphs previous to
this, he declares bluntly words we need to hear:

"Beware of false prophets, who come to you in sheep's clothing but inwardly
are ravenous wolves. You will know them by their fruits. Are grapes gath-
ered from thorns, or figs from thistles? In the same way, every good tree
bears good fruit, but the bad tree bears bad fruit. A good tree cannot bear

bad fruit, nor can a bad tree bear good fruit. Every tree that does not bear good fruit is cut down and thrown into the fire. Thus you will know them by their fruits.

"Not everyone who says to me, 'Lord, Lord,' will enter the kingdom of heaven, but only the one who does the will of my Father in heaven. On that day many will say to me, 'Lord, Lord, did we not prophesy in your name, and cast out demons in your name, and do many deeds of power in your name?' Then I will declare to them, 'I never knew you; go away from me, you evildoers.'" (Mt 7:15–23)

These are not the portions of the gospel that we read often, but we need to take them to heart. We are in need of conversion always, and should continually strive to take the words of Jesus and incorporate them into our flesh, blood, and bones, and into our ways of practice and of being with others in the world. We are in need of communities that hold us accountable—each and every believer is in need, including those who preach, teach, minister, rule, and use any sort of power in the name of the Church—the criteria are clear: by our fruits all are known. This constant conversion is not just for individuals, it is for groups—within the institutions of the Church and systematically or systemically converting and holding accountable the structures that maintain the Church and the leaders who work as much to enforce the structures and maintain existing modes and practices in Church—all of which basically contradict the words of Jesus on how his followers and friends should live together and in the world as witness and example of his hope and revelation of God present in the Body of Christ—those who are his presence on earth.

The structure of the book is simple. The opening chapter describes how to listen to and hear the Word of God in the gospels. It is, in a sense, trying to prepare us to be ready to hear the Word of the Lord aloud in the midst of a community of believers seeking to put the Word into practice and hold one another responsible for making the Word a reality in our lives, each in our own way and together in small groups. It is written in hopes of learning a new/old way of listening to and obeying the Word and becoming the Word Made Flesh ourselves. To quote the monk Thomas Merton again: "We all exist solely for this—to be the human place God has chosen for his presence, his manifestation, his epiphany ... we are God's words. We echo him, we signify and contain him."

After the introduction and the opening chapter that looks at the Scriptures and the gospels and how to read them aloud in small groups for conversion, there are eight chapters looking at each of the gospels in the order they were written: Mark, Matthew, Luke, and John. The chapters are written in sets of two: the gospel as it was proclaimed then (more than two thousand years ago) and the same gospel as it needs to be heard anew now. Basically it is Mark then and Mark now; Matthew then and Matthew now; Luke then and Luke now; and John then and John now. The tenth chapter, however, deals with a reality that surfaced in looking at the gospels then and now. There is a need for new gospels—a good number of them, in fact; this last chapter offers a number of suggestions, places to start thinking about additional gospels, written by believers/ communities today in the power of the Spirit ever present among us. From the early Church, Paulinus of Nola wrote: *Let us listen to what all the faithful say, because in every one of them the Spirit of God breathes.* We need the contemporary Spirit's wisdom, too. Each gospel and the last chapter are followed by somewhat extensive bibliographies on the gospels themselves for background reading regarding the issues brought to light in the closing chapter. And the last entry is an afterword written to draw the book forward and to fill in the gaps between the time the book was written and when it was published (three years).

I once saw a copy of the four books of the gospels that were carefully scribed in exquisite handwriting but left with huge margins on both sides of the texts. The idea was that the reader would write his or her own commentary while reading and studying the text, interpreting, contrasting, and commenting on it in the margins in relation to his or her own contemporary situation. The Jews, of course, do just this on all the books in their canon—so that alongside the original material are the thoughts and struggles for meaning of all those who have studied and gone before them in faith; in essence, creating a dialogue back and forth across generations, languages, and cultures. This is what we need to do today, but not primarily as individuals—we need to do it as small communities struggling together to absorb the Word and the Spirit of Jesus into our own words and spirits and in our world today so that we might together still learn to live and witness with our lives as did the first followers and friends of Jesus.

We end with another quote from the only Syrian Doctor of the Church (declared to be one in 1920, also referred to as the Harp of the Holy Spirit).

> The word of God is a tree of life that offers us blessed fruit from each of its branches. It is like that rock which was struck open in the wilderness, from which all were offered spiritual drink.[1]

May this book and those who read it and seek to put it into practice echo and resound with the force of a hammer breaking rock, the intensity of fire, the faithfulness of breath, the refreshment of living water, the fierceness and power of a double-edged sword, the penetration of an arrow to the heart, the music of hope, and the freedom of possibility for all, especially as Good News to the poor, as the gospels convert us and transform us again and again into evermore surprising Words of God spoken aloud in our world. May it be so. Amen.

Chapter 1

THE GOSPEL

The Word of God Made Flesh Dwelling Among Us

> A word is dead
> When it is said
> Some say.
> I say it just
> Begins to live
> That day.

EMILY DICKINSON

FOR CHRISTIANS THERE ARE TRADITIONALLY FOUR GOSPELS: Mark, Matthew, Luke, and John (in the order they were written down). These are the canonical gospels—the four accepted as universally comprising the core of belief within the Church. In reality, historically there were many more—some say nineteen or twenty, others as many as thirty-four. Others say that many communities wrote their own gospels, perhaps as many as two hundred in the first couple of hundred years of Christianity being preached to all the ends of the earth. In Luke's gospel we read in the very first line:

> Since many have undertaken to set down an orderly account of the events that have been fulfilled among us, just as they were handed on to us by those who from the beginning were eyewitnesses and servants of the word, I too decided, after investigating everything carefully from the very first, to write an orderly account for you, most excellent Theophilus, so that you may know the truth concerning the things about which you have been instructed. (Lk 1:1–4)

Out of the sheer abundance and diversity of the gospel—orderly accounts of events that have been fulfilled and passed on to others, concerning the truth—these four eventually became the foundation and universally preserved tradition that has been handed on by the institutional Church over the last two thousand years. A gospel is simply "good news," from the Greek *euangelion*. There were earlier oral traditions and lost written ones besides these four accounts, and there were myriad others. There are many called "lost gospels" and fragments and variations that belong to the category of noncanonical—meaning not usually accepted or included in the core teachings and beliefs of the Church. By the end of the second century these four gospels were chosen and used over the others. It is generally believed that no one really knows exactly how the four were singled out or how the canon was selected. The process seems to have happened at the grass roots, and spread across the Christian world along with the Church, drawing others into the practice and belief of Christianity. In other words, one could say that it was the work of the Spirit. There is mention of the list in 367 by Bishop Athanasius of Alexandria and in *The Ecclesiastical History* by Eusebius (early fourth century). It is thought that in 325 at the first Council of Nicaea, Constantine established the canon and put an end to the writing of more gospels.

The gospels are collections of Jesus's sayings, stories about Jesus, stories Jesus told, and reactions to these events and words. The practice of writing a gospel is not unique to Christianity; in fact, during the time of Jesus and the early Church, the most common gospel was that of Rome—the good news of the empire and of the emperor who saw himself as and decreed that he was indeed a god. This gospel of Rome was sent out periodically through the entire realm to inform the populace, those conquered, and those who wielded power in its name what Rome was doing and to stir up enthusiasm for the emperor and his edicts and decisions.

None of the four gospels are meant to be read as eyewitness accounts—they are belief statements of the early Christian Church. These are believers' creeds, so to speak: catechetical teaching texts to both prepare people for initiation—the receiving of the sacraments of baptism, confirmation (sealing in the Spirit), and Eucharist—as well as further lifelong instructions and exhortations to believers after the initiation rites, called the mystogia, or the ever-deeper entrance into and experience of the mysteries of revelation and belief.

Generally speaking, the gospels were written within the first hundred years after the death and resurrection of Jesus. This book is not interested in the historicity of the gospels, or specifics on their relation to other gospels. The diversity and the depth of the four we have as a foundation are rich and powerful wisdom for anyone who calls himself a believer in Jesus, to be counted among his followers and alive in the community of the Risen Lord. This book is interested in the Truth of the gospels and what they meant and should—and could—mean to believers today. In the last two thousand–plus years, it appears that the Church no longer preaches the gospels of Mark, Matthew, Luke, and John but instead preaches its own gospel: what it has developed into historically and culturally, even politically and economically, rather than the Good News to the Poor, the Good News of the present reality of the Kingdom of God in our midst, and the Good News of Love as I Have Loved You as its essence, meaning, practice, and reason for existence in the world.

This book hopes to look at issues including: If the gospels were written today—Mark, Matthew, Luke, and John—would they say the same things, emphasize the same teachings, the same exhortations on how to live and be in relation with others and the world, and with God? Or is there need for a new gospel? What is gospel truth? How do you read the gospels? What is the connection between Word and practice in the gospels and in the community? How do you take words off the paper, put them into your mouth, and make them live again in a community? If the gospels were originally an oral tradition, how do we reclaim and recover that tradition—read between, under, and over the lines on the pages today? And perhaps most important of all—how does the Word in the gospels in the power of the Spirit continue to convert as radically as it did in its beginning century; to transform human beings' lives, attitudes, decision making, choices, and beliefs on how to be human and like God in the world today?

Basically I am saying that there isn't a need to rewrite the gospels, because we have already done that in many ways: interpreting them to suit our needs, our power, and our agendas rather than letting the Word transform us. We have not lived the gospels or steeped ourselves in their mysteries, their power, and the presence of the Risen Lord among us. We have used the gospels to proof-text other statements and laws. We have taken lines and phrases out of context and often misused them and, in doing so, have often contradicted some of the primary and foundational teachings of Jesus. We have ignored whole pieces of the gospel because they are too difficult and too demanding, too convicting of us as not believing and not practicing what we claim in our words. We have betrayed the gospels as individual persons, as communities, as groups, as institutions, and as leaders—even as Church, the Body of Christ.

The next eight chapters will look at each of the gospels in the order we have them, as they were written, in sets—then and now. We will look at their cores, at their hearts, and at what Jesus is saying, demanding, confronting us with, and summoning us to live. Each chapter will look at the gospel then and will be followed by a look at that gospel today. Each was written for a particular community coping with history, with persecution and peace, with economics and other religions, with governments and cultures, and even with languages. Each has moral principles, values, and commands that are simple, clearly stated, and come with the expectation that they are to be obeyed—along with what to do when they are ignored, disobeyed, and twisted to destroy the integrity of Jesus's words and actions. They were written for believers—some already baptized, others preparing for the sacraments of initiation—and for those who were seeking reentry into the community after betraying their belief or committing such actions that tore the community to shreds religiously and spiritually.

Each chapter that looked at a particular gospel then will be followed by a look at that gospel now, in light of history today, at national, universal, and local church levels. We'll analyze the struggles we are confronted with today not only as individuals but primarily as communities of believers who are to become Good News to all, but especially to the poor, the outcast, the fringe, the excluded, the "other" in all societies. Each gospel will reveal a piece of the larger puzzle of values, and ways of life and meaning that are found at the heart of the gospels—beliefs about Jesus and what it means to proclaim and become the words that we speak aloud to others. Hopefully we will experience the gospels as the living, breathing Word of God, the double-edged sword of truth, laying bare and exposing what is evil and yet as living water and the presence of the Spirit of God breathing life into us still.

The last chapter will look at suggestions for other gospels for the twenty-first-century world, and some issues that are alluded to in the four original gospels but now need to be spelled out: the demand that there be no war, no violence; the relationship between science, technology, and religion; interreligious dialogue; the universe, its resources, and state of being in the two thousand years since Jesus; and the understanding of the world, the arts, and their connection to the gospels. Lastly we will look at the structure of the institution and how it contradicts and has become a stumbling block and scandal for many, even those who already believe. We will examine the position and devaluation of women, of sexuality, of marriage, and the Church that is not the hierarchy as the norm either for holiness or for a life lived in community following Jesus as disciples and friends.

For the remainder of this chapter we will look at how to read the gospels—and reclaim the oral tradition that lived in people's mouths and in the communities of believers before the words went down on paper. We will look at a few underlying assumptions— that the gospels are written for believers and are not to be used to "prove" anything, let alone threaten or harm anyone, or allow others to be harmed in the name of the gospel. We will also examine the necessity of reading the gospels in communities of belief, together and out loud, to provide accountability for our words and the intention to put our understanding of those words into practice, as the norm for studying and knowing the Scriptures; in other words, reading the gospels as wisdom for living. Finally, we will look at Jesus as alive today—in the Word Made Flesh dwelling among us—in the gospels and in the communities that seek to incarnate his words, insights, commands, and hope into their own lives and realities in the here and now.

I will try to avoid documents, doctrines, dogmas, and teachings over the historical development of Christianity as a world power, nation, institutional structure, and global economic reality. But I *will* quote from past believers and contemporary disciples who struggle with putting the commands of Jesus into practice, being prophetic as Jesus was, and being constantly re-converted to and becoming the Good News for and with others.

PERHAPS THE PLACE to begin in earnest is with a question and a story. How did Christians get so far removed from the teachings of Jesus, ignoring Jesus's Words and actions and altering them to serve their own ways in the world rather than being a visible sign of power, of hope, of "life ever more abundantly for everyone" (John 10:10)? How did the religion of Jesus become an individualistic work for saving one's own soul, of the morbid fear of sin, death, sex, and of being holy without loving the world and all that God created, with the narrow concentration on the me-and-Jesus mentality, alongside the judgmental attitudes of who is saved and who is damned?

And at the same time, how did the followers of Jesus become those who dominated the world, history, the rise of nations, economics, and politics, steeped in blood, war, violence, torture, and the only religion that has value and meaning? It seems that by the third century, the Church was no longer just the Body of Christ, the followers of the Crucified and Risen One, but instead was the religion that had become the torturers, the empire, the force that dominates, manipulates, and demands that all become believers— or else.

This may sound overly damning and simplistic—but for many this is reality, and those who profess to be believers have betrayed Jesus by past and present behaviors, actions, and teachings. They are indeed both sinners and saints—but it seems the public face is more the sinner, more unrepentant and stubborn in resisting the gospels than in making them come true today worldwide.

What is the situation today? There is an old story, traditionally told in Eastern European and Muslim circles. Sometimes it is called the Lodestone, named for the mythical stone that while in one's possession held the wisdom and power of what it means to be human, to be holy, to be in right relation to others, to understand the mysteries of the universe, and to be in communion with God.

Once upon a time a man was obsessed with searching for and seeking knowledge, wisdom, and understanding. He studied with masters and read every book that he could lay his hands on—and this is at a time when books were rare, expensive, and hand copied. One day, he was finishing up a book on philosophy and got to the back cover. As he was closing the book, he noticed that there seemed to be another page in the binding that was loose—once glued but coming undone. Intrigued, he carefully separated the thin tissue of paper from the cover and found words written there.

Painstakingly he deciphered them and copied them down, and when he read them back to himself out loud he couldn't believe what he was hearing. The words spoke thusly: If you are serious in your intent to discover the Lodestone, the stone of truth—you must be diligent but it is not hard to do. Walk along the sea—the Black Sea—daily, without fail, and pick up stones, one at a time. Hold each in your hand briefly. If it is cold to the touch, throw it back into the waters. But if it is warm, even fiery, to the touch, as you hold it, grasp it firmly and hold it dear. It will lead you to all goodness and knowledge, to truth and life. Do not be afraid. I assure you, you will have it in your hand before long. Be blessed along the way.

Immediately the man set out for the Black Sea, gave away most of what he owned, left his job, family, friends, and got a small hut near the sea. Early in the morning, for most of the daylight hours and sometimes even in the moonlight, he walked the edge of the shoreline, his feet in the water. He bent and picked up a stone, held it briefly, squeezed it, and then threw it back. He did it for days, weeks, months that led into years. It became a ritual, a dance, a way of living. Pick up a stone (he rarely even looked at them anymore), grasp it firmly, and turn and lob it back into the waters. The stones were invariably cold, even frigid to the touch—never was there one that was hot, even warm. He persevered and was faithful, never doubting even when he was cold and tired that he would one day find that stone that would change him and everything in his life. He mused, wondered, questioned his previous life, thought of the future and what he would do when he had the stone and returned to his other life. He daydreamed and night-dreamed and imagined, hoped, and kept on.

And then one day—it was a bright, beautiful, crisp, and clear day in late autumn and the sea was casting light that was almost blinding—he walked along the edge of the waters, bent, picked up a stone, grasped it, and automatically turned to throw it once again back into its vast bed—but it was not cold, it was flaming in his hand! But he had grown accustomed to the pattern and the routine and before it could register in his mind or his heart that it was hot, he had thrown it back into the sea!

No, everything in him cried out, NO!... How could I have missed that one after so long? He dove into the waters, scrambling in the frigid waves, dragging his hands and feet along the sandy bottom, hoping that he would find it again.

Hours later, near-frozen, he crawled forth from the sea. It was over—he'd never find it again—years had passed in his fruitless search. And they say: who knows what he did or if he ever went back home? And they ask: how many times have you grasped the Lodestone, the stone of Truth, and mindlessly thrown it back—and are you still searching for the Truth alone?

Sadly the story is far too close to home and the way we routinely seek the Truth: alone and without accountability, wanting it, but unaware of all the Truth that is around us already. That moment of lost awareness, the dislocation from where we are, our present realities, and our moment in time, contributes to our sense of never having the Lodestone, or of grasping the Truth.

This is in manifold ways what many of us have done with the gospels, the Word of God, the Scriptures: we seek understanding of them singularly, read them to ourselves, share them with no one, or use them to get what we want or desire. We may even change or become converted, but on our own terms, in our own ways, and for our own ends. What began as a conversation with the reader and the book, and perhaps another who had read the book previously, becomes not even a monologue but a proscription, a habit, or a routine and mindless thing to do—missing the elements of dialogue with others, the journey, the seeking, the awareness of the present moment and reality, and that somehow the practice itself is meant to reveal and share the Truth with the one who obeys and seeks to be faithful.

The rise of individualism and the cult of knowledge for oneself as the use and justification of power, often divorced from the world around us, devoid of responsibility and accountability, turning us inside ourselves—all has led to this perception of how to read and use the Scriptures. But it has also led to misuse, abuse, and misinterpretation of the gospels, the stories, the words and accounts of Jesus, too. While reading the gospels, we must keep our singular mind open and not let our *monkey-mind* (as Buddhism calls the mind that strays from the text and the breath) run rampant. The corrective for this is simple—other people. Originally, the gospels were *all* oral traditions. They lived, huge pieces of each gospel, in people's mouths, proclaimed, repeated, prayed, intoned, chanted, spoken reflectively—all OUT LOUD, with others listening. The others were crucial to their meaning, insight, power, and how to put the lessons of the gospels into practice and in making sure that the one who spoke the words, as well as those who heard them, actually put them into practice. It was mutual accountability, reminding, remembrance, and exhortation to become true—to intimately connect the words and their lives.

The words of the gospel should be learned by the heart—not memorized or obeyed blindly. They were incorporated—embodied and enfleshed in those who spoke them out loud and put into practice alone and with others, discussed, mulled over, studied, struggled with, and taken to heart. The power of THE WORD of GOD in JESUS is in the text and in the community that believes and seeks to make the Word a reality in their flesh and blood and lives. The sound of the Word of God was the beginning of the transformational process of belief, and becoming what was proclaimed in ritual and prayer. It was a lifelong process, adhered to with others, and these others demanded that each and all live up to the meaning of Jesus's Good News. The words, when spoken out loud, never ceased to astonish, amaze, and bring those who listened and those who spoke them up short!

The gospels are, in a sense, nuts to crack, dig out the meat, and then eat—together, each one getting a taste of it, digesting it, and then becoming it. They cracked open the Scriptures, the gospels, and delved down into layer after layer of meaning that was inspired. To believe that the gospels are inspired is to stake one's life on the reality that the power of the Spirit of God and the Word of God in the text hides and reveals all that believers need to know to become holy, truthful, the Body of Christ; to allow the Word to seize hold of our flesh today so that the Good News is still proclaimed in our gestures, decisions, deeds, practice, and presence together as a community. If one takes hold and takes to heart the meaning of the gospels with others, and begins to put Jesus's words, exhortations, and deeds into practice, then another level will reveal itself: the conversion of Word into flesh, of Word into practice, of Word into change singularly and as a community of believers. This is the process of inspiration becoming transformation, and it is never ending—in depth of perception, behavior, and practice—becoming like the Word Made Flesh among us.

Sometimes you hear a voice through
the door calling you,
as fish out of
Water hear the waves or a hunting
falcon hears the drum's come back.
This turning toward what you deeply love
saves you.

RUMI (TRANSLATED BY COLEMAN BARKS)

I learned by chance—or perhaps by accident or serendipity—while trying to teach others to read and reflect before speaking to one another that you *hear* meaning drastically differently and more deeply when you read out loud. I told them to put their hands over their ears and hear the words in their own head as they read the text out loud. They heard and listened to their own voice echoing throughout their own body. They began to hear themselves and remember that sound, that sensation, that knowing, and were confronted by the words, the intent, and the understanding of the text in ways you cannot "get" if you read it off the page in your head. Then I spoke the words out loud, looking right at them—and they knew and heard the power of the words coming off the page and echoing through their ears and into their hearts. The words and the sound of them in my mouth caught them off guard and even stunned them. They not only could hear and understand the words I was speaking on many different levels of meaning, they also touched another kind of truth released through a voice, my sharing knowledge and belief with them through eye contact, resonance, and communion. There was more than content or even comfort or affirmation of what one already knows or thinks—there was wisdom voiced and revealed in breath, in orality, and in words that could be known intimately—the words lived in my mouth and in their ears and in both our hearts and our bodies.

The words became reality, invitation, expectation, command, possibility, warning, comfort, familiar, strange—an echo resonating truth and faith. The words on the page of the gospels, especially if you believe that they are inspired as well as finely crafted, are arranged so that speaking them out loud affects breath, pace, rhythm, the phrasing in one's mouth, sound, depth, cadence—it all moves through the speaker's body out into the bodies of those who listen. It echoes in the mind, stirring insight, triggering memories, calling forth emotions, and even, it is said, altering brain-wave patterns. When the words are spoken out loud and repeated over and over again in the presence of others, they become distilled in the mind, easy in the memory, and they begin to have a life of their own—singing and moving—giving one the sense of the words singing through you, moving through your arteries and veins, sinews and muscles. They move inside you and stay there—move in and dwell, making a home within you. Or as Catherine of Siena said: "There the soul dwells—like the fish in the sea and the sea in the fish.¹

Speaking the gospels aloud by heart allows them to become intimate friends. In some ways they are two sides of the same hand/reality: some demand (and you can hear it in your stomach and throat and lungs) short breaths, even gasps; some become drawn out, like singing or sighing (note: even the cartoon character Snoopy had seven levels of sighing!); still others become hard breaths that can sometimes be heard along with the words, cadenced, rising, falling, pulsing, steady, returning breath—like waves on the shore, building in power, even terror, fear that is awe inspiring and mesmerizing—until breath and words stop just before they hit you—then the waves recede and stay with you. It all sounds very poetic, and it is—like reciting a poem that has become you and it tells you almost.

In Buddhism, this learning by heart and speaking out loud is very close to what is called "writing on the bones," the process and experience of taking phrases, stanzas, and lines from the sutras, prayers, and koans of the masters, and learning them by heart— from Buddha's mouth to your own—and learning what they are like in your mouth. This is from Jesus's mouth or the mouth of the Spirit and the Word to your mouth, and learning what they sound like in your mouth now. When you have learned a little of this practice of knowing and speaking out loud by heart the words of the gospel texts, it's like the Spirit borrows your voice, your sound, your body, and your soul and the Spirit—the Breath of God—comes through you in a new and startling way. Or as Hildegard von Bingen, a medieval mystic, said: "When the inner and the outer are wedded, revelation occurs." This is the telling of the gospel as manifestation of God's presence, as epiphany—the showing forth of revelation that can almost be seen, sensed, and certainly can be felt and heard singularly and with many others around you.

What happens between the one who utters the words by heart and the ones who listen is communion. And if both believe that the words and the text itself are inspired by the Spirit, and that the Word Made Flesh in Jesus is present when two or three are gathered together, then the community is inspired and inspirited by the presence of the Risen Lord. This communion is as sacred and holy as the communion of Eucharist that is taken into one's body, chewed on, digested, and taken as nourishment. Both forms of the Word of the Lord, in the gospels and in the Eucharist, are meant to be taken inside, shared so that they become a communion of flesh/bone/breath/blood and hope that is expressed in obedience (what the word *listen* actually means) and worship and practice shared as one.

In one sentence it can be said: in the hearing is the meaning. When the gospel is spoken out loud, by heart, in a community that holds one another accountable to actually put the words into practice and enflesh or incarnate them today in those who believe them, many of the problems of understanding Scripture, like literalism (word-for-word meaning without context), fundamentalism (it only means this and this alone), and the use of Scripture as threats on others can be avoided. Interpreting Scripture becomes more solid, more engaging, and more demanding! The Jews believe that there are forty-three different ways of interpreting Scripture: the whole Bible—each book, chapter, verse, sentence, phrase, word, punctuation, even empty spaces on the page! For Christians this mystery is infinite; there is always more to know and understand of the mystery of God's Word in the human flesh of Jesus and the Word of Scripture in the gospels. The image I use is baklava—a good Greek cook knows that this rich dessert has 122 layers (at least) of thin phyllo dough, ground nuts, honey, lard/butter, sometimes a bit of jasmine or mint pressed down tightly and is then cut and served in an inch-by-inch square. That is all one can digest with good strong dark coffee! And the Scriptures, the gospel of Mark, Matthew, Luke, and John are just like that—packed densely with meaning that can often only be heard in the power and breath of the Spirit, in the text, in the community out loud, in those who know pieces of it by heart.

Much of the theology and the interpretation of the gospels in this book comes from speaking out loud and by heart segments of the gospel and sharing that with others—the listeners who have heard and taken them to heart so that they can put them into practice, live them, and enflesh them in their lives together—in communion as the Body of Christ the Church. This method and process, this experience, is life altering, filled with dread, terror, amazement, and promise for understanding and conversion. It is not as easy to get away from the breath and voice of a word of the heart that is heard in communion with others struggling with its meaning, knowing that you will be challenged on putting it into practice, as it is to read it to yourself.

As you read this book, try to learn bits and pieces, phrases, sentences, parables and stories, prayers and commands by heart, and say them out loud to yourself and share them with others, studying them for meaning. A good way to start and persevere is to use the readings from the Lectionary—the Sunday readings worldwide, just the gospel—with a small group of others struggling for meaning and practice. Ask after listening and some silence: What does this mean, and how do I put this into practice in my life today? What does this mean for us as a community, and what are we to be preaching and practicing in public today? How do I make this come true in the world now? How do I come true and take this Word into my flesh so that I—and we—become Good News, a gospel for the world today?

To encourage you in learning the gospels by heart and to return to the gospels of Mark, Matthew, Luke, and John to delve into them more deeply and truly and let the gospels upend your life, here is the old Irish story of Caedmon, who lived around AD 660 and is sometimes considered the first poet, singer, or storyteller of the English language. It is a story that is part true, part historical, part mystical, part mythical (telling truths that cannot be spoken in mere words and concepts—you must use images to convey the meaning).

Once upon a time there was a simple peasant, a shepherd and day laborer. He lived a lonely life, mostly by choice, but also of happenstance. He was mortified to speak out loud—he stuttered terribly and it was nearly impossible to understand his words or know what it was he was trying so desperately to say. He lived in shame and silence, listening to others or stealing away whenever he could to be out in the fields with the birds and the animals, the air and the wind, the vast night and the stars. He loved, though, to listen to the songs and the tales, to others who could speak with such fluidity and ease, weaving words effortlessly and having others listen to them. Because he lived in a country of music, sound, songs, harps, stirring ballads, heroic deeds, chants of praise and holy words, the sounds were both a delight and a torment to him. At night when the work was done, everyone would gather and talk, and the words would send them to bed and rest. And when there was a celebration like a wedding or a good harvest, when there was a funeral and death, when war threatened, when there was uneasiness in the land—there was more reason to gather, and all shared in the merriment or grieving, or waiting for what would be.

He would be teased sometimes—cajoled and pushed to speak, to give his ideas or feelings, to sing the praises or to pray, but he just couldn't. He whispered and muttered so that no one knew what he was saying, and as soon as he could he escaped from others. He loved the animals, but best of all he loved the night air: the stars and the dome of sky above him—and the sounds of night, from the trees and their limbs, the sheep and lambs, footsteps, the wings of birds that breathed all around him, sighing and sloughing and speaking their own languages. And it is said that one night an angel came to him and commanded him to speak, to stand alone in the field and raise his voice to the heavens and let all the creatures of earth and sky hear him—to praise the Holy One. He stood and trembled and nothing came out, but the angel was insistent: speak your own words, another's words, the words of psalm or song, any sounds, begin by humming, but lift your voice. He tried—such strange and unfamiliar sounds issued forth from his mouth. His tongue slurred, his throat constricted, his lungs were dry, his mind wouldn't put words in his mouth.

He stood silent before the angel. He was miserable but the angel demanded again—speak out loud. Finally what came forth was a question: "What shall I say? What shall I speak?" And the angel replied: "Speak! Sing! Tell the story! Breathe out, breathe in, let the Spirit borrow you and come through you! And speak of all things, as it was in the beginning!" And he did!

From that night forth Caedmon spoke out loud. He said it just didn't come—he had to work at it—at breathing and throwing his voice, at pulling it up from his abdomen, and casting it forth like bread on the waters. He had to reflect and make sure it was what the Spirit wished to say. He had to make sure the words were clear, understood, taken to heart—he had to put his heart and soul and all his body into the speaking. That first night only the stars, the animals and the field, and his own ears heard his voice (and the angels!) but now it was other human beings, and all that he spoke must be good, must be holy, must draw others to truth and to God's ways and to open the door to God's kingdom. He was only to praise God and all the goodness God made, and call that forth in others, call them back, call them home, in whispers and chants, songs and stories, parables and questions, and with the words of the Scriptures—the gospels—Jesus's own words in his mouth!

Word spread and people from all the local villages and towns came to hear his voice and words . . . word came to the local abbess of the monastery and she sent word for him to come—to come and speak, to preach and teach and say the holy words of the gospels out loud, and he did. His memory grew stronger and he would listen to those who could read and learn all the words he heard by heart, cherishing them and holding them dear. In his voice, people could hear meaning, hope, consolation, freedom, passion, grace, the need for conversion, reconciliation, restitution, justice, mercy, and especially no harm to anyone or anything, no violence, no war— his words, the words of Jesus were of peace and truth. His words were like water, like balm and dew, like thunder and lightning, like music, and sometimes often they led straight into silence, deep and abiding.

And always he reminded people that he was a stutterer, without grace, and that it was God's command that he speak out loud. It was God that opened his mouth and loosed his tongue and kissed his lips that night and that all creation and the angels and God had heard his vow—to speak only the Truth, the peace, and Good News of the Word of God until he spoke no more. And Caedmon did.

Chapter 2

The Gospel of Mark Then

Someone once told me that saying certain words, phrases, lines of poetry, Scriptures was a way of making peace in time of war.

The gospel of Mark presents us with the beginning of the tradition of these accounts of Good News from the believers of the early Christian communities. The historical time frame of the writing of Mark's gospel is between AD 55 and 65, about twenty-five to thirty years after the life, death, and resurrection of Jesus. The times were not easy, though they were rich in the presence of the Spirit of the Risen Jesus and in the deepening of the communities' understanding of what it means to be a follower or a disciple of Jesus. Originally, these groups were primarily Jews who were called "the Followers of the Way" (Acts), and over time they became more separate from the Jewish communities they were born into, belonged to, and considered themselves still to be part of. But within those years, history contrived to change that reality and push apart those who were Jews but now believed that Jesus was the Messiah—the one long awaited—and that he was more than Messiah, and so they turned more and more to their own path and followed this new way that Jesus preached and lived.

It was a rocky transition and one fraught with personal difficulties for many who had been practicing Jews all their lives and for those who became followers of this new religion and were baptized. While experiencing conversion within their communities, many rulers began faith-based persecutions; these persecutions shattered the daily lives of believers and added confusion to Christian life—with torture and death, with loss of property, with the need for silence and fear of whom to trust, as well as what to do when those who had been welcomed into the community and baptized gave up their faith, betrayed the community, and caused despair and discouragement within the young Churches. It was a volatile, violent time filled with enthusiasm for their newly accepted belief and community life, a time of martyrdom and fierce faithfulness that braced those who lived in fear, but it was also a time of terrible loss of faith. Many who chose to give up their belief to save their lives, their families, their possessions, and their reputations often saddened and broke the faith and unity of their community. As time went on, many of them wanted to return—to repent again of their failure in courage and faith and begin again to try to live Jesus's teachings in a world that was becoming more and more hostile to their very presence.

By the year 60, Peter and Paul, two of the strongest personages of the early Church, were martyred in Rome during Nero's persecution of the Christians. The Jews were arming and again planning to try to overthrow the Romans, drive them from Jerusalem, and reclaim the Temple for their own. The Jews were pushing sects of Christians to join them in this endeavor—to fight with them against the Romans to recover the Temple for worship—but meanwhile Christians were struggling with their own beliefs and whether or not to join the Jewish nation. For now they believe that the new temple is the Body of Christ—the community of believers—and Jesus's strongest teachings and practice are against any form of violence. This problem led to the separation of Jew and Christian and to the sect within Judaism becoming its own religion, because the Christians decide there is to be no harm, no violence, and no fighting against anyone, to protect any piece of property, even the Temple. Instead, Christians believed they must stand in solidarity with the Body of Christ alongside other human beings. They may lay down their lives for what they believe if need be, but they cannot do violence to anyone because of their belief in Jesus.

Each of the gospels is a catechetical text—a teaching tool for those preparing for baptism and for those after baptism who begin to study and experience the mysteries of their religion more closely and intimately, but this first gospel of Mark is also a primer on discipleship. It is a manual that seeks not just to prepare people for the internal rituals of the sacraments and liturgy (worship), and daily prayer and life as a believer, but also to remind them of the Cross of suffering and the need to stand fast and remain firm in their belief in the face of rejection, persecution, and even possible loss of their very lives and loved ones. It was written to help the community take back those who had failed in their baptismal promises to the community and God, and to help those returning to admit their failures and how these failures had impacted their brothers and sisters. The gospel of Mark also discusses how to be re-converted, do restitution for the harm they had caused, and once again seek to live in unity and communion with others seeking to be faithful as disciples of Jesus, the Crucified and Risen Lord of Life.

Though it may seem difficult for us to imagine these circumstances, a story told in South America from the 1960s (and even now) demonstrates what life in the communities of believers among the Romans might have been like. The Romans sought to blame the Christians for the destruction of Rome by fire, and wanted to eradicate them from the empire politically and religiously, and this caused distress in the communities themselves—among families, husbands and wives, friends, and even the leaders. The story from South America also takes place at a time of unrest, with small communities trying to survive between the government forces and guerrilla groups—both sought the allegiance of the people and the Church groups, and the people were caught in the middle between the practices and ideologies of both, a no-win situation for most ordinary folk. This is the way I heard the story told in a community that was studying the gospel of Mark during one year's gatherings.

Once upon a time there was a community like ours, seeking to be disciples of Jesus. They were farmers, peasants, small landholders, craftspeople, weavers, and potters, raising families and trying to take care of one another in hard times. There was a civil war and many were struggling for their rights: for their land and a chance to live as freemen and -women in a country that treated them as slaves. They met weekly to read the Scripture, and when a priest could come they all gathered in the small adobe church they had built for mass on Sunday. One Sunday—it was a feast day—the priest came and the church was crowded, packed with people who had come in from many other villages. There was a festive air, and the mass would be followed by a celebration with music and food and time for everyone to gather, to share news of what was going on in the country and in their small villages.

The mass began with music and singing and readings from the Scripture. There was time for reflection and then they discussed what these words of Jesus might mean for them today in their lives. The priest gathered their thoughts together, and added some ideas of his own and what he had heard from various other groups that had met with him during the week—they preached to one another. They were preparing to bring the gifts up to begin the Eucharist—the offering of the bread and wine and flowers, incense, copal, and food for the poor—when suddenly everything stopped. The doors to the church were thrown open and the guerrilla commander and his men stood in the doorway. The music stopped. He strode down the aisle and stood next to the priest at the altar. There was silence.

He spoke: "You all are here worshipping and claiming to be Christians, yes?" There were nods and a few mumbled affirmations. "Well," he said, "let's see how many of you really are Christians!" He turned and looked at the priest and the leaders who had read and the altar servers, a few young boys and girls, and said, "You obviously are believers since you're in charge here—go outside"—and they all walked down the aisle and out. There was silence again and then shots rang out—one for each of those who had left.

The silence now was deadly and laced with terror. "Okay," he continued, "how many more of you really are Christians? Stand up if you believe: because if you're Christians you are committed to not fighting—no violence, not against us or against the military—doesn't Jesus say that?"

There was whimpering now, children crying, picking up on their parents' fears, and everyone knew it was going to be awful. One by one a few stood up—young men and women who said they would not kill, that they were trying to love their enemies and do good to those who persecuted them and forgive those who harmed them and betrayed them. A few older men and women stood and said that it had been hard for years to try to obey the words of Jesus, to share what little they had with so many in need and to try not to hate, but they were going to keep trying. One or two even said that they would try to pray for them—their own people who had decided to fight the government troops—that they understood why they had chosen to do this, but that they themselves could not—they would share their food with them, and water and medicine, but they could not kill. They were told to go down the aisle, too—and go outside. They did, holding hands, their arms over one another's shoulders, helping the elderly.

And there was silence, but not for long—the shots rang out again and again. And then there was nothing. Husbands and wives looked at one another and at their children. Catechists who had taught children and adults, and who had read at mass and brought up the gifts—the leaders of the community looked down at the floor. And the commander said, "Anyone else believe?" And no one moved. Out of more than three hundred people maybe twenty altogether had stood up and left the church; he didn't count the ones he had just told to go first—they didn't decide, it was decided for them because they were the obvious leaders of the group who had professed publicly who they were by their roles in the assembly. People sat ashamed, weeping, raging in their hearts, too—some wanting to fight back, no one else moving a muscle.

And then he shouted at them, "Look at me! You claim to believe in Jesus! And you don't—or if you do, you don't have the courage to stand up for what you believe out of fear, out of feeling responsible for your children or your husbands and wives and elderly, or because you just don't know how much you really believe. I'm ashamed of you. If you were united, if you were together—in communion—you'd stand together, not just separate with every believer for themselves like you just did. What kind of example are you giving your children—or just to each other?" Then he signaled to the men at the back of the church and everyone almost panicked. But instead, they were amazed to see all of those who had walked out walking back in, and up the aisle to stand before the altar and before the community—their faces shining and looking right at them.

"Here are your disciples of Jesus," the guerrilla leader proclaimed. "These people are your Good News—when you see them coming and when they're in your midst you know they will speak truthfully and they will act upon those words. These are your leaders— though you might question the ones I sent out without letting them choose to go, when we're gone, to see if they would have walked outside. We all live in fear. We all live in hard times. But we must make decisions and we must decide with whom we stand—to whom we belong and who holds us accountable. Or else when the time comes we will not choose or we will outright betray one another. I respect all of you who chose, but I am angry and saddened by all of you who wouldn't—most of you here. Who knows—the next time someone interrupts your worship and singing praise to God, maybe they won't be here to teach you a lesson in believing, but it will be the moment of declaring whether or not you do belong together to God. I—we—will pray that you will be converted to the words you hear in the gospel and become what you declare to stake your life on—every day." And with that he and his disciples marched out the door, closing it behind them, and the congregation could hear them singing as they left the village.

This stark story sets the tone and the situation for the gospel of Mark and how a community deals with all those issues, as individual believers, as people in places of leadership, and as those who betray their faith—for many different reasons—as well as those who seek to stand fast. This is why the gospel of Mark was written.

The gospel of Mark has often been described as a primer on the Cross, on suffering and struggle, or a passion account with an introduction. Another way to look at Mark's gospel is as a series of calls to conversion—three in particular: the first a call to initial discipleship with Jesus and in a community of believers who "go off in his company" (Mk 1). Then the second call to conversion of life is the call to "deny yourself, pick up your cross and come after me," often called the call to the Cross (Mk 8). The last conversion demands a life of resurrection, hope, resisting dominance in a community that holds one another accountable for continuing conversion to the practice of being Jesus's brothers and sisters, living the kingdom of justice that brings peace to the world today (Mk 16).

In Mark's gospel, the person who models the one who needs to be baptized or the one trying to return to faith after betraying Jesus and their community is Peter, the disciple first called to follow Jesus and, when Jesus is not around, the acknowledged leader of the disciples. Peter is chosen by Mark because Peter fails and fails and fails yet again to stand up for Jesus, to stand with Jesus, or even to admit that he is Jesus's friend and follower. And yet, Peter does learn faithfulness and in fact dies a martyr's death, crucified upside down—probably around AD 60—and becomes the model for a disciple, though it takes some time, a lot of trying, and does not happen until after the resurrection of Jesus. Peter is a good model for so many who turned away from the practice of their faith and betrayed their baptismal promises and family of other believers. The sense is that if Peter can finally become not only a true disciple of Jesus but also a leader in the community, then anyone can repent and turn again, and again, and again, back to following Jesus and living with grace, freedom, and power in Jesus's company of friends.

There are a few stories in the gospel of Mark that characterize the issues and dilemmas facing these early Christians, and reveal core commands of Jesus: his followers are to not only give lip service but put faith into practice, not only as individuals but as a community that serves as an alternative to how others live—as Jews, as

Romans, as Greeks—as anyone who is not a follower of Jesus might act. Some of the stories are what would be termed "in-house," which are stories of Jesus within the leadership of the Jewish religion, and how he perceives and practices the law and worship differently than they do. Many such stories involve people who were considered "lost," or beyond saving, and excluded by the religious people and even persecuted because they were public sinners. And other stories deal with those outside the Jewish religion—pagans, those who worshipped other gods and those who were seemingly without a religion. It is within these stories that we experience how Jesus worships, makes decisions, and puts into practice his understanding of what it means to believe in God, to be ethical, and to practice one's religion with others; to be a follower of the law and the Spirit of the law that attests to true belief in a person and in the Church. We will look at some of these stories to learn the commandments Jesus is teaching and what he is demanding out of his followers— the core of what it means to practice the religion of Jesus as found in Mark's text.

Mark's gospel is about liberation, about freedom and hope for justice and peace, about fulfillment of the promises of Isaiah the prophet (chapters 40–66) and the possibility of life without fear, without domination by others, and without captivity—to any form of evil, external or within one's own person. It is Jesus's authority and his assurance about who he is, who God is, and how we are to treat one another that give Mark's gospel its power and attraction. Jesus is intent on "grasping people by the hand for the victory of justice, and wresting them away from the forces of evil" (Is 42:6ff) so that they can rise up to a life of hope, forgiveness, justice, and truth.

The wrestling match starts early. Jesus is baptized by John in the Jordan River and immediately begins to call followers to come with him in his work to catch others for this kingdom that is God's place on earth. In the first chapter, Jesus calls a demon out of a man in the synagogue, commanding it to be quiet. Then he moves from exorcising or freeing someone religiously from their inabilities and confusion to healing and calling forth Peter's mother-in-law to more integrated physical health. Word spreads so that "the whole city is gathered at his door," and Jesus leaves because he must "go on to the neighboring towns [and] proclaim the message there also; for that is what I came out to do" (Mk 1). When lepers approach him, he stretches out to touch them and reintegrate them into the community.

This is God's kingdom on earth—where no one is excluded, all are drawn back into wholeness, and there is integrity of life for all. Jesus heals a man lowered by his friends through the roof of the house where he is staying, forgives him anything he has failed in, and makes his body whole again—once more revealing the wholeness, or the *holiness,* that is not categorized or separated from living. All of life is sacred, all human beings are holy, and there is no more distinction between clean and unclean ritually or socially. He continues to call others to come after him, but now he calls public sinners, some of whom are despised because of what they do for a living, or because of the fact that they make money off their own people's suffering—but Jesus is clear when questioned by his own religious superiors that "those who are well have no need of a physician, but those who are sick; I have come to call not the righteous but sinners" (Mk 2:17).

This breaking of social and religious norms, worship, and cultural taboos comes to a confrontation level in chapter 3: the story of the man with the withered hand in the synagogue on a Sabbath—and the leaders want to see what Jesus will do.

> *Again he entered the synagogue, and a man was there who had a withered hand. They watched him to see whether he would cure him on the Sabbath, so that they might accuse him. And he said to the man who had the withered hand, "Come forward." Then he said to them, "Is it lawful to do good or to do harm on the Sabbath, to save life or to kill?" But they were silent. He looked around at them with anger; he was grieved at their hardness of heart and said to the man, "Stretch out your hand." He stretched it out, and his*

hand was restored. The Pharisees went out and immediately conspired with
the Herodians against him, how to destroy him. (Mk 3:1—7)

Mark's gospel throws believers into the midst of the lion's den,
so to speak, because that is where they find themselves: between a
rock and a hard place. They are caught between the Romans, who
are persecuting them for trying to live as Jesus did, and their own
people, with whom they are having difficulty living because they
interpret the law differently than they do. Because of Jesus's words
and actions, Christians not only cannot do harm to others; they
must break laws that allow suffering and violence to continue in
their midst. They cannot just stand by and watch others suffer and
do nothing—even or especially on the Sabbath. For worship and
life are not to be separated out—to worship the God of life on the
Sabbath must be followed by worshipping the God of life every day
of the week. No law can excuse a Christian from bringing life, protecting life, and sharing life with others—not even the law of resting on the Sabbath.

The story is short and stark—as is much of Mark's gospel—and
blunt with the message of Jesus's words of truth. It is a setup between religious legalism and human compassion; between what is
ritually acceptable and what is demanded of one who is a follower
of Jesus. It is the Sabbath—and there is a man with a withered
hand. He cannot work, and most probably he cannot take care of
himself. There is no mention of family, friends, anyone who is with
him or helps him. And the leaders are cold-blooded—let's see what
he's going to do? Does the law rule over the Sabbath exhortations
that are the heart of Judaism, or does the Spirit of the law engage
believers to step beyond what is required to break the lesser law and
move toward the depths of compassion, solidarity, freedom, and a
possibility of life, health, and hope for others?

Jesus is blunt in his questioning of them: "Is it lawful to do good
or to do harm on the Sabbath?" There is a law beyond particulars—
the law, the internal demand to do good beyond what is specified

or normal. The religious leaders refuse to commit themselves and Jesus becomes angry. They do not care for the man; they are lacking in any level of simple human compassion or concern. They do not care about life, only about legalities. In Jesus's grief he tells the man to stretch out his hand—the Sabbath is for stretching and deepening all of life, life in the Spirit, in the body, and in the community—and the man obeys Jesus and he finds restoration. This is the underlying and true meaning of the Sabbath—to restore the community, the people of God, and life to all, but especially to those most in need. It is because of Jesus's concern about people, life, health, inclusion, and hope that crowds begin to follow him.

Immediately (everything happens at breakneck speed in Mark's gospel) the Pharisees and the Herodians—enemies of Jesus and factions of religious power—decide to conspire together against Jesus. Both groups see him and his compassion, his interpretation of the law, and his alliance with groups of people who have been controlled and contained by the law and their power to interpret it, as dangerous to their own positions. From this point on, they will work together to find a way to destroy him. If anything, Mark's gospel is about being realistic and facing up to what one's beliefs and practices can call forth from others in opposition—because of fear of loss, anger, threat, or intent on protecting positions and ways of being religious. Someone once said that Mark's gospel adamantly proclaims that there is nothing worse than self-righteous religious people who decide that you are evil rather than ever wondering if they themselves might be in need of some personal and communal conversion of life or change of attitude and perception. In Mark's gospel, Jesus is clear: one's worship of God must be reflected primarily in one's care for other human beings, not primarily in the correctness of religious ritual or practice. To insist on law, custom, and what is religiously important at the expense of human beings is a "law" that can be ignored and disobeyed; one must side with those excluded and considered unclean and unworthy of the sphere of perceived holiness and what is sacred.

There are many other stories where this theme is repeated,

extended, and deepened: the story of the Gerasene Demoniac in the tombs (chapter 5) and less dramatic ones like those of the young girl restored to life and the woman who was hemorrhaging for twelve years (chapter 5). He will restore pagans like the Syro-Phoenician woman's daughter to wholeness and a non-Jewish deaf man in the region of the Decapolis (chapter 7). Jesus is concerned about people and restores them to health, wholeness, life within the community, a sense of their own identity and worth, and a future that is filled with hope. He continues to disagree with and confront the teachers, lawyers, scribes, and other groups about how they interpret the law—whether it gives life or whether it burdens people and makes their lives more difficult, excluding them while at the same time giving excuses to those who think they are religious so that they don't have to sully themselves through interactions with those whom they have ruled unclean sinners—unlike themselves who obey the law and are holy. The stories are many: being accused in chapter 3 of doing what is good by the power of Beelzebul (a term for the power of evil), and even in the previous chapter, when Jesus takes it upon himself to forgive the sins of the paralytic, when only God can do that, he is accused of blaspheming.

Jesus also seeks to teach them with parables—turning their way of seeing God and what they are to do in imitation of how God acts inside out—but they refuse. Jesus uses his parables and the experiences of everyone he meets to try to speak truthfully about the nature of God, and what it means to try to obey God and act like God—in compassion, with the power of life and solidarity with all, and with forgiveness. More and more, Jesus is rejected outright by the leaders and factions of the religious community and even by his own family and his hometown of Nazareth (chapter 6).

Jesus's actions in the first ten chapters of Mark reveal his priorities: health and well-being of the bodies of human beings; feeding crowds who are hungry for food, justice, and a chance to live with dignity; and the care and inclusion of all, especially those poorest and in need of the basic necessities of life: food, clothing, shelter, medicine and health care, freedom, dignity, the chance to live without fear and insecurity, and a chance at a future for themselves and their children. Jesus demands truthfulness and integrity of life beyond just words, but also in relationships, public connections, worship, and in dealing with those who are not considered worthy of respect. Almost halfway into the gospel Jesus stands and boldly contradicts the elders of his own people, saying to them:

> *"Isaiah prophesied rightly about you hypocrites, as it is written,*
>
> > *'This people honors me with their lips,*
> > *but their hearts are far from me;*
> > *in vain do they worship me,*
> > *teaching human precepts as doctrines.'*
>
> > *You abandon the commandment of God and hold to human tradition."*
> > (Mk 7:6–8)

This relationship continues to deteriorate with Jesus winning when it comes to making clear what God expects and demands of those who call themselves his own people. Many of the healings that Jesus performs on those who are blind, deaf, mute, paralyzed, etc., reflect the inner world and resistance of those to whom he is preaching—those who are resisting the coming of the Good News of God in the world, and the kingdom where God's priorities of caring and feeding of the hungry and for the health and well-being of the poorest and weakest and hospitality to all is practiced. Many, including Jesus's disciples do not catch the awesomeness of what he is saying or the power that he is teaching. When he asks the disciples whether or not they understand, they glibly say, "Yes we do," though they don't at all. Even the disciples begin to reject his words, his actions, and his associations with sinners and pagans because Jesus is becoming dangerous—and to be connected with him will be dangerous, as well.

Chapter 8 is the turning point, when even his disciples reach a point where they will not listen to Jesus and in their own fear, confusion, and anger begin to deliberately reject what Jesus is saying and seek to turn his words into what might be more tolerable teachings that they must endorse and practice as his disciples. This turning point begins with the story of a blind man from Bethsaida (where Peter is from), who is brought to Jesus by others, and they beg Jesus to touch him. Again, the story is short and stark:

> They came to Bethsaida. Some people brought a blind man to him and begged him to touch him. He took the blind man by the hand and led him out of the village; and when he had put saliva on his eyes and laid his hands on him, he asked him, "Can you see anything?" And the man looked up and said, "I can see people, but they look like trees, walking." Then Jesus laid his hands on his eyes again; and he looked intently and his sight was restored, and he saw everything clearly. Then he sent him away to his home, saying, "Do not even go into the village." (Mk 8:22–26)

The blind man is Peter, who is representative of all of Jesus's disciples and those who initially believe in Jesus's words but then as time progresses and they begin to realize how difficult following Jesus can be, they go blind again. For the blind man's sight is restored when Jesus puts his spit/saliva on his eyes and lays hands on him—a baptism, bringing the light of the Spirit of God, the Spirit of the Law, and the Spirit of Truth to the believer. The man has seen before, because he describes what he sees as people who look like walking trees! Jesus touches him again and then he can see clearly. But he is warned not to weaken his faith and resolve and go back to his old ways and to those who would blur his sight once again. And this story is followed immediately by Peter's declaration that Jesus is the Messiah—which Jesus keeps telling the disciples not to say to anyone because it is so far off who he is as the one who brings justice and peace to Israel, and sight and truth to the people; Jesus rejects the political and economic power that many were expecting the Messiah to utilize. Peter can't believe that Jesus is rejecting his words of who he is and tries to remonstrate with Jesus—an old word denoting a parent with a stupid child who must be corrected. Jesus turns on Peter and the rest of his disciples, telling them to face reality.

In the next chapters (8–10) before Jesus goes to Jerusalem to die, he will repeat over and over again—three times—that he is going to be rejected by his own people: the leaders of the community, his own family members, and even by them, his disciples. He tells them he will be tortured, man-handled, and given over to those who will crucify him and he will die—and that he will rise again after three days. Though all the gospels were written long after the resurrection—which is the foundation stone of belief in Jesus—at the time of persecution, when Jesus is in mortal verbal combat with his enemies, all the disciples can hear is the rejection/torture/crucifixion announcements, and they are terrified and repulsed beyond even being able to speak about it or respond to Jesus. Jesus's words in Mark 8 are the cornerstone, the fulcrum, and the benchmark of what it means to be faithful as a Christian and what it can entail in a world of religious, political, and economic powers that resist this kingdom of the poor, of justice, and of peace:

> He called the crowd with his disciples, and said to them, "If any want to become my followers, let them deny themselves, and take up their cross and follow me. For those who want to save their life will lose it, and those who lose their life for my sake, and for the sake of the gospel, will save it. For what will it profit them to gain the whole world and forfeit their life? Indeed, what can they give in return for their life? Those who are ashamed of me and of my words in this adulterous and sinful generation, of them the Son of Man will also be ashamed when he comes in the glory of his Father with the holy angels." (Mk 8:34–38)

The gauntlet has been thrown down. Jesus is doing hard reality-therapy on his followers. To believe in Jesus's words, to practice his way of bringing God's power, presence, and rule into the world today, requires single-hearted attachment to the Word of God, laying down one's life if necessary, and accepting suffering, torture, and persecution, but in return saving one's soul, integrity, and humanity. There is to be no violence, no retaliation, no hatred, no harm to others—this is the Way that they are to follow—coming after Jesus, and they must live faithfully and rely on God's compassion and power to endure whatever the future holds with grace. Jesus is telling them that they are stumbling blocks for one another and for the coming of the kingdom in its power on earth, and they are to take heed of his words.

He then teaches them what constitutes the basic elements of being his disciple: faithfulness in relationships, especially in marriage; taking care of the least, the children, the poorest—all those with no power or authority among the powers of the world; of sharing their excess with the poor so that they lay up treasure in heaven here on earth; and exercise control, power, and authority not the way the nations of the world do, but the way Jesus does—as a servant of all, even giving your life as a ransom so that others might be saved (chapter 10).

And again there comes a story about another blind man, this time named Bartimaeus, the son of Timaeus, a beggar by the roadside. He is named, so he is actually a person in Mark's Church community! He becomes a model of faith, unlike Peter who keeps misreading Jesus's words because of his fear, his ignorance, and his reluctance to be converted. And the story reveals what is going on in the community as well as how individuals are following Jesus in spite of others who would hold them back and stop them from being faithful. This story is the way of the Cross, the way of Jesus, the way of the Kingdom of Good News, the way to God, the way home here on earth.

They came to Jericho. As he and his disciples and a large crowd were leaving Jericho, Bartimaeus son of Timaeus, a blind beggar, was sitting by the roadside. When he heard that it was Jesus of Nazareth, he began to shout out and say, "Jesus, Son of David, have mercy on me!" Many sternly ordered him to be quiet, but he cried out even more loudly, "Son of David, have mercy on me!" Jesus stood still and said, "Call him here." And they called the blind man, saying to him, "Take heart; get up, he is calling you." So throwing off his cloak, he sprang up and came to Jesus. Then Jesus said to him, "What do you want me to do for you?" The blind man said to him, "My teacher, let me see again." Jesus said to him, "Go; your faith has made you well." Immediately he regained his sight and followed him on the way. (Mk 10:46–52)

This story is devastating in many ways. Someone in desperate need is crying out to Jesus because he has HEARD his Word, and he is being silenced and told to shut up by the crowd—but we also get the sense that it is some of Jesus's own followers who have decided Jesus does not need to listen to or respond to this man. When Jesus stops and there is silence, he orders those who initially told Bartimaeus to be quiet to call him over, rather than do it himself directly. Their tone shifts with the words: take heart—have courage, get up—he is calling you now! Those who think they are close to Jesus, in proximity and as followers, are far from him while Bartimaeus is far closer to Jesus. He springs up (the words have echoes of Isaiah the prophet—when he cries out—see I am doing a new thing—do you not perceive it?), drops his cloak, giving up all he has to protect himself from others as a beggar with no home, no resources, and no privacy or dignity, and approaches Jesus. In many of the translations he runs to Jesus! How? Through the crowd that parts before him, and once in front of Jesus it is Jesus who asks him with respect and equality, "What do you want me to do for you?" This is one who believes and who is ready to be baptized— yet again, in a sense—because his answer is: Lord, let me see again! He wants to return, to follow again, to once again commit himself to being faithful. And he is welcomed back, encouraged by Jesus, and we are told that his sight, his light, his freedom and hope are restored and he begins to follow Jesus once again, on the way—the way up to Jerusalem, to the Cross, and perhaps to death—but also to the power that is sourced by resurrection.

Again Jesus's authority will be questioned yet another time

when he attempts to teach that his power is found not in tradition, law, force, fear, or threat but in forgiveness, love, and the
mercy and faithfulness of the Father God's Word. He will tell more
parables—of those who reject and those who accept his Word, and
who repent and convert and who refuse. And late in the gospel,
Jesus will condemn outright the scribes and Pharisees for their
outward practice and their inward rebellion; their interpretation
of the law that burdens and breaks the resolve of others while they
themselves reap economic, political, and even public religious ad-
vantages. Jesus will respond with two side-by-side tracks—on one
side the coming destruction of Jerusalem, the Temple, and all the
leaders stand for (which is already a reality by the time this gospel
is being preached—the Temple falls in AD 70); on the other, hopeful, side he points out who is really a disciple already in his kingdom
and a faithful follower, one that all his male disciples should watch
closely and imitate—for *she* is like Jesus! It is probably the shortest
and most powerful story of Mark's gospel:

> He sat down opposite the treasury, and watched the crowd putting money
> into the treasury. Many rich people put in large sums. A poor widow came
> and put in two small copper coins, which are worth a penny. Then he called
> his disciples and said to them, "Truly I tell you, this poor widow has put in
> more than all those who are contributing to the treasury. For all of them
> have contributed out of their abundance; but she out of her poverty has put
> in everything she had, all she had to live on. (Mk 12:41–44)

The widow is the true disciple of Jesus. There is no pretense, no
public display of piety or devotion. There is silence. There is true
worship. It is anonymous and not attention seeking. She gives of
her very livelihood, what she needs to survive on—to the glory of
God—not expecting any return for her generosity. She is, in essence, giving her life, her soul, her heart, and all she has to God
daily. She is picking up her Cross, living life that burdens her, yet
living it with gratitude, with openhandedness and freedom, and she
is giving her life over. And Jesus's community is to be made up of all

these people—poor, struggling, but honest and faithful, day after day, no matter what is going on around them in society and how it impacts them. His disciples are to look to her to get a glimpse of him!

The gospel comes to an abrupt end after this: preparations for the Passover, the betrayal of Jesus by one of his own disciples, indeed from the inner circle of believers, then Peter will betray him loudly in public and deny his faith, and the others will all scatter in fear and terror. Jesus is caught in the net of intrigue set in motion at the very beginning of the gospel, when all factions decide together to destroy him. And he will be handed over, tortured, brutalized, and crucified, and he dies and is buried. In the first eight lines of the last chapter of Mark, some of his women disciples (barely mentioned except in passing) go to the tomb and attempt to prepare his body more decently for burial; they find an empty tomb and run in terror from an announcement of hope and life beyond death.

At this point, it becomes obvious that the gospel primarily makes sense for those who already believe and are struggling to put that belief into practice in spite of their own failures and the climate of fear, indifference, and sometimes hate around them. The women run to tell the other disciples that Jesus's tomb is empty—by now there are probably at least thirty or more of them, men and women who were with Jesus from the beginning or picked up along the way, and they go back home to Nazareth. It is a ninety-mile journey filled with joy, expectations, hope, fear, wondering, skepticism, and questions. They share their stories about Jesus, and things they heard him say and do, and they share what happened in their own lives because of his words. They walk and talk their way through their fears and bond together as his followers, as those who belong to "his company" that share words/stories, bread, and life together—even their failures and weaknesses as well as their moments of faith and life. The story ends, hanging by a thread, but it is meant to be picked up at the beginning and read again—lived through and struggled with over and over. Because the gospel of Mark is a spiraling circle in and down and in and out and in again, deeper and truer each time. The community together tells the story of Mark and their own stories. Together they catch sight of what they were blind to earlier, and they now face more truthfully what they rejected earlier. It is a lifelong process, a lifelong telling and listening, and a lifelong becoming of the Good News for one another and the world.

The monk and writer Thomas Merton had a voluminous correspondence even as he was cloistered in a monastery and in one of his many letters—to Czeslaw Milosz in February 1959, he writes:

> Milosz, life is on our side. The silence and the Cross are forces that cannot be defeated. In silence and suffering, in the heartbreaking effort to be honest in the midst of dishonesty (most of all our own dishonesty), in all these is victory. It is Christ in us who drives us through darkness to a light of which we have no conception and which can only be found by passing through apparent despair. Everything has to be tested. All relationships must be tried. All loyalties have to pass through fire. Much has to be lost. Much in us has to be killed, even much that is best in us. But Victory is certain."[1]

Mark's gospel is for those who become stumbling blocks for others: for those who fail miserably yet stand up and learn to see and walk again and again; for those who betray, even knowing Jesus, let alone commit out loud to being his follower or his friend; for those who need to be forgiven in public, and welcomed back—they know they must repent and do restitution so that others will not fail because of their cowardice, ignorance, or self-righteousness. Mark's gospel is for everyone but especially for those in leadership positions and those who are teachers and preachers; for those who do rituals and sacraments in the community and whose public lives are supposed to reveal to others the core teachings and demands of Jesus—and to remember that true disciples are unlikely folk, not necessarily noticed by those in charge, but appreciated and singled out by Jesus.

Mark's gospel is about the Cross—as the sign of freedom, of hope, of possibility in everything, most especially in the hard, grinding, and terrifying moments of life in confrontation with others, in times of violence and hate, and in the presence of war, rejection, persecution, and possible loss of all that is dear to us, including our very lives. But under no circumstances are we to react or respond with violence or harm. The disciple is called to compassion, solidarity with the other, the one in most need—even to the sinner and the enemy. This is the heart of Mark's gospel.

Chapter 3

THE GOSPEL OF MARK NOW

War is as outmoded as cannibalism, chattel slavery, blood-feuds, and dueling, an insult to God and humanity . . . a daily crucifixion of Christ.

MURIEL LESTER

MARK'S GOSPEL, THE FIRST OF THE FOUR GOSPELS HISTORI-cally, provides a background for all of Jesus's words and work. Mark's Jesus is born in a very specific time, place, culture, race, and religion. Those particulars provide the backdrop, the foundation, and what has been called "the matrix" of Jesus's message and person. We often relate to Jesus very singularly as individuals, and yet Jesus drew followers around him and situated his message in the context of a way to live together in society. The early Christians were first called the "Followers of the Way"—the way of the Cross, the way of Jesus the Crucified One, and the way of the Good News. Jesus and those who believed in him made their way through Palestine, from Galilee to Jerusalem, a distance of about ninety miles. They traveled through occupied territory to the city of Jerusalem, the center of Jewish religion, culture, nationalism, and the site of the hopes of the Jewish people once again being a sovereign nation. It was along roads of commerce and enmeshed among other nationalities, cultures, and religions.

It began as a way steeped in the testament of the Jewish people, including their history and hopes, but it forged a way that developed and branched out universally. The development was precipitated by historical events. The most dramatic and far-reaching was the Judean revolt against the Roman occupying army in the years

AD 66–70 and the destruction of the Temple in 70. The way led in time through oppression, stark poverty, slow starvation, humiliation, terror, and imperial domination that overshadowed every area of life: economics, politics, the practice of religion, and daily survival of not only individuals but a people and their traditions.

This backdrop or matrix is described by Ched Myers in realistic and shuddering detail.

> A series of Herodian dynasties loyal to Caesar ruthlessly exploited the peasant majority: debt burdens forced many subsistence farmers off their traditional lands, imperial economic policies disrupted village life, and grinding poverty increased while the elite lived in luxury. So the historic matrix of both Jesus and Mark was shaped deeply by the "spiral of violence": structural oppression, reactive violence, and counter-reactive military suppression. It is a scenario, sadly, that remains all too familiar in our world.[1]

Mark's gospel begins like a bat out of hell, to use an old expression. It leaps off the page and demands immediate attention. HERE begins the Good News!

> The beginning of the good news of Jesus Christ, the Son of God. As it is written in the prophet Isaiah, "See, I am sending my messenger ahead of you, who will prepare my way; the voice of one crying out in the wilderness: 'Prepare the way of the Lord, make his paths straight.'"
>
> John the Baptizer appeared in the wilderness, proclaiming a baptism of repentance for the forgiveness of sins. And people from the whole Judean countryside and all the people of Jerusalem were going out to him, and were baptized by him in the river Jordan, confessing their sins. (Mk 1:1–5)

The opening line isn't even a sentence! It interrupts history and breaks into reality. It situates the narrative of Jesus in the line of prophets—fiery, unorthodox, revolutionary, truth-telling, and demanding change—figures who appear in Israel's history when God is not being worshipped or honored, the poor are neglected (the criteria for faithfulness in the covenant God has with the people), and justice is disdained. The prophets all come to a harsh end, exiled, tortured, murdered, butchered, all hated and feared because of their words. Jesus is initiated—baptized into this tradition by John, who will be butchered while Herod is at a dinner party, beheaded after time in prison on the whim of Herod's wife. John is clear that he goes before another—one with power beyond anything he knows. John works with water but this one coming will work with fire and the Holy Spirit! This is crucial because when Jesus begins his own ministry, he calls men and women to follow him in this prophetic, truth-telling, and demanding tradition. This is the way it begins. Listen:

> Now after John was arrested, Jesus came to Galilee, proclaiming the good news of God, and saying, "The time is fulfilled, and the kingdom of God has come near; repent, and believe in the good news."
>
> As Jesus passed along the Sea of Galilee, he saw Simon and his brother Andrew casting a net into the lake—for they were fishermen. And Jesus said to them, "Follow me and I will make you fish for people." And immediately they left their nets and followed him. As he went a little farther, he saw James son of Zebedee and his brother John, who were in their boat mending the nets. Immediately he called them; and they left their father Zebedee in the boat with the hired men, and followed him. (Mk 1:14–20)

The message seems disarmingly simple and engaging—the Good News of God and now is the time—turn, let go of the past and your old way of life, your old ways of thinking and perceiving reality, and believe! Yet every word is subversive. There already was "good news." It was Caesar's and it was delivered on a regular basis throughout the empire, detailing the number of soldiers, the number of acres planted and harvested (to feed Rome and the army), the number of people enslaved and conquered, and the Pax Romana that ruled the land with a heavy hand. It was the good news of the conqueror, the oppressor, the empire.

With the words "the time is fulfilled," the announcement is one of hope—all the promises, all the waiting, all the suffering of generations before and now would soon be over. Now the prophet's announcements would become reality. Now it will be God's domain, God's justice and peace that will prevail—not Rome's or any other nation's or army's. There are only two things necessary—or really, three: repent and believe. Repent means to come full circle so as to face in the opposite direction; to believe is to stake one's life on a word, a person, a hope, and make it come true in your flesh and blood and history. Finally, the third necessity is that all of this is done together with others, in a company, a band that models how to do it right here and right now.

John comes from the wilderness. Jesus is driven into the wilderness. The Israelite people were born in the wilderness. The wilderness is the mysterious realm and locus of God's power of Spirit and Word. Out of the wilderness they came into the river Jordan, and then to the cities, like Tiberias, built overlooking the Sea of Galilee, and Sepphoris, about an hour's walk from Nazareth and Jerusalem. They are all cities of kings and emperors and are there to oversee, to enforce Rome's domination, and to extort as much money, food crops, labor, and trade as possible out of the people. Every aspect of life was controlled so that Rome benefited from local labor—endless taxes and tithes on food, fish, water, transport, land (seeded or not), wine, animals, slaves. Fishermen and farmers were the hardest hit and among some of the poorest—Jesus calls fishermen and their families first! He comes from Nazareth but makes his home in Capernaum, on the main road from Galilee to Jerusalem for traders and commerce.

The beginnings of Jesus's ministry and calling others to move with him occur among the poorest, and his intent is prophetic. The first chapter of Mark echoes the forty-second chapter of Isaiah both in its description of the prophet Jesus and in his preaching—his words and presence announce: "See, the former things have come to pass, and new things I now declare; before they spring forth, I tell you of them." Some of these new things are spelled out: it is God who gives life and breath to the earth and all the people who

walk on it. The words summon others to move and change and alter
their circumstances and transform the way the live. Listen:

> I am the Lord, I have called you in righteousness, I have taken you by the
> hand and kept you; I have given you as a covenant to the people, a light to
> the nations, to open the eyes that are blind, to bring out prisoners from the
> dungeon, from the prison those who sit in darkness. (Is 42:6–7)

This is the work, the dream to be pursued in public together on
behalf of others. Earlier in the text the Way is carefully crafted and
described—the way of no violence, no harm, no destruction, no
killing, and thus, no war. Jesus will be a force to be reckoned with
continually, but he will not use the methods of Rome or those in
collusion with its power. This is how he will bring God's ways into
the world.

> Here is my servant, whom I uphold, my chosen, in whom my soul delights;
> I have put my spirit upon him; he will bring forth justice to the nations.
> He will not cry or lift up his voice, or make it heard in the street; a bruised
> reed he will not break, and a dimly burning wick he will not quench; he will
> faithfully bring forth justice. He will not grow faint or be crushed until he
> has established justice in the earth; and the coastlands wait for his teaching.
> (Is 42:1–4)

This is the style of Jesus, his spirituality and soul, and this is
what he will attempt to share and seed in his followers so that they
can redeem and save the soul of their people, their nation, and all
the cities and coastlands. Justice is the core, heart, foundation, and
method of God's ways on earth. Where there is justice, there are
no poor and there is abiding peace. This is Jesus's Good News
of God's ways on earth. It is a revolution but not one that calls
people into the streets to attack and destroy—it is the opposite.
Whatever is weak is to be strengthened. Whatever waivers is to be
made firm. Whoever is in pain is to be given solace, healing, and

companionship. Whatever flicker of hope and life is there is to be nurtured and encouraged. Faithfulness and enduring grace characterize all of life, though it will know suffering and death, rejection and failure. But God is in the world now, and the die is cast—the call and summons has been voiced—and immediately you have to respond.

The call comes to two sets of brothers first, who had probably listened to Jesus in the crowds on the shore, and he stirred their hopes. They respond. Peter (Simon, later called Peter) and Andrew, laying aside their livelihood, fall in behind him as he hits the road. James and John leave their father and the hands hired to continue the family's struggle to survive and cast in their lot with Jesus. He has four fledgling followers.

Peter will emerge as a sort of leader when Jesus isn't necessarily present, while James and John (dubbed the "sons of thunder") will play their part in stirring up controversies among the other followers; by now the followers include twelve named men and at least eight or more named women. But Peter will also be constantly seen as failing to understand what Jesus is teaching and saying, though the others are with him in that regard. The acknowledged disciples close to Jesus seem dense while others not so positioned get the message and practice it immediately. Peter, in his role as spokesman for the group, will get himself into trouble, though he is often only speaking what the others feel but do not say. It begins. Jesus will ask them repeatedly after he preaches or something has happened: "Do you not yet understand?" (Mk 8:21). But they do not yet understand—and won't until after Jesus is raised from the dead.

HALFWAY THROUGH THE gospel it becomes apparent that Peter and the disciples are pulling away from Jesus. When Jesus asks them who the people say he is, they are quick to answer correctly: "John the Baptist; and others, Elijah; and still others, one of the prophets" (Mk 8:28). But when he pushes them for an answer it is

Peter who pipes up with "You are the Messiah." Jesus responds by sternly ordering them not to tell anyone about him (Mk 8:29–30). Peter thinks or hopes his answer is correct, but it is so far off base; Jesus is about God's kingdom, not driving the Romans out of Judea and setting up another Jewish nation-state. He is about driving hate, division, nationalism, fear of differences, harsh judgments of others, and anger out of people's hearts. He does not want them to make his mission and teaching problematic for others—he is trying to seed a revolution of heart, mind, soul, lifestyles, and community, not build a kingdom. They are not getting it.

Peter, however, begins to verbally reject Jesus's words after Jesus begins to teach in public that he will be rejected by his own nation and its leaders, handed over to be tortured, crucified, and raised up from the dead. We are told: "Peter took him aside and began to rebuke him. But turning and looking at his disciples, he rebuked Peter and said, 'Get behind me, Satan! For you are setting your mind not on divine things but on human things' " (Mk 8:31–33). This is the turning point in Mark's gospel. From here on, Jesus is on his own—rejected by his own people, the people of his hometown, Nazareth, his family, and now by the ones he called to follow him and be a part of making this dream of God come true. The translation would better read: you are not thinking like God but thinking like everyone else in dominant culture, your peer group, and those in power. Peter, and everyone else from here on out, fails Jesus and fails to be his follower. This is crucial—not only for them in their becoming those who will be Christ-bearers, but for all who have any leadership position or place of prestige or closeness among the followers of Jesus today. This is what Alan Jamieson says about the meaning of Peter's failure to live up to Jesus's words and what that tells us today.

> The failing of Peter and many other biblical characters is not just a peripheral issue but failure that strikes at the very heart of their place of strength and conviction. Failure at the very point where they felt they were able to achieve. Failure in the most important areas for them. Perhaps it is only

as we encounter, own, acknowledge, and grieve this personal failure that we know the desert of failure and the grace and growth that God offers through it.[2]

Peter will continue to fail, and all the disciples will be a part of that failure. Whenever they hear Jesus speaking about what will happen to him—reality therapy for them—they ignore what he has to say. They don't understand, but they don't ask him about it, either: they are afraid. In fact, they begin to play games of power among themselves. When Jesus is not around (though he questions them about it), they begin to discuss and argue about which one among them will be the greatest and have the most power. Jesus rebukes them again with these words: "Whoever wants to be first must be last of all and servant of all" (Mk 9:33–35). They hear but they do not take his words to heart.

When he has three times tried to get them to listen to him as he speaks of what will be done to him, James and John become even more insensitive to Jesus's sideways invitation to accompany him and stay with him when he will lay down his life for his words, for God's way, and for all people of the earth. They approach him and want a favor—they want to sit at his right and left hand when he enters his glory. They are oblivious to the fact that if he is crucified that would put them on either side of him when he dies, and they are still convincing themselves that he will be ruling as the Messiah, king in Jerusalem, and they will be sharing earthly power with him. He questions them on whether or not they can share in his pain—drink the cup he will drink and be baptized with his baptism (of pain, suffering, and death). They answer, of course—but of course they can't and won't. No one will stay with him when he is taken to die (Mk 10:35–40). This request causes dissension among the others, and so Jesus tries to be clear with them about their role in God's way.

So Jesus called them and said to them, "You know that among the Gentiles those whom they recognize as their rulers lord it over them, and their great

*ones are tyrants over them. But it is not so among you; but whoever wishes
to become great among you must be your servant, and whoever wishes to
be first among you must be slave of all. For the Son of Man came not to be
served but to serve, and to give his life as a ransom for many. (Mk 10:42–45)*

When Jesus tries to warn them all that they will desert him at
the moment when they should stand with him, Peter protests that
he will not! With bravado he declares: "Even though I must die with
you, I will not deny you." The rest of the disciples said the same
(Mk 14:31). But they all do, and Peter most vehemently, again and
again—not before a tribunal, a court of law, or anyone with any
power, but to a serving girl in the courtyard where they wait trying not to be noticed while Jesus is convicted in a sham trial under
cover of darkness.

Jesus is betrayed by one of his chosen followers with a kiss. He
calls him friend still, knowing the bitterness of such isolation and
loneliness. One of the group (traditionally it is Peter) grabs a sword
and cuts off the ear of the slave of the high priest. It is an act of
violent rage and frustration, reactive and brutal—the slave lived
in a position worse even than that of a freeman like Peter. Jesus
responds with power and dignity, once again revealing the utter
strength of never using violence—even to save himself from torture
and death. He will not let his followers use violence. It is a total
contradiction of everything he is, preaches, and lives—everything
he reveals about God.

> *Then Jesus said to them, "Have you come out with swords and clubs to ar-
> rest me as though I were a bandit? Day after day I was with you in the
> temple teaching, and you did not arrest me. But let the scriptures be ful-
> filled." All of them deserted him and fled. (Mk 14:48–50)*

Jesus is spit upon, struck, humiliated by religious leaders and
their followers. False witnesses are paid to condemn and lie about
what he has taught. He has been set up by one of his own, and now
those who find him dangerous to their carefully controlled positions

of power (even under oppression) infiltrate his inner group. They condemn him to death, though they do not have the power to enforce the decision. But they do have their own soldiers, and they are allowed to mock and blindfold him, beat and torture him for the rest of the night. Jesus will go through it all again with Pilate, who lets his soldiers brutalize and torture him again before the actual execution begins with Jesus carrying his Cross through the city and outside to the garbage dump. Even as he dies he is derided by people passing by and those dying with him. But then there is one line—a sliver of hope is given. Listen:

> *There were also women looking on from a distance; among them were Mary Magdalene, and Mary the mother of James the younger and of Joses, and Salome. These used to follow him and provided for him when he was in Galilee; and there were many other women who had come up with him to Jerusalem.* (Mk 15:40–41)

Oddly enough, in the gospels, it is not the twelve named disciples of Jesus who are seen as models of believers or even as followers: it is the women, some named and some not, and individuals singled out as those the disciples should learn from, imitate, obey, and follow their practice. Jesus uses a child to indicate how they are to see themselves in the community. Children had no power—they had to obey anyone, from their own families, village, synagogue, and even strangers. They had to obey anyone bigger or stronger than them. Jesus compares himself to that child who gives his life as ransom and does not lord it over anyone.

He singles out the widow who gives so little and yet it is her sustenance and so he says that she is like him, giving even what she has to live on as worship and as obedience to the covenant (Mk 12:41ff). Days before he is betrayed he praises an unnamed woman at a public dinner party for her public anointing of him, wasting a year's wages on a small vial of ointment, standing with him. She has done what she could, anointing his body for burial while others dismiss her, are infuriated and enraged with her. But she's his follower in public. At another point he praises a Syro-Phoenician woman, an outsider to Judaism, for her great faith, her endurance, and her compassion on behalf of another (Mk 7:24–30).

Now, three more women are named. They stand at a distance, but they are there and they will be among the women who will go to the tomb in the morning, seeking to anoint his body for burial and will instead be given the Good News of God—the resurrection of Jesus and that he is going before them all into Galilee. They will be the first preachers, teachers, evangelists. It is said that the unnamed woman who anointed him earlier at the dinner party is Salome—she is a watcher near the Cross and she will be there in the morning light, too.

But this is a reality throughout the gospels. There are many who do follow Jesus who are not privy to being one of the chosen/named. It begins early on, in the first chapter. After Jesus calls Peter, Andrew, James, and John, teaches in the synagogue on the Sabbath, and heals someone who is unclean (having a psychotic episode, perhaps), he leaves. But immediately everything around him begins to shift.

> As soon as they left the synagogue, they entered the house of Simon and Andrew, with James and John. Now Simon's mother-in-law was in bed with a fever, and they told him about her at once. He came and took her by the hand and lifted her up. Then the fever left her, and she began to serve them. (Mk 1:29–31)

The story is so short it can easily be lost in more striking accounts, but it is remarkable in its own right. The first thing Jesus does after the Sabbath synagogue service is to go to someone's house—there would be a Sabbath meal shared with friends, neighbors, and family. But when he goes into Peter's house he is told immediately that Peter's mother-in-law is ill. In those days a fever was life-threatening and joined with poor diet, slow starvation, and unclean water it was often a desperate situation—unfortunately common. We are told that Jesus goes to her. In the Greek translation, he grasps her by the hand and raises her up. The language is biblical and strong. It harks back to Isaiah 42:6–7, where the prophet declares: "I am the Lord, I have called you in righteousness, I have taken you by the hand and kept you; I have given you as a covenant to the people, a light to the nations, to open the eyes that are blind, to bring out prisoners from the dungeon, from the prison those who sit in darkness." Jesus is grasping her, out of illness, out of her darkness and life in Capernaum, in a fishing village, in occupied territory, and claiming her, raising her up to work for the justice and righteousness, the holiness of God!

Immediately the fever leaves her and she rises up and serves—waits on them! The Greek word *diakonos,* meaning *deacon,* in fact, means one who both serves at the table in liturgy and worship and serves the poor and is the presence of God's Good News in his or her flesh and words. Now Jesus has five followers! The first four were summoned, and the fifth responded in gratitude. Her house, more like a hut, becomes the gathering place for those desperate, like her, for healing, hope, a word of encouragement, and the Good News of God present in Jesus and now in those who believe in him. The threshold of her house becomes the doorway to God's way on earth. This is the household of God, a fledging Church where Jesus and his disciples will return again and again—home base.

Peter has a mother-in-law! This means, of course, that Peter, like most of the disciples, excluding perhaps John, who is referred to as young (maybe age twelve to fifteen), was married. But there is no mention of his wife; the general understanding of the Scriptures is that if you are not named either you are not a follower of Jesus or you have died. Most likely Peter's wife has died. One out of every two women died in childbirth in those years, and availability of food and water, the harvests, sickness, and general strength and health were also factors. Peter's mother-in-law lives with Peter's family, tending to their needs, meals, clothing, gathering water, dung, and so on. If his wife died in childbirth, then Peter's mother-in-law is also raising the child, most likely a girl.

All of this essential information has often been lost as the

Church grew and spread beyond Jewish boundaries into the Gentile world and later into the Roman world, becoming synonymous with the Holy Roman Empire. The Church became an institution, sanctioned by the state, and it was law that everyone would be Christian, and the structures, the "system," of Church became Roman in culture, law, domination, liturgical practice, ministry, mission, preaching, teaching, and lifestyle. It became, in essence, the good news of Rome again, swallowing much of Jesus's Good News of God and making Jesus's Word and presence and way and hope serve the empire.

By the third and fourth centuries the structure of Church with the hierarchy in total control is not recognizable as anything Jesus preached. There is a priesthood that has become as entrenched and exclusive as that of the Jewish community. Leaders, teachers, theologians, bishops, and deacons have become more interested in what you believe as a Christian—in doctrines, dogmas, and what others teach about Jesus—rather than what is practiced in obedience to Jesus's Word. And law—canon law—takes the place of any Jewish legal system alongside Roman law. Women practically disappear, except as extremes of what is good and what is evil, with no one in between. Ordinary people are dumped into a category, the laity, when in reality THEY ARE THE CHURCH, THE BODY OF CHRIST. The leadership that decrees one must be celibate or virgin to have any role in the Church no longer practices being servants—they are now those who "lord" it over all the others.

Today there are 7 billion people on earth. Among those billions are 1.1 billion Catholics. That number is less than the population of the continent of India. Catholics are about one-seventh of the world's people, concentrated primarily in Western countries: in northern and eastern Europe, in North and South America, a modest number in Africa through colonialism, and very few in Asia, where the majority of human beings live. The majority of those 1.1 billion people—approximately 98 percent—are the actual Body of Christ the Church. The other 2 percent comprises the pope, cardinals, bishops, priests, deacons, and members of religious orders of men and women. And yet ordinary people, believers, find themselves with very little power within Jesus's community and with no leaders to serve them. The structures of the institution of the Catholic Church throughout the last two thousand years have become comfortable with being a nation-state and the dominant power within Europe and often the dominant power of religion (within the larger groupings of Christians). It has been the undergirding and vanguard of colonialism, slavery, nationalism, capitalism, globalization, wars, both civil and worldwide; the structures of prisons, the place of torture; and the seat of those who blessed the armies of both sides, siding in the end with whomever won or allowed them limited freedom to continue to be Church—generally speaking. The Cross became inverted and indistinguishable from the sword, forcing baptism on the population, or else. Violence, murder, enslavement, and all the usual practices of the systems of power in the world became common practice in the Church.

In each generation, there have always been preachers and prophets within the Church who sought to temper the collusion between the Church and the state, calling all believers, those who yield power and those without love of one's enemies, to forgiveness and compassion—these prophets stood alone, a voice crying out in the wilderness much like John the Baptist. There have been those who cried out and sought peace in each generation, like Francis traveling during the time of the Crusades to the Muslim caliph, going into the lion's den, so to speak, to open a door to dialogue and the cessation of war—in vain. One courageous lamb cannot alter the face of war—he or she can only herald the cry of the prophets of old, like Isaiah and Jesus, the Lamb of God. More recently, in the last fifty years, the bishops of the United States wrote a Peace Pastoral seeking to call the Church to examine its stance in support of nuclear weapons and contemporary warfare. Similarly, in the months before John Paul II died, he sought to reexamine the concept of Augustine's oft misused "just war theology" that begins with the reminder that there is no such thing as a "just war" but allows that war is is permitted only under stringent conditions. But even Augustine ignored and left out the four-hundred-year teaching and practice of the Church to not baptize soldiers until they left the army, and then advise them to do penance for the rest of their lives to atone for killing a beloved child of God. Sadly, Augustine's writing on this topic does not refer to any of Jesus's strong words about loving one's enemy and doing good to those whom we fear or who might hate us. It seems by then there is already a disconnect from Jesus's words: "Love one another as I have loved you."

The Church fell into the trap of bending and twisting and ignoring Jesus's Word of the Good News of God and the Spirit of no violence, no harm, and no killing, and being content rather with preaching the bits and pieces of the gospel that were convenient. It turned the Good News of the ways of God on earth into private/personal salvation and focused its attention on the next world, using the Word of God to proof-text its own words rather than as a call to conversion, both collectively and for individuals within the community.

It removed the gospel and the sacraments from most of its members and isolated the leadership from the members of the Body of Christ until the twentieth century. Holiness was modeled in those who were celibate, virgin, monastic. In the early days, martyrdom would automatically get you into that privileged group, though it seems in the twentieth and twenty-first centuries you can be killed, martyred, tortured, or made to disappear and that doesn't necessarily merit recognition of faithfulness or holiness for others. Sometimes children or teens merited the title of saint, but most of the time it helped to die young, be pious, or be killed. Clerics and members of the hierarchy, especially popes, cardinals, and bishops, and religious orders seem to be much holier than all others. Sometimes the leadership held up those who were wealthy or powerful enough in society to get a member of their family or group canonized. It's an enormously expensive prospect. And it's amazing how many men are holy but not women!

All of this—while the rest of the 98 percent of the human race had to deal with sexuality, gender, marriage, family, children, and the support of extended families outside the confines of an ecclesial culture that reflects the wealth, power, and prestige of Western countries. Most people struggle to survive and long for ever more abundant life. Most people struggle to know justice and abiding peace in their lifetimes. Most want to grow old and live without terror and fear for their children in a time and a place without war. Most people, like the majority of the people at the time of Jesus, are dying of slow starvation, with little or no health care or clean water. They find themselves caught in war, drafted, consigned, forced to be soldiers or victims; being unfortunate enough to live in occupied territory or on the run, running for their lives, with no country— migrants, gypsies, tribes, immigrants, refugees—or they belong to the wrong caste, ethnic group, language group, religion, economic bracket, sexual orientation, or gender.

As Archbishop Oscar Romero said: "We cannot separate God's word from the historical reality in which it is proclaimed. That would not be God's word. The Bible would be just a pious history book in our library. It is God's word because it enlightens, contrasts, repudiates, praises what is going on today in this society." But we have made just this separation.

Today, as in Mark's time, the first and primary teaching of Jesus is about life. God is the God of life. We belong to God and all life is to be cherished, protected, encouraged, raised up, healed, brought forth, sustained, and no one is to harm another human being, let alone take his or her life. In the early days of Christianity, John Chrysostom, a preacher, said: "It is certainly a great and more wonderful work to change the minds of enemies, bringing about a change of soul, than to kill them!"

Today this wisdom comes more often from sources other than Christians. For instance, this is a story about the Dalai Lama. He was teaching before a huge audience. When it was time for questions, someone asked him, "Why didn't you fight back against the Chinese?" The Dalai Lama didn't immediately reply; instead, he looked down for a moment, swung his feet back and forth a bit (he was sitting up high), then looked at the person who asked the question and at the whole audience, and smiled. "You know," he said, "war is obsolete." There was more silence, and then his face grew solemn and he said, "Of course the mind can rationalize fighting back . . . but the heart, the heart would never understand. Then you would be divided in yourself, the heart and the mind, and the war would be inside you."

The Church has made statements on war and on all sorts of conventional and nuclear and biological weapons, but it hedges—the Church maintains you can have the weapons, and you probably can design new ones, and then it hedges some more. Some members of the hierarchy have also made statements like abortion is always wrong, but war is always understandable and allowed. I quoted that statement once in a church and a ten-year-old girl got up and yelled out, "No, that's wrong. I read a book just this week called *The Arm of the Starfish* by Madeleine L'Engle. It's for eight-year-olds and up. It talks about the ability to regenerate the arm of the starfish and what would that mean if we could do it for humans, too. It's about a man and a woman, both scientists, who learn how to do it, and everyone wants their secret—some want it for good and medicine and to relieve people's pain, and others want to use it for evil, to distort and destroy. And their children have to save their parents and protect their secret and make sure it doesn't fall into the wrong people's hands. They have a friend who helps them who comes into their life at just the right time, and one of the things he tells them is this: 'If you are going to care about the fall of the sparrow, you are not allowed to choose between your birds.'" The entire church was stunned into silence. She turned around and said, "Don't you see? We're not supposed to kill or harm anyone. You can't say killing some people is OK, and—oh, those you can't."

I was stunned—what more would there be to say? Jesus would have cheered her on and probably said, "You go, girl." And she had absorbed more wisdom of Jesus's way than anyone else in that church and more than most of its leaders and teachers had.

Now more than ever, we must return to the words of Jesus and study them in small groups—not for information primarily but for conversion of heart, mind, behaviors, practices, and in relationships, economics, politics, prayer, and worship. The gospel of Mark ends with the women sent by the young man in white in the tomb to "my disciples and Peter" to tell them to return to Galilee—to go home, to go back to where it all started—and when they get there they will see him! Mark's gospel ends abruptly, but later writers added on another couple of paragraphs because it was so awkward and uncomfortable. The original ending is Mark 16:1–8, with these words: "So they went out and fled from the tomb, for terror and amazement had seized them; and they said nothing to anyone, for they were afraid." The gospel shocked people—those who knew Jesus in passing as well as those who sought to follow him in their lives before he died and rose, and afterward, as well. It's supposed to shock us, too.

The Church is born in the death and resurrection of Jesus, but it begins to live and learns to walk in the way of Jesus when the stragglers, those terrified women and the frightened disciples (which would have included the ten to twelve each of men and women named as followers and as many as seventy to eighty others, families, friends, individuals who had come to Jerusalem to celebrate the Passover with Jesus), head back along the way to Galilee—to home. It's ninety miles, so they walk maybe ten miles a day maximum— there are old and young, rich and poor, babes in arms, the sick, probably lepers, people from all classes and economic levels, bound in grieving and in hope. As they walk, they talk—they talk gospel. They tell stories: the ones they heard Jesus tell and the ones that had been passed along, parables and other stories of people touched, changed, healed, accepted, drawn into a group, forgiven, challenged, told the truth, and exhorted to do justice, be merciful, and learn to pray and to live in the way of God's Good News. Most important, they learned they needed one another to do that. It was Martin Luther who said: "A Christian is no Christian." To be a follower of the way, to believe in the Good News of God and to live without violence or harm, revealing to everyone the love and mercy of God, requires that it be done with others.

The women are described as those who followed and provided

for Jesus when he was in Galilee, as well as the many other women who accompanied him to Jerusalem. This is a good description of Jesus's early households, like the home of Peter's mother-in-law, where the whole town gathered to hear Jesus, get a glimpse of him, hoping that he might touch them. They all do go home—do they see Jesus there, as he said they would? Mark's gospel is abruptly worded, but is written in a circle and returns to the first lines: the cry of "HERE" begins the gospel of Jesus Christ. Here, once again, today. Here in the United States (as in Galilee or wherever the gospel is preached); here begins the Good News of God. Here we repent again, turn again, and believe again. Here we hear the gospel and catch what we missed the first time around and the second time and the hundredth time. It is concentric circles, spiraling down and in—or as C. S. Lewis says, "Further up and further in."

The gospel is food for the way, taken in daily doses and meant to be shared with others in feasts, picnics, banquets, and around tables. Jesus's altar was always the table, and the talk is as nourishing and as essential as the food—not just the bread and wine, but the actual food—so that the ritual reflects the mystery celebrated in the world: that all are fed in body, soul, mind, and heart. Along with the talk and food is the community itself that is held together by the Spirit of the Risen Lord—and we can see him most clearly in others, with others, as they need to see the presence and the face of the Lord in our own persons and lives. Thomas Merton wrote:

> We all exist solely for this—to be the human place God has chosen for his presence, his manifestation, his epiphany. . . . We are God's words. We echo God, we signify and contain God.

There is an old medieval story that presents us with the summons that Jesus brought to earth—to repent, turn, and believe in only God's Good News, not any other on the earth. Mark's gospel is about making us choose, decide, and act again and again to walk the way of God in the world. It is no easier for us now than it was for Peter, James, John, and the other disciples—or for Peter's mother-in-law, Mary of Magdala, Salome, Mary the mother of James and Joses, the widow in the temple, the Syro-Phoenician woman, or the mothers, fathers, and kin of the disciples. The story has a number of titles: it's been called "Two Mirrors," "Have You Checked Your Glasses Lately?," and "The Hinderer." I've been told it sounds like a tale from Hans Christian Andersen, but I cannot find it.

Once upon a time the world was very young. There had been a battle in heaven and the angels of light won. But they had forced Lucifer (The Light), now called Satan (The Hinderer), out and he and his followers had nowhere else to go but earth. (Why didn't angels think of that?) Satan loved to make trouble, to confuse people, cause chaos, and generally just make life harder for everyone. That was his name now—the one who hinders others from living, from being the children of God, from knowing and living out the truth.

One day, while trying to think of things to do, Satan chanced upon an idea. He was intrigued by mirrors—anything that reflected back to the viewer what he or she was looking at. What if he made a mirror that didn't reflect back everything as it was but instead reflected back a shrunken version of what was good and beautiful and an enlarged version of what was distorted and violent? It took awhile but the mirror was made, and now Satan roamed the earth letting people catch a glimpse of what they could see in the mirror. He traveled the length and breadth of the world and in no time at all everyone had caught a glimpse of what was seen in the mirror. They all got a good look at the violence, the anger, the distortion, lacks, and what they took to be ugly, which was often only something different or what they'd not experienced or seen before.

The Hinderer took great delight in spreading this sense of horror, of what could be inhuman as stronger and more true than anything good, beautiful, filled with light, or creative and new. And one day he dropped the mirror. First he was annoyed—his toy was broken—but then he realized it had shattered into millions of tiny fragments. Just then a great storm rose and the wind began to scatter the fragments everywhere. Satan was overjoyed. Why hadn't he thought about that before? Now the bits of the mirror would work anywhere and anyone could pick them up. The bits were as fine as sand and grit, and they could lodge in people's eyes, causing constant irritation until they were washed out.

Later, when things like spectacles and mirrors, small and great, were made, many of the pieces were ground together with other substances and made into glasses—to see through, to drink from, to reflect images large and small, and everywhere people's vision was damaged. Now God was aware of all this and knew what needed to be done; in fact, he had had it in mind when the angels cast Satan and his followers down to earth in the first place. God decided it was time to send his own image, his beloved child, a human one like all the others who, of course, saw truly and did not see or do evil, or distort, or do violence. This child/man/human being would be the reflection of God's own justice, mercy, truth, and peace, and once you had seen the face of Jesus, then you would know what God intended the world and every human being to look like and to see.

Jesus came, was born, and grew. There was Good News spoken and stories told of hope and why we were really created—we were to give delight like his firstborn child did and to draw all people into the way of God, the way of justice for all, abundant life and abiding peace. If you glanced into the eyes of Jesus you saw yourself reflected back and what a glory that was! No matter who you were or what you'd done or said you were seen with the eyes of glory, of true sight and clear vision—with the eyes of acceptance, love, and challenge to be God's-eye view of you.

There were those who loved the mirror and those who sought to shatter the mirror. The mirror threatened as well as encouraged people. But you could not stand before the mirror and not react or respond. The mirror was broken, and buried. But now the mirror was raised to life again and the Spirit still lives and wanders the world—there is no place on earth where the light and the sound of the mirror's shattering is not! It is found in all of creation, in the eyes of all human beings, and especially in those who were once considered ugly, sick, enemies, strangers, different, threatening, poor, even sinners and outcasts. For now the mirror reflects the truth—that there is darkness and light and both are beautiful. All that God has made is fashioned of glory. But it still helps if you have a pair of those glasses! But it's easy to find a set: the wisdom and the eye of God is still found in Jesus—in the gospels and in the words you hear—and you hear better with your eyes open!

Perhaps a way to end this chapter is with a long quote about Jesus. The gospels all give a portrait, a lens through which to see the face of God in Jesus. Each is colored by the place, the time, the people, the situations, and the needs of the community that was seeking to reflect and incarnate in their own lives, singularly but especially together in common, the wisdom, the truth, and the way of God that was in the flesh and heart, the mind and soul, of Jesus. Each of us singularly reflects some aspect of Jesus, and each small community and the communities together reflect something of Jesus—but there is always more to absorb, and to be incarnated in our bodies and the Body of Christ universally. This piece is called "Christianity's Gift" by Walter Wink:

All Christianity has to give, and all it needs to give, is the myth of the human Jesus. It is the story of Jesus the Jew, a human being, the incarnate son of the man: imperfect but still exemplary, a victim of the Powers yet still victorious, crushed only to rise again, in solidarity with all who are ground to dust under the jackboots of the mighty, healer of those under the power of death, lover of all who are rejected and marginalized, forgiver, liberator, exposer of the regnant cancer called "civilization"—that Jesus, the one the Powers killed and whom death could not vanquish. Jesus' is the simple story of a person who gambled his last drop of devotion on the reality of God and the coming of God's new world. In the process, he lived out, in his flesh and blood, the archetype of the son of the man, the Child of the Human One, Sophia's Child, the New Being, the Sisterchild—call it what you will—as the intimation of what that new humanity might entail. In doing so, he not only incarnated God, he changed the way the people experienced God. In short, the gift of Christianity to the world, as the Hindu Gandhi saw with such lucidity, is not Christianity, but Jesus, revealer and catalyst of our true humanity.[3]

The first words of Jesus in Mark's gospel ring out again and again. All who claim to be Christian, to be Catholic, to be the Church as individual believers and as communities, begin again here: "The time is fulfilled, and the kingdom of God has come near; repent, and believe in the good news." Here we begin with every moment to walk in the way of God, with Jesus in the Spirit, together. All else in our religious belief, practices, devotions, and structures must once again serve this conversion and radical shift to live without violence, harm, killing, war, or the sanction of any form of death, and instead to live sharing all that has been given to human beings. The Church should not be a system or an institution but a movement and a people who together image God as a community that serves, includes, and welcomes all. And Jesus will keep saying to us, "Do you not yet understand?"

Chapter 4

THE GOSPEL OF MATTHEW THEN

If you want to build a ship, don't herd people together to collect wood and don't assign them tasks and work but rather, teach them to long for the endless immensity of the sea.

ANTOINE DE SAINT-EXUPÉRY

THE GOSPEL OF MATTHEW WAS WRITTEN, IN THE FORM WE have, about twenty-five years after the gospel of Mark. Historically much ensued in the duration. The Judeo-Roman war ended disastrously with the destruction of the Temple in Jerusalem—the rebuilding process had just been finished around the time of Jesus's death and resurrection—and the Jewish people were forced to change their Sabbath worship into synagogue worship. The wait for the Messiah who would restore Israel and the Jewish sense of identity as God's chosen people, and now restore the Temple, was ongoing. The fledging Christian community, originally a sect within Judaism, split from Jewish believers and surged out into the known world along trade routes and through slave and merchant society alike. Prior to the war, the Jews had sought the presence and the power of the Christians to fight with them against the Romans to protect the Temple in Jerusalem. The Christians agonized over whether to align themselves with their own people or with the Jewish population, and ultimately decided wholeheartedly that they could not join the Jews and fight with them.

When the war was finished and the Temple no longer existed (only the Wailing Wall remains to this day), open hostility formed between the Christians and the Jews, even while the Romans continually persecuted both groups. Along with this bombardment from outside the community, inside the community itself there were growing factions and dissension. Followers were no longer considered Jewish by the Jewish religious and economic leaders, but if they were not Jewish, then who were they? Meanwhile, the Christians were being mercilessly attacked by the state of Rome as traitors, who just by their existence were a danger to Rome and all of its values and national ideals. In many regards the gospel of Matthew is about identity: just who is a Christian? What values characterize the community's behavior and lifestyle? If they are no longer waiting for the Messiah, then what are they waiting for, or living in expectation of, as they proclaim Jesus as Lord and seek to draw others to become his disciples?

There are three things that the gospel of Matthew seeks to balance and juggle: the violent climate the community finds itself trying to live gracefully within; the tensions and need for an identity among themselves as the followers of Jesus; and how to live the teachings of Jesus among themselves as well as among those who betrayed them, tortured them, and made their lives difficult by exclusion, persecution, physical harm, and hatred. The answers to these questions are simple, stark: Christians are to live a life without violence or harm to anyone, no matter what circumstances they find themselves a part of; this is fleshed out in the mystery of Jesus's teachings on forgiveness. Who are the Christians? They are the beloved brothers and sisters of Jesus, the beloved children and servants of God, and in the power of the Spirit they live to be peacemakers, bridge builders, and reconcilers within their own communities and in connection with the larger world. What are they living for in hope? They are uncovering, revealing, and building the kingdom of justice that brings abiding peace upon earth now, though it will be a long time coming in its fullness.

A Buddhist story puts a number of these realities into perspective, revealing their power and the problematic nature of trying to integrate them into personal life and in communal contexts in the midst of a world that looks upon religious people as a dangerous threat to the dominant culture and society.

Once upon a time Buddha decided to go on a journey to see some of his friends, do a pilgrimage, and preach, as he always did, to anyone he met along the way. But his plans were changed, and he needed to get to where he was going more quickly. After thinking about it for a while, he decided to go straight up and over the mountain instead of going around it. As soon as his followers and friends heard what he was intending to do they confronted him. "Master, you can't—it's not safe. That mountain is filled with thieves and bandits. In fact, it's said to be the home of the leader of them all— he's vicious and without any sense of shame. He robs everyone, rich or poor, and shows no mercy. Don't go."

But Buddha just smiled and said to them, "I have nothing worth robbing and I won't stand out on the path." And so in spite of all their concerns and warnings, off he went.

The journey was lovely. He traveled for two days and nights, sleeping in caves and admiring the shift of the seasons—it was autumn—and delighting in being alone. However, on the third day he heard the pounding hooves of a horse. Suddenly, right in front of him was a heavily armed horseman, sword in hand, shouting at him: "Your money or your life!" Buddha looked up at the man, put his hands in the pockets of his robe, and pulled them inside out— empty! And he said to him, "No money, so I guess it's going to be my life!" The bandit was startled but regathered his wits about himself and leaned forward, sword in hand, to take Buddha's life.

"Wait just a minute!" Buddha roared. "You know the rules! If you are going to take my life, then you owe me one wish before I die." The bandit hesitated. He did know the rules, but no one had ever thought to invoke them before now. "OK—what do you want— what's your last wish, old man?"

Buddha gestured toward an old tree alongside the road. "My wish has two parts to it. See that tree! I want you to hack off its largest limb."

The bandit laughed, swung with his sword, and it was done! "Good," said Buddha, "now for the second part—I want you to put the limb back on the tree." The bandit was stupefied and just sat on his horse. Then he started laughing and screaming, "You stupid old man. That's impossible! No one can put a limb back on a tree."

But Buddha looked sternly at him and replied, "You are the only one here who is stupid! Fix what you have destroyed. Any ignoramus, even a thoughtless child, can destroy and chop off things, but it takes power and creativity to undo such idiocy." The man grew wrathful and angry, cursing Buddha.

Buddha calmly continued, "Anyone can kill, or maim, or destroy—it takes no thought or intelligence whatsoever. Real power is found in being able to undo the harm that you and others do. Real power is found in healing what has been broken, in standing in a breach and drawing both sides together, and in imaginatively bringing life and possibility where there was nothing before. That's the only real kind of power."

The bandit now was silent. He got down off his horse and approached Buddha and then fell to his knees before him, saying, "I want that kind of power—can you teach me?"

Buddha answered, "Yes, I can teach you, but it is the hardest discipline of all, bringing life and wholeness out of death and despair. It is a lifelong struggle."

And they say the bandit rose from his knees, dropped his sword, and followed after Buddha. And eventually, long decades after his meeting with Buddha, the bandit became his first disciple, the one who would carry his tradition and teaching beyond Buddha's lifetime.

The story is a teaching koan, or parable, and it is a rare one because it ends "happily ever after," so to speak, whereas in real life this isn't always the case. But the story illustrates some of the issues the early Church of Matthew was struggling to put into practice. The overarching issue of doing no violence in a violent world and meeting violence with creative and imaginative, even life-giving, responses is the first reality. This is the power of Jesus's words, teachings, practice, and the announcement of the presence of the Kingdom of God now abiding in the world, and it is found first most clearly in his own communities. In the story, the bandit responds positively to Buddha's exhortations and explanations, just as many did to the teachings of Jesus, but in reality there were many failures, small and great, after the initial commitment to learning to live and use that kind of power—the power of no violence, no harm, along with gracious and life-sharing relationships and connections. Each individual had to learn to incorporate the teachings into his or her own lifestyle, and this precept of putting the Good News of God's power and reign into practice in the community's affairs and relationships was easier said than done.

The gospel begins with intimations of the extent and depth of the violence that believers would have to contend with consistently. Matthew's gospel begins with the announcement to Joseph, who is engaged to Mary, that she is with child. The law dictated two responses to such a situation: (1) the young woman, as yet unmarried, was to be stoned to death so that both mother and child were killed; (2) the aggrieved man could put away the woman quietly, leaving her without support, economic aid, or a place in the community—reducing the woman and the child to be born to the status of slaves, concubines, outcasts, and public sinners. In other words, the aggrieved man was lawfully able to sentence such a woman to death without actually killing her himself. Thus the violence begins within the community.

It is Joseph who is the image of the catechumen and new believer within the Jewish community. He shifts into a way of living that keeps with the Word of Jesus and is converted as a disciple. The story contains many of the issues, ethics, and teachings that will be core to Matthew's gospel and to how the Christian community is to live in the face of moral dilemmas, danger from others, and what appears to be a life stuck between "a rock and a hard place."

Now the birth of Jesus the Messiah took place in this way. When his mother Mary had been engaged to Joseph, but before they lived together, she was found to be with child from the Holy Spirit. Her husband Joseph, being a righteous man and unwilling to expose her to public disgrace, planned to dismiss her quietly. But just when he had resolved to do this, an angel of the

Lord appeared to him in a dream and said, "Joseph, son of David, do not be afraid to take Mary as your wife, for the child conceived in her is from the Holy Spirit. She will bear a son, and you are to name him Jesus, for he will save his people from their sins." All this took place to fulfill what had been spoken by the Lord through the prophet: "Look, the virgin shall conceive and bear a son, and they shall name him Emmanuel," which means, "God is with us." When Joseph awoke from sleep, he did as the angel of the Lord commanded him; he took her as his wife, but had no marital relations with her until she had borne a son; and he named him Jesus. (Mt 1:18–25)

The paragraph is layered with what has become theological issues and dogmas about who Jesus is, about Mary, and about the mysteries of the Incarnation (God becoming human), but interestingly enough, Joseph's actions have not become the focus of ethical decision making or moral priorities and practice in the Christian community. The story is about law and obedience to it, what constitutes righteousness or justice, and how to decide on a course of action that will have life-or-death consequences for all involved. Joseph is described as a righteous man, high praise indeed for any Jew or Christian. And what does this just man do? He breaks the laws and interprets what the law might mean in a wildly creative and life-giving way—a way that demands much more of him than the law ever did before. Joseph was a Jew, and so he lived on the Word of the Lord as found in the law and the Scriptures. He awaits the coming of the Messiah who will be the presence of God as Justice in the world so clearly that all nations will one day stream to Jerusalem to learn the wisdom of the law and the prophets. In a sense, he eats, sleeps, drinks, and so dreams the Word of the Lord, while he is seeking the will of the Lord in his own life and choices. Joseph dreams about a messenger of God quoting the Word of the Lord to him in a highly unusual and never-before-heard context. In his dream, he's also given an interpretation of that Word that instructs him to disobey all previous interpretations of the law and to act responsibly, freely, with regard for others, and in love. It does not excuse him from obedience to the law, but it gives him a perspective that is larger than his own life, couched in the context of his nation and his religion's belief, one filled with promise and hope. And he names the child—another break with tradition (it was the domain of the woman to name the child).

This story of Joseph learning that love trumps all other interpretations of the law, and that obedience sustains life while demanding new and vibrant relationships in place of what existed previously, all based on the Word of the Scriptures and the prophets, sets the stage for what will happen in Matthew's gospel and how he presents Jesus's core teachings on community life: on forgiveness, reconciliation, restitution, and communion with others for his own disciples, his communities, and their life in the world.

The context of violence continues. The child is born in Bethlehem and wise men (astrologers or scientists) come from the Far East (Persia/Iran) to pay homage to the newborn king of the Jews. Matthew's gospel is all about a kingdom, a domain that is encompassed by justice, welcoming to all, and characterized by abundance and peace that endures. They travel and come to Herod's kingdom asking for directions. Their ignorance in matters of state, coupled with a lack of awareness of Herod's habit of dealing with anything that disturbs him with brute force, triggers what is called the slaughter of the innocents—the massacre of children who are around the age of Jesus and who might be in the vicinity of where he was last thought to be dwelling. Herod is ruthless in wiping out any claims to usurp him, regardless of whether the threat is in his own family or part of an outside rebellion. When the wise men, who have seen Jesus and learned to dream of an alternative to their routes and lives, fail to return to Herod with any significant information, he decrees vengeance and sets in motion a bloodbath.

> When Herod saw that he had been tricked by the wise men, he was infuriated, and he sent and killed all the children in and around Bethlehem who were two years old or under, according to the time that he had learned from the wise men. Then was fulfilled what had been spoken through the prophet Jeremiah: "A voice was heard in Ramah, wailing and loud lamentation,

Rachel weeping for her children; she refused to be consoled, because they are no more." (Mt 2:16–18)

Jesus escapes because his father Joseph dreams again and they flee out of Israel into Egypt, returning only after long years and Herod's death. But this shadow of death and a violent streak of killing will be the backdrop of the gospel, of Jesus's own life, and of the lives of his disciples. Matthew's gospel is incredibly realistic— one must face the power of violence, madness, and armed national power; one must be aware of the evil in the world that is intent on wiping out what it fears and hates. Jesus will eventually be caught in the snare and crucified, and many of his followers will find themselves in the same predicament.

After Jesus's baptism, Matthew inserts a story about the temptations in the desert that teaches his disciples the three things that must undergird their own discipline of life if they are not to be caught in violence or succumb to fear as they seek to uncover and reveal the Kingdom of God, as opposed to the empire of Caesar. The temptations are tests to discover personal weaknesses and areas of strength and power; they show that one has to be aware of these factors throughout one's lifetime, and not simply when initially discovering faith and the Good News of God in Jesus.

There are three tests. The first is to take care of one's own personal needs—and thus of one's family, friends, and community— and to do this in any way possible. In Matthew's gospel, this is shown when Jesus is hungry after fasting and is summoned to turn stones into bread. Instead, he proclaims the Word that people do not live on bread alone but on every Word that comes forth from the mouth of God (Mt 4:4). Jesus does acknowledge that we do need bread and the sustenance and the necessities of life, but even more so we need integrity and respect for others, and in all things we must honor God and chew on the Word of God to know how to live day to day.

The second test is on a larger scale. Jesus is taken to the highest point of Judaism—the top of the Temple—and is baited: he's told to throw himself down. If he really was so closely related to the Holy One, then nothing would happen to him. This is the temptation to use religion to keep one from suffering or even death—to practice one's religion as a safeguard, a security blanket, and a self-righteous crutch that God is there for us when we do what we're supposed to do. Again Jesus's response comes from earlier passages in the Scriptures and he declares: "Again it is written, 'Do not put the Lord your God to the test'" (Mt 4:7).

For the followers of Jesus, religion is about living the fullness of life in the presence of God but not expecting God to protect you from others, from harm, or from your own stupidity on occasion. Religion for Jesus's disciples is trust that God is present in all circumstances, places, relationships, and that God's power is available but is not a given—and is certainly not given as a protection from living in the world or for proving that we're right where others are wrong.

The third and final test is the most inclusive and extensive. Jesus is shown the larger world, including religious groups and structures in culture and institutions. He is told by the forces of evil that he can have it all—the power and the splendors—if only he submits to worshipping false gods, the idols of violence, selfishness, greed, isolation, individualism, hate, racism, nationalism, capitalism—all the isms that demand constant sacrifices of other people's lives and integrity—rage and adherence to law, institution, and worship. Jesus's words are delivered with blunt force: "Away with you, Satan! for it is written, 'Worship the Lord your God, and serve only him'" (Mt 4:10).

These lessons are the basis of Jesus's teachings, his words, his gestures of defiance with some and solidarity with others, and the source of how he sees power, uses it, shares it, and renews it within his life. The first priorities are worship of God: the God of life, of truth, of universal family, of forgiveness, of freedom—and liberation from all the other idols of power and destruction—and of justice, peace, and even mercy, as God has always sought to share with the people who belong to the Holy. His first public words are: "Repent, for the kingdom of heaven has come near" (Mt 4:17). This kingdom of heaven, of God, and of justice and peace for all, is Jesus's vision, hope, work, ministry, and attitude, and it is found first in him and then, hopefully, within his disciples. Glimpses and sights of what Jesus's vision might actually mean can be found by looking at the circle of those who believe in it, seek to bring it closer in all places, and let it be revealed in their relationships, choices, and priorities of life.

In the beatitudes, Jesus praises and encourages those who practice and seek to make this kingdom touchable here and now. They are described as belonging to eight groups: the poor in spirit, who are also the poor in reality, who must rely on one another and God for basic necessities and sustained living; those who mourn, whose sufferings make them act compassionately toward others struggling with lack, indignity, and pain; the meek, meaning the nonviolent and humble, who know their right relation to others and God; those who hunger and thirst for justice, righteousness, and integrity for all, and stand with them in solidarity until they are given their just due; those who are merciful, living with openness to forgiving others and returning to relationships as God is merciful in forgiving and restoring them to the community; the pure in heart, the single-minded who seek God's will first and see all things, people, and situations in the wisdom of God; the peacemakers, whose relationships and work are for unity, communion, understanding, and living as human beings gracefully in the midst of sadness, horror, and joy; and lastly those who are persecuted for doing what is right and just, for standing with those who are the victims of hate, despair, poverty, and violence and boldly—or even timidly—proclaiming that God's will and God's presence is with them. The teachings of Jesus in the early portion of Matthew's gospel are often called the Sermon on the Mount, where the laws of the earlier testament of the Jewish people are upheld but extended to be practiced not just among one's own people but universally; and that obedience to the law must go beyond lip service or interpretation that limits what must be done, or defines what is to be done by others and done by oneself or one's group selectively and differently.

There is much more material in Matthew's gospel on what is to be done and what is to be avoided and on one's attitude toward others than what is found in Mark's gospel. There are many more demands, and Jesus bluntly tells his disciples that they are not above him and that they should expect to be treated as he was treated—maligned with force, lies, rejection, and physical suffering (Mt 10:24). Many core teachings from Mark are repeated again and extended and shifted to connect to the experience of the Christian community fifty years after the life and death of Jesus, facing problems in society, with the Romans, the Jewish leadership, their own families who did not always become Christians, and in-house, in church: "Whoever loves father or mother more than me is not worthy of me; and whoever loves son or daughter more than me is not worthy of me; and whoever does not take up the cross and follow me is not worthy of me. Those who find their life will lose it, and those who lose their life for my sake will find it" (Mt 10:37–39).

Matthew reiterates and reminds the Christian community that their primary relationship is to God the Father in Jesus by the power of the Spirit—as the Body of Christ, the community of believers, bound by water, the Spirit, the Word, and Bread—but expressed in forgiveness, reconciliation, and mercy. They are family beyond blood and marriage ties; beyond mother, father, children, and kin ties and duties. His own family stands outside, not coming into his circle of disciples, and he does not go out to them. He speaks forcibly, almost shockingly, to everyone in hearing range (including his family): "Who is my mother, and who are my brothers?" And pointing to his disciples, he said, "Here are my mother and my brothers! For whoever does the will of my Father in heaven is my brother and sister and mother" (Mt 12:48–50).

Practically all of Jesus's stories/parables begin with a variation on the words "the kingdom of heaven" or "the kingdom of God." This relationship, this place of gathering and dwelling together here on earth has very specific parameters and demands. They all begin with hearing the Word—either his teaching, or a story, or something Jesus has done or a person he has eaten with or touched—and then an image is thrown forth, a seed that grows by the power of the Spirit, which can bring forth a wide range of fruit and expression (Mt 13:18ff), or again, a seed that grows amid other weeds, darnels, and thorns but is allowed to remain for all must grow together. The harvest will reveal the fruit that can be eaten and shared, and what is useless will be burned (Mt 13:24ff). It can be a mustard seed, tiny and easily dismissed, or something that can spread like weeds and take over everything, including well-tended gardens, vineyards, and orchards. While this seed is growing, it attracts birds, which were often considered a danger, but on that patch of ground, the birds find security and hospitality, a dwelling place (Mt 13:31ff).

All of the parables reflect daily life, with its troubles, violence, political and economic realities, strata of society, and how religion either serves this dominant ordering of things or calls it into question and proclaims an alternative that offers freedom, hope, and a newness not perceived before. There are parables of one lost sheep amid ninety-nine that don't stray; of a lost coin off the belt of a woman's dowry; of lost sons and daughters all unaware of their parents' faithful love and devotion to them. The stories speak of those who are greedy and unforgiving: servants who cheat their masters and make deals with other houses and masters, and then beg for forgiveness. There are always surprising reactions and an ending that throws everything up into the air. Many of them are about forgiveness—and what can be if that forgiveness is accepted. But forgiveness must be shared: it cannot be taken and hoarded. Once it becomes a part of your life, then it becomes a lifestyle in relation to everyone else in your life. It is not just a onetime thing, or for a specific group or event; it is communal, constant, and relentless in its practice.

Chapter 18 provides the fulcrum of what a community of disciples is to look like and how they are to live with one another. It shows, layer by layer, what it means to be a disciple, to follow

Jesus with other disciples, and how to deal with evil, sin, dissension, and broken relationships within the group, as well as how the group deals with others who do not belong to it. It begins with the exhortation not to give scandal, and that the greatest in the kingdom are children, meaning the children of God—beloved servants and all those who, like children, have no power in society. But this category of children included pagans, sinners, the sick, the lame, the infirm, women for most of their lives, lepers, and those who disobeyed the law and didn't live up to the expectations of the leaders, the scribes, the Pharisees, and the priests: basically the majority of people. To be a child is to be like Jesus—in relation to God the Father, and in relation to others—waiting on all others, at the beck and call of all others, and servant to all.

The exhortation is extended in hyperbole to not causing scandal—to new believers, to those weak in faith, to actual children, and to all those in the groups above. It demands that we remember the deep connection that we have to all others whenever we are held responsible for our own actions and words. They always impact others and either call them to faithfulness and hope or send them into discouragement, despair, and doing what is wrong. This harsh hyperbole is followed immediately by the parable that is either loved or hated—about a man who had one hundred sheep. This is the way it is told:

> *"What do you think? If a shepherd has a hundred sheep, and one of them has gone astray, does he not leave the ninety-nine on the mountains and go in search of the one that went astray? And if he finds it, truly I tell you, he rejoices over it more than over the ninety-nine that never went astray. So it is not the will of your Father in heaven that one of these little ones should be lost." (Mt 18:12–14)*

This parable/teaching sets up all that is to follow about how to live in community—with failure and with those who betray you or do you wrong or harm you, and with those you love—and about what is the attitude of the community, as individuals and together, toward the wayward wandering one. When this story is told to shepherds they are appalled: they would think twice about leaving the flock behind without supervision and heading off to chase the errant sheep. Sheep are notorious for straying and scattering. A look at any hillside and a shepherd's flock reveals that whatever their community status is, it is at best loose and widely spread out. If a shepherd does go after the one that has left, he hopes there is nothing in the vicinity that will scatter his sheep: no oncoming thunderstorm that would spook them or any predator that would take advantage of the shepherd's absence. The joy, though, in the shepherd's return, and the catching of the stray sheep is easily accepted. But there is always consternation over the last saying: that somehow the rejoicing over the return of the lost means more than the staying power of those who don't stray. Obviously God's vantage point and priorities may not match our own.

This story is definitive in all that follows. There were many who strayed on large issues from giving up one's faith and just running away to actively turning in one's own friends, even family, to the authorities. There were disagreements, marriage difficulties, lying, stealing, and all the usual things humans do when they are together over a period of time. Being baptized or becoming religious doesn't stop it all from happening, and the situation that often develops in the Church is postulated in the following scenario:

> "If another member of the church sins against you, go and point out the fault when the two of you are alone. If the member listens to you, you have regained that one. But if you are not listened to, take one or two others along with you, so that every word may be confirmed by the evidence of two or three witnesses. If the member refuses to listen to them, tell it to the church; and if the offender refuses to listen even to the church, let such a one be to you as a Gentile and a tax collector. Truly I tell you, whatever you bind on earth will be bound in heaven, and whatever you loose on earth will be loosed in heaven. Again, truly I tell you, if two of you agree on earth

about anything you ask, it will be done for you by my Father in heaven.
For where two or three are gathered in my name, I am there among them."
(Mt 18:15—20)

In dealing with altercations or even with issues that are serious enough to call for a trial and a public hearing, there is an agenda to follow and attitudes that must be practiced in community. The underlying premise for all that will happen isn't specifically noted at this point in the gospel, but earlier Jesus taught his disciples to pray. Part of that prayer (the Our Father) clearly states: "Forgive us our debts, as we also have forgiven our debtors" (Mt 6:12). This petition comes immediately after the prayer that God's kingdom come on earth as it is in fullness with God in heaven, and that God's will be done on earth as it is in heaven. God's will is always about life, freedom and unity, forgiveness, and sharing with others.

It seems simple and straightforward enough: first go one to one—good communications theory and skill. Try to work it out together. If that fails, go and get two or three others who are not connected to either of the opponents so that there can be some impartiality and outside input for both to bend, dialogue, and come together. The language is stronger—they are referred to as witnesses, which suggests that this is not a trivial issue but something that impacts many and is concerned with something of import, something that could cause scandal or harm to others. If that fails, then go to the Church. In some renderings of the text, it reads: go to the elders—those who would be deacons/deaconesses, teachers, prophets, and administrators in the community—another level of discourse, interpretation, and exhortation, so that the opposing people could come to some agreement. If all else fails go to the Church—to the assembly of believers. In those days, the communities were small, maybe a hundred or a couple of hundred individuals, and most or many would know by now that something was happening. The issue would be put forth and the Spirit in the community would discuss, talk together, and hopefully draw the person or persons back into the community's embrace. The understanding would have been stated at the beginning that we are all sinners. We all fail. We all need forgiveness. We have all been forgiven. We all need to forgive. But what is most important is that we bend, we submit to one another, we work it through, and we try to undo the harm done and come up with some sort of resolution that restores the integrity of the individuals and the Church.

The agenda becomes problematic at this point. If the Church fails to reconcile the parties, what is to be done? It seems clear: "let such a one be to you as a Gentile and a tax collector" (Mt 18:17). Responses to this and what it might mean pragmatically are found along a spectrum of reactions, often very strong reactions at that. Shun them. Cast them out. Refuse them entrance to prayer, to breaking bread and participating in Church rituals. Impose a penance on them. Do not talk to them—tell them you will pray for them (this always elicits groans—many find it insulting or pompous or self-righteous). And yet, what has Jesus been teaching in parables and practice throughout the entire gospel? How does Jesus treat Gentiles and tax collectors? Not only does he treat them as he does Jews and everyone else in his community, he often singles them out for praise; he heals them, invites them in, goes out to them, and points them out as those to be imitated because somehow they sense how radical what Jesus is saying and doing really is for life. The stories of the Centurion begging a healing of his servant (Mt 8:5–13); the insane, despairing man at the tombs (Mt 8:28–34); the dialogue with the Canaanite woman outside the house of Israel (Mt 15:21–28); and Jesus's teaching and healing and feeding of Gentiles scattered from the district of Tyre and Sidon (Mt 15:29–38) all attest to his way of treating Gentiles and tax collectors with continued care, truthfulness, compassion, words of encouragement, sharing of his resources and his beliefs. In fact, Jesus goes out of his way to show them attention and kindness.

Jesus's words seem to demand that the community bear the responsibility for approaching and keeping in touch with anyone who has strayed, and that they must not act as others do but as he does: seeking them out and rejoicing when they do return. This can be a long trek and struggle, and it impacts the community as much as it impacts those who are seeking the lost and bringing them home.

The rest of chapter 18 is about forgiveness: Peter's question of how many times he should forgive—seven?—and Jesus's retort is no, seventy times seven times, a sharp way of saying stop counting and start practicing. This is the lifestyle and the discipline of Jesus's disciples. The chapter ends with a parable of a man forgiven a huge debt that he could not repay even if he worked his entire lifetime and his total lack of gratefulness or responding in kind to someone who owed him peanuts in comparison. The community is shaken, and it is the community that calls attention to the gross inappropriateness of the behavior of the one forgiven—and instead of forgiveness, whose only tag is sharing that forgiveness with others as you have known it, there is justice. One is given what one deserves, and some sort of restitution is called for as much for the benefit of others as for the benefit of the one treated so crassly by one who had been shown forgiveness. The last line is a stern warning that puts it all in perspective from God's point of view: "So my heavenly Father will also do to every one of you, if you do not forgive your brother or sister from your heart" (Mt 18:35).

Matthew's gospel is adamant that forgiveness is a necessity of life, the defining practice of disciples, and that it must be consistent, continual, and practiced with others as surely as it is practiced individually. There is always an alternative in every situation and a relationship that gives life, restores, heals, does restitution, and opens up breaches allowing for new life to emerge. Everything is redeemable. Jesus's words are clear and filled with hope: wherever just two or three agree on something together—something that is Good News, that echoes his own words—then it will be done. His own presence in the community will draw forth the Spirit's power of living without harm, violence, vengeance, or making others pay.

The Spirit will be given in words, in gestures, in long suffering, in meekness, in peacemaking, in struggling for justice, in seeing things as God sees them, and in living with the poverty of what community often demands.

Matthew's gospel is laced with violence: parables that speak of the violence of refusing to forgive or share what has been given to you; of the death of John the Baptist, and the reminder that like him, his disciples will be called into courts and false testimony will be given against them, and they will suffer rejection, torture, and sometimes death because they are bound to Jesus and the Kingdom of God. The parables at the end of Matthew's gospel grow even more violent: tenants refuse to pay their leases and instead murder those who are sent to collect what is lawfully owed; they even murder the son of the landlord, thinking they'd get to keep the son's inheritance (chapter 21). There are wedding banquets where the invited guests all make excuses about why they can't come, and though everyone is invited, some of them are thrown out for not being dressed properly, which dishonors the wedding feast (chapter 22). Matthew's gospel also includes the parable of "the talents," which was the largest amount of money in Roman society at the time. The parable is about economics, politics, bribes, and giving power to those who are in the pocket of Rome and appointed leaders. If you do well, you get more. If you only perform like those in second place, your rewards reflect that; if you fail, then you lose everything. If you disagree with those in charge, you will be cast out, worthless at playing the power games and participating in the violence of dominant society and nations.

The confrontations between Jesus and lawyers and members of the various factions and parties within Judaism kick up a notch and become cold-blooded. It becomes very clear they are all intent on taking him down one way or another. Jesus becomes increasingly blunt in his words and refusal to spar with them. Chapter 23 of Matthew is not often read; it includes all of the curses, woes to various groups in Jesus's own religious communities, and warnings and words about what they actually are—hypocrites, blind guides, and fools, how they twist the law and lay heavy burdens on others without any compassion or sense of what is justice. He accuses them of being greedy, self-righteous, and selfish, whitewashed tombs full of rotting flesh and dead bones that look good on the outside and are vile on the inside, and delivers the coup d'état—that they murder the prophets. This careful tirade ends with him telling his own followers not to be fooled—they, too, will suffer as he suffers at the hands of self-righteous religious practitioners conspiring with people they despise within their own communities and with enemies beyond their borders to use religion to eliminate him and silence him brutally.

After Jesus's words and last stories about judgment, about justice and what is due all the beloved children of God—both in this world and in the world to come, and in his own community—the forces of violence move quickly. The account of Jesus's betrayal in Matthew is set up as a ring of circles. Each circle tells the story differently and reveals belief, resistance, or outright choices for evil and violence. There are the Romans, Pilate, and the soldiers. There are factions of leaders within Jerusalem and various groups: the Pharisees, scribes, Caiaphas the high priest, elders, and members of the Sanhedrin and the soldiers who work for them; there are his disciples, all men, and specifically Judas from the inner circle, who meets with the chief priests and betrays Jesus for thirty pieces of silver; and there are his women disciples and Joseph of Arimathea (another Joseph!).

Though they detest one another, these groups lie, conspire together, set a price on a human being's life, arrange for torture, hold a mock trial, and commit physical violence against Jesus, who has been arrested, bound, and dragged before their own inner group; it is not public and the people are not involved or even included. Jesus is handed over to Pilate, who repeats the process but more viciously than they could—using his power to have Jesus nearly flogged to death, humiliated, and used as someone to scapegoat, giving his soldiers some blowing-off-steam play. When questioned on whether he is a king, Jesus only says, "You say so," and then stands silent before all who accuse him. The verdict has been decided already; there just has to be a semblance of some protocol so that the execution can start.

In the background the story is played out with Jesus and his disciples, at his last meal with them, and in the garden where he takes them to pray and is kissed, embraced, and betrayed by Judas. Even in this situation, Jesus calls Judas "friend," leaving the door open for him to return. When the mob and those sent from the high priest's house seek to grab Jesus, fights break out and there is violence. Peter, who carries a sword, cuts off the ear of one of the servants of the high priest. Jesus responds almost furiously: have his disciples learned nothing? Jesus's last words to his own followers are a clear reiteration of all of the gospel of Mark and Matthew regarding never using violence: "Put your sword back into its place; for all who take the sword will perish by the sword" (Mt 26:52). It is a statement about no violence in a moment when many would try to justify it. In the courtyard of the high priest, and among the crowds waiting for Pilate to make his decision, his disciples all deny him, betray him, even curse him, and run.

The account of the crucifixion is short and brutal. Someone is dragged from the crowd to help him make it to the dump outside Jerusalem: Simon of Cyrene. Two thieves crucified on either side of Jesus and in excrutiating pain themselves even join in the mockery. Jesus cries out in agony and dies.

After Jesus's death, there are glimmers of hope. Like Joseph, Jesus's father and the dreamer from the beginning of Matthew's gospel who breaks laws to protect and give life to a woman he loves, Mary, and a child he takes as his own to raise, protect, and care for—teaching Jesus what it means to be a man, a Jew, and a just and righteous believer—others now gather. When Jesus dies it is told that "many women were also there, looking on from a distance; they had followed Jesus from Galilee and had provided for him. Among them were Mary Magdalene, and Mary the mother of James and Joseph, and the mother of the sons of Zebedee. When it was evening, there came a rich man from Arimathea, named Joseph, who was also a disciple of Jesus" (Mt 27:55–57). There aren't many of them, and they watch from a safe distance. Only one makes a public move that could put him in danger—Joseph, who goes and asks for Jesus's body and buries him in the tomb he had prepared for himself.

This story doesn't just jump straight to the Resurrection, though. Jesus's death and burial give people the shakes and undermine their sense of power and control. The leaders go to Pilate yet again and want a guard at Jesus's tomb. Pilate bends to their requests, but instead of placing a guard at the tomb, he seals it. Whoever opens it will be traitors to the Roman authority and empire. They are still in collusion with one another, doing evil and trying to cover their tracks. Judas has hanged himself and the other disciples are in hiding. The violence is over for now, but it has destroyed Jesus's life, their hopes, and whatever sense of identity and community that they might have had.

The Resurrection will change that—the women who watched will come after the Sabbath to anoint Jesus's body and will find he is not there. On their way to proclaim this Good News, they are met by Jesus himself coming toward them with the words "Peace be with you" (as much a command as it is a blessing) and "Do not be afraid; go and tell my brothers to go to Galilee; there they will see me." With that form of address and reference—"my brothers"— and in speaking with his sisters, the bond is sealed, their identity is proclaimed anew, and the community begins to live in the kingdom with a vision of peace and no violence among themselves. They seek to make it a phenomenon that the world must at least acknowledge as a reality.

The gospel will end with Jesus sending his disciples out into the world to make disciples from every nation; to teach his words by example and continue to live what he has taught them through their own actions and relationships, assuring them that he is with them, that the kingdom is here, and that what was his vision—in

Matthew's gospel—is now on its way to becoming reality in them. This is Matthew's community of Jesus's disciples, and the vision of forgiveness begins to seep out into the whole world and all of history. In our immediate past the words still echo, too:

> *"Forgiveness is not just an occasional act; it is a permanent attitude."*
> (MARTIN LUTHER KING JR., 1929–1968)

Chapter 5

THE GOSPEL OF MATTHEW NOW

Honor the tradition but expand the understanding. That's what religions must do right now if they hope to be helpful to humans in the years ahead.

NEALE DONALD WALSCH, *Tomorrow's God*

THE TWO MOST FAMOUS AND OFTEN-QUOTED SEGMENTS OF Matthew's gospel are probably the Sermon on the Mount (Mt 5, 6, and 7) and what is typically known as the parable of the sheep and the goats, but in actuality is called "the judgment of the nations" (Mt 25:31–46). In a way these two pieces bracket the entire gospel. First is the sermon; all in between is the practice that results in the uncovering and living of what is called "the kingdom of God." Finally, last is the judgment on how well the content of belief and imitation of Jesus have been incorporated into the members of the community of believers.

The parable of the sheep and the goats reveals that Jesus's words, stories, and practices are not just single individual acts of rebellion or disobedience against the usual interpretation of existing rules, constructs, mores, and the dominant structures, or simply suggestions for behavior in the community. Instead, they seek to reveal the way God perceives reality and acts accordingly with justice, judgment, and mercy for all; Jesus insists that his disciples act in this manner of God our Father. Sometimes it sounds like a threat—do it or else suffer the consequences. Familiar to many, the parable is set in an unknown future: "When the Son of Man comes in his glory, and all the angels with him, he will sit on the throne of his glory. All the nations will be gathered before him, and he will separate people one from another as a shepherd separates the sheep from the goats, and he will put the sheep at his right hand and the goats at the left" (Mt 25:31–33).

This is a story about what will happen, with the sense that it will happen whether or not you believe it will, no matter what nation you find yourself a member of, or even if you are a believer in Jesus, his words, and the Father's kingdom. The stage is set and then comes the judgment. It is clear about the criteria put forth on six fronts, how you pragmatically deal with the six issues of justice: food, drink, clothing/shelter, sickness and health care, strangers being welcomed, and prisoners. The entire judgment rests on actions on behalf of and with others—all these being in need, outcast, other, or just human beings who found themselves with less than what they needed to live as human beings with some sort of dignity. The criteria will be applied to nations, religious groups, churches, societies, families, and individuals.

The first group, the sheep, are told: "Come, you that are blessed by my Father"—echoes of the beatitudes so early on in the gospel—"inherit the kingdom!" Why? It is decreed: "Truly I tell you, just as you did it to one of the least of these who are members of my family, you did it to me" (Mt 25:40). Other translations read: "Whatever you did to the least of my brothers and sisters, you did it to me." This is God's close association and alliance with the members of the human race who are most vulnerable, closest to us in proximity and possibility yet lacking what is essential to be human.

The second judgment is the same, but to the goats—whole nations, groups, churches, families, and individuals are told: "Truly I tell you, just as you did not do it to one of the least of these, you did not do it to me" (Mt 25:45). Other translations read: "What you did not do to the least of your brothers and sisters, you did not do it to me." In the first judgment the emphasis is on the least of Jesus's family, and in the second judgment the emphasis is on the least of our own brothers and sisters. The shift of focus is the fulcrum that changes everything—do we see ourselves one with God in Jesus and so with everyone else in the human community? Or do we see ourselves as separate and distinct from all others, when we see ourselves in relation to God?

There is a marvelous story told in China about this parable and its centrality to the gospel. It is told by Father Eugene F. Thalman, of Maryknoll, in Hong Kong[1]. Due to a shortage of priests and personnel, the only person available to do the preaching and teaching in a parish was an old catechist—a ninety-year-old who could only whisper because of illness that destroyed his voice. So someone in the community would read the gospel aloud to the congregation, after which there would be ten minutes or more of silence; finally, everyone would engage in intense discussion of the gospel. As you looked around the church there were people squirming, uncomfortable, distracted by others, adding their thoughts, and whispering to one another across the seats.

What was so strange about his leading of the worship service was that the old man chose the same reading every single Sunday: Matthew 25:31–46 about the sheep and the goats! The man would stand, welcoming people into the church as they arrived, and he would whisper to each of them as they entered: Did you give food to Jesus this week? Did you welcome Jesus the Stranger this week? Did you go and visit Jesus in prison or take care of his bodily pains? And based on their answers they were directed to the right side of the gathering—the sheep side—or to the left side—the goats' domain. If they made excuses or said that Jesus wasn't there, they would be steered to the goat section with an exhortation to open their eyes and see Jesus crucified everywhere waiting for them.

The talk after the gospel was the same every week. The goats talked about what they had to do to get over to the sheep side next Sunday, and the sheep talked about what they had to do to stay on the right side and not end up with the goats. They would share their blessings and talk of how they and others lived in God's kingdom this week, or reflect back on those whom they ignored or refused to treat as their brother and sister in God's house of creation under heaven.

The story is amazingly simple and to the heart of the matter.

Jesus's preaching, when put into practice with others, uncovers the Kingdom of God. However, the word *kingdom* is problematic in our modern world and cultures. Nearly all of Jesus's parables and teachings begin with these words: "The kingdom of God is like . . ." This kingdom, this realm, this dream of God, the hope of God for humankind, the community of God, the relationship of God with us, the will of God—all are trying to speak of the same reality: the dawn of the new age, the new millennium, the new society that Jesus's presence in the world has begun. Perhaps its first and undergirding characteristic is the universality of love, beginning oddly enough with one's enemies, strangers, those who are not part of your economic, religious, or political group; it is the call to "be as compassionate and loving as our Father is with all of us" (Mt 5:43–48). These three chapters of the Sermon on the Mount contain Jesus's vision of the way humans were created to live in the world. It is not something anyone can do independently. It assumes you belong to a community that is struggling together to make this vision a reality in a world beset with violence, injustice, anger, and all manner of weakness. Furthermore, it assumes that all follow the demands that such a vision rooted in no harm, no violence, and no killing presents daily. There are no "ifs, ands, or buts" regarding violence; it is not acceptable, and any act of violence is a failure to obey and believe in Jesus's power of the Spirit to make human beings like God—to make Christians. This is not an optional piece or a sidebar of belief: it is the foundation stone and the heart of the person of Jesus. To be a Christian and bear the light of Christ in the world is to bear that light in the shadow of the Cross, as Jesus himself did.

In a paper entitled "Living the Proclaimed Reign of God: A Sermon on the Sermon on the Mount," Stanley Hauerwas writes this:

> Gene Davenport, in his wonderful book on the Sermon on the Mount, Into the Darkness, reminds us that "when the first hearers of Matthew's Gospel heard Jesus' call to suffer rather than to inflict suffering, to accept death rather than to inflict death, to reject all efforts to save themselves from

their plight by military action and to leave their deliverance to God, they knew that the one who gave such scandalous instruction had himself lived and died in accord with that call." [Into the Darkness: Discipleship and the Sermon on the Mount *(Nashville: Abingdon Press, 1988), p. 15.]*

The Jesus of the Sermon on the Mount is not one who extols an esoteric or naïve or idealistic ethic—a way of life never tested or tried—but is one whose instruction sets forth the way of life that he himself embodied, the way of life that manifests God's own life. (p. 154, 152—58)

This is God's dwelling place on earth, and Jesus's work is to uncover it and extend it to be the reality of the whole world, and if not, then to have its presence a reality in the world that serves as an alternative of hope for all to see, visit, experience, and know that God's vision—in contrast to the realities of nations, armies, and economies—is possible and God's will can be known and lived here and now. These are its beginnings, and one day it will be known ever more completely by all.

Jesus's hearers knew the kingdom of the Herods, the kingdom of Caesar Augustus, and the reign of Pilate and invading and occupying armies, and they heard the shocking alternative that Jesus was presenting them. Do we ever catch the demand and the power of God's Word in Jesus? It is God's way of dwelling upon the earth with us and it's for here and now. It is one of the first petitions in the Lord's Prayer: may your dwelling place come; your will be done, on earth [now] as it is in eternity. This is to be the end result of our belief, worship, and practice for those who call themselves Christians. This coming of God's dwelling place among us is fraught with politics, economics, power, brutality, armies, nationalism, and all sorts of institutions, including religions that live in collusion with every kingdom except God's on earth now. Political and economic salvation is part of being saved and "grasped by the hand for the victory of justice" (Is 42). This is the way C. S. Song, an Asian theologian, speaks about God's reign and dwelling place with us:

Not surprising, Song grounds his theology of the reign of God in the message of the Hebrew prophets and the preaching of Jesus, especially the parables. From these sources he derives the conviction that salvation includes political and economic salvation. The God of the Hebrew-Christian faith, he says, is a "political God." "God's politics" means two things: it is a "politics against the barbarism of power," and it means that "the God of the prophets, and . . . the God of Jesus Christ, is a God who takes . . . the side of the poor against the rich."

Song is quick to point out that God's politics does not mean that Christians should replace secular power and government with another, perhaps sacred, power and government of their own to bring about the kingdom of God. Rather, "it aims at . . . the transformation of power . . . And in this transformation, or metanoia of power, is found the essence of God's politics." [2]

In a nutshell, Christians must confront every form of violence, injustice, and rage with good, with peace, with justice, and with compassion—in imitation of Jesus's own words and actions, and in imitation of God, with the power of the Spirit. This is the Christian's stance in regard to law, authority, and power in every form, whether practiced by individuals, institutions, economic systems, governments, militaries, or religious leaders. The law is necessary, but what the law protects must be protected first. No law may be obeyed or used to harm another, or given as an excuse not to help and transform the lives of those in danger.

Violence is simply never an option. In the words of Martin Luther King Jr., "Returning violence for violence multiples violence, adding deeper darkness to a night already devoid of stars." In the sermon, those who work for peace will be called the children of God with Jesus (Mt 5:9). Jesus's proclamation of the presence of God's dwelling among us is that of abiding peace in the midst of warring nations. It is refuge and sanctuary.

The second cornerstone of the coming of God's vision in practical terms is justice. The beatitude reads: "Blessed are those who hunger and thirst for righteousness, for they will be filled" (Mt 5:6).

The image of hungering and thirsting implies daily devotion to this practice, and is as necessary as what sustains human beings. The word *righteousness* in the Scriptures is interchangeable with justice and with holiness. But what is justice? A definition I use often is this: justice is love expressed in terms of sheer human need; it encompasses food, water, shelter/clothing, medicine, health care, education, work, human dignity, freedom from fear and violence, a sense of basic security, the right to practice one's religion, to assemble and organize, to be protected in a court of law, to speak the truth, to immigrate, and to have hope for the life of one's children. It is what every human being deserves just by being human. There is a grand story about John XXIII that puts justice in its proper place: soon after he was elected, he wanted to make some phone calls but found all connections severed in conjunction with the rules of the conclave, which wasn't technically over yet. A repairman was summoned, and he worked on the wires and set things up so that John XXIII could call out of the Vatican long distance.

The new pope was standing around and waiting while the man worked, and started to make conversation with him: "How are things going with you these days?" He was concerned when the man answered, "Not really well, in fact, poorly." The man who had been the cardinal of Venice and was now the pope was immediately concerned because he heard in the man's voice that he wasn't talking about the wiring problem but something more pervasive. John XXIII persuaded the man to talk about his large family and how the less-than-adequate pay for working in the Vatican was a source of great hardship for him and all the workers. After a while, the man finished, looked up, and said, "Your Eminence, the phone now works."

John XXIII replied, "Oh, that's not my title anymore—I'm the pope." The man's jaw dropped and John embraced him warmly and thanked him.

Within a few months changes were made. John XXIII increased everyone's salary by 25 to 40 percent across the board. Of course, the pope had run into a brick wall with the finance people in the

Vatican. It was too much; it just couldn't be done. The only way they could come up with that kind of money immediately was to take the money out of the funds that were used for charity. John's response was: "Well, take the money from there. This raise for these people is long overdue and necessary. It will feed their children. I came from a family of fourteen and I remember how hard it was for my parents to make ends meet. This is justice and justice always comes before charity!"

This is what it means, perhaps, to be a "living tradition"—one who honors the teaching of the past in our Jewish roots, along with Jesus's own words, and puts them into practice pastorally, with the same intensity of compassion and the need to be just. We are called to this wisdom of God both in our personal lives and in our public connections with others. And so the third cornerstone is that of forgiveness. Again this demanding reality is found as one of the petitions in Jesus's prayer that is intended as our own: "And forgive us our debts, as we also have forgiven our debtors" (Mt 6:12). It comes immediately after the petition for justice: "Give us this day our daily bread" (Mt 6:11). Mark Twain wrote: "Forgiveness is the fragrance that the violet sheds on the heel that has crushed it." These stones are literally hard as rock, to serve as foundation and support and to hold those who are bound to Jesus together. This forgiveness is a given—it is the Good News of God that Jesus announces—we are bound once again, all of us, to God. We are beloved of God. Because we are forgiven always, in all ways we are to forgive in the same manner those who offend us, harm us, and make our lives difficult.

When I was in Israel more than a decade ago, one of the women in the group I was traveling with needed a doctor on the Sabbath. We were staying at a convent and the young woman at the desk told me that she could bring her father over from the West Bank, but I would have to go with her and bring him back, stay with him while he saw the woman and prescribed whatever was necessary, and then go back over with him through the checkpoints to make sure he got home safely. After all of which I was welcome to stay with her family until the next morning, when they would bring me back into Jerusalem through another checkpoint rather than try again at the same one for the fourth time in one day. This is what I did, spending the night with the family in their home, which became the highlight of my whole trip to Israel and Palestine. While I was there I was told an unbelievable story.

We were sitting in the ground-floor level, not yet finished because of regulations, sipping coffee and eating a pastry while watching the children playing. There was music playing and the usual shouts and screams and noise of the street. The children came in to eat, and as they gathered around I watched them, trying to match each to a photo that held a place of honor on the table, taken from its usual spot upstairs by the family's grandmother. I told them I could place some of them, but others I couldn't. So they all lined up and pointed themselves out to me. There were two in the picture who were not in the group, and I asked where they were. It was very silent, and I realized I had stepped into a realm of sorrow.

One of the girls said, "They are dead. The soldier shot them."

I was stunned and inanely stumbled out, "How old were they?" "Three and seven," were the responses. It became more awkward, and the man I had accompanied back and forth earlier that day spoke. I will never forget what he said: "We keep telling the children that they are not really dead. You see, when they were shot we took them to the nearest hospital and their hearts, their eyes, their livers, and their spleens were used as organ donations. They live in six different people now. I know that one of them lives down the street from us here and two children on the other side, Israeli children, have their eyes and their hearts. We must remember that and perhaps one day we will come together."

In light of his words, all other acts of forgiveness take on a different meaning. The act of forgiveness, no matter how trivial or great, brings life to all, though that life may be startling in unforeseen ways and expressions. But this is the cement that allows the community and all people to build and grow, no matter what might happen among them, or to them—or what they might do to others.

Forgiveness is a moment, a word, a gesture, a possibility; it is a long process of integration, healing, and making something new out of what has happened. What follows is reconciliation—the walking together again—developing a way of being together that takes what needs to be forgiven and transforms it into a new thing through the Spirit of truth, grace, freedom, and hope. This happens in many ways, but it must include restitution and creative responses that seek to undo the harm that was done and to plot a new course in the relationships.

The more devastating the harm, violence, unfaithfulness, or lies, the more public the restitution must be. When it involves the leadership of a community, group, or church, then not only must it be public, it must be ongoing—a shift in lifestyle that acknowledges the depth of hurt and how it affected not only the individuals involved but created scandal and discouragement in the larger community, and directly caused the Body of Christ, the Church, to be seen as hypocritical, lying, and despicable, causing ridicule and disdain of Jesus's words of what it means to belong to his community.

When the violence or evil is public and committed by those in power, then the repentance and restitution is not just a personal responsibility: the forms of atonement must look at the cause and roots of the failures. The conversion must take place in structures, in organizational rules, and in the methods for choosing leaders, and be held accountable for what is lacking and missing in the existing frameworks. The future, and what was in the past called "the firm purpose of amendment," cannot be consigned to the individual alone but must be reestablished in a new structure and dismantling of what situations, rules, and training of people caused the harm, violence, and evil to be practiced and perpetuated.

This must happen on a systemic basis if there is to be atonement. The root meaning of the word is *at-one-ment*, meaning communion or unity—once again, so that the community of believers, in small groups and in the universal Church, can be made whole again. That reality of communion is paid for at a great price: the Cross, which was laid on others who were the innocent victims and suffered indignity and violence and felt the effects and harm long after they were sinned against. In a like manner, those who did violence to others must bear their share of the undoing of evil and live in such a way that they are held accountable for their actions and how they now seek to live still in the community.

That means that the first step in any conversion process is to step down from all places of authority and power previously held, and to turn to a life of service, penance, and anonymous restitution in places that will remind them daily of what they have done. Public power and public sin demand public penance and public restitution that restores some semblance of public rightness. Lifetime service in places where they can pick up others' crosses and share in others' pain—in prisons, mental hospitals, institutions for the criminally insane, hospitals for those with Alzheimer's and other terminal diseases, homes for the aged and infirm, refugee camps, and houses of detention can connect those who commit harm to compassionate counterbalances in the larger community. This accountability cannot be done "in house," so to speak. It must be entrusted to the care of others who can demand what will restore unity and hope among all involved.

All this reflects a number of lines from people around the world. From Archbishop Dom Hélder Câmara: "Watch how you live. Your lives may be the only gospel your brothers and sisters will ever read." From another tradition: "The sign of the friend of God is that he/she has three qualities: a generosity like that of the ocean, a compassion like that of the sun and a humility like that of the earth" (Bayazid in 'Attar). Even the Mayan people have a greeting that fits this scenario: "en Lak'esh." It means "I am another yourself." It is in confronting evil that the mettle and heart of those who are leaders is revealed and seen in truth. The entire Sermon on the Mount and Matthew's gospel of Jesus seek to teach one how to live and to reveal what is essential in those in leadership positions. The human race is adept at self-deception and a standard outside of individual choice must be the basis for choosing leaders publicly. It cannot be done in secrecy, with no external input, and they cannot be chosen from a select group that basically appoints and regulates themselves apart from the majority of people in the community. At the very end of the sermon Jesus says:

> *"Not everyone who says to me, 'Lord, Lord,' will enter the kingdom of heaven, but only the one who does the will of my Father in heaven. On that day many will say to me, 'Lord, Lord, did we not prophesy in your name, and cast out demons in your name, and do many deeds of power in your name?' Then I will declare to them, 'I never knew you; go away from me, you evildoers." (Mt 7:21–23)*

Jesus has many words for those he has chosen to be leaders as well as those who are his many followers. He also has strong words for those who are in leadership positions and how they will be judged on how their lives, words, and decrees have affected those they were to teach, not only in law but in modeling life as one who follows in Jesus's footsteps. Many leaders are more into language about God, demanding that others obey the laws of God, judging others' worthiness, and enforcing restrictions and penalties on others, than they are concerned with actually living the essence of what constituted being part of the covenant of God with the people.

It is no different in society today. External traditions and rites are trivial and indicative of what had become acceptable practice at the demand of leaders, and were often only inaugurated within the previous 50 to 150 years. These decisions, laws, and practices were dealt with on the same level as greater commands and the primary commandment: to love the Lord your God with all your heart, your entire mind, and all your strength (meaning resources), and to love one's neighbor as you loved yourself (Mt 22:37–39).

Since time immemorial, those in power (including those who exercise religious power) often use religion and the words of their founders to serve their own purposes, or in failing to obey the original precepts themselves, bend the laws, add to the rules, and muddy the waters on what is essential and what is the truth. Jesus is blunt with the leaders of his own tradition, and he would be equally as blunt today, twenty centuries later, to those who lay claim to his tradition.

> *Then Pharisees and scribes came to Jesus from Jerusalem and said, "Why do your disciples break the tradition of the elders? For they do not wash their hands before they eat." He answered them, "And why do you break the commandment of God for the sake of your tradition? For God said, 'Honor your father and your mother,' and, 'Whoever speaks evil of father or mother must surely die.' But you say that whoever tells father or mother, 'Whatever support you might have had from me is given to God,' then that person need not honor the father. So, for the sake of your tradition, you make void the word of God. You hypocrites! Isaiah prophesied rightly about you when he said: 'This people honors me with their lips, but their hearts are far from me; in vain do they worship me, teaching human precepts as doctrines.'" (Mt 15:1–9)*

Rachel Naomi Remen, a doctor, counselor, and healer from the Jewish tradition, tells a startling story about an Orthodox rabbi and his young daughter. The story reminds us that what holds up the law is compassion, and the law is never to be used or practiced for its own sake or just because it is—it must serve human beings and it must be used to ease the life of others. A young girl, twelve, with Hodgkin's disease, cancer of the lymph nodes, would come in regularly for her radiation treatments when Remen was a pediatrician in New York. Her father obeyed the many laws and traditions proscribed by their religion. It so happened that one of the treatments was scheduled for Yom Kippur, the Day of Atonement, the holiest day of the Jewish year. It is the day when the whole synagogue gathers and prays fervently for forgiveness for all their sins committed in the past year. There are many specific rules decreed for that particular day: one cannot ride in a car, wear leather shoes, have any financial dealings—or even handle money—or use electricity. And so the rabbi came to Dr. Remen to suggest that his daughter's treatment be canceled in obedience to the laws.

As a doctor, she was appalled—no, she told him. The scheduling and timing of the treatments are crucial. You can't just skip one. It could have disastrous effects. The rabbi listened and then decided—his daughter would not go. It was more important to obey God's law than any human law, no matter the consequences. It was decided. When she argued with him, he quoted her the story of Abraham and Isaac. They argued more, and he said he would go to the rabbi in New York who was the leader of his particular branch of Orthodox Judaism.

She did not hear back from him and her heart sank. His poor daughter was being used to prove a religious tenet at the expense of her life. Yom Kippur came and to her surprise the young girl showed up for her appointment. She often came with her mother, but today both her mother and her father were in the waiting room. Dr. Remen asked him what had changed his mind. He was subdued and answered that he had written to his rabbi and explained the situation and what he had decided was right. He was surprised when he got a phone call from the rabbi himself! He was told to call a taxi and take his wife and daughter to the hospital for her treatment, as scheduled. He had been shocked—his rabbi was telling him to break the laws on Yom Kippur? He argued and was told that he must accompany his daughter and go so "that she would know that even the most pious and upright man in her life, her father, may ride on the holiest of days for the purpose of serving life. He continued to say that it was important that Shoshana (the girl's name) not feel separated from God by breaking the law. Such a feeling might interfere with her healing."[3]

Holiness, righteousness, obedience to the law are always at the service of life: preserving it, encouraging it, nourishing it, and upholding it, and true wisdom and courage are found in knowing when to break the laws and to tell others to lay them aside, as well. This is the tradition, the solid foundation, of the law in Judaism and even more so in Jesus's teachings on the Spirit of the law. The law is always to draw us closer to God and never to shame and humiliate anyone or give them the sense that they are apart from God.

Jesus often harshly denounces the scribes, Pharisees, and those who interpreted the traditions and laws and enforced them on the people—and he would do the same today. Here are selections from chapter 23, which is devoted to attacking them for their many transgressions while demanding others live up to standards not found in the teachings of the law and the prophets—add-ons, human demands that are extra and designed by those with authority at a particular time in history.

> Then Jesus said to the crowds and to his disciples, "The scribes and the Pharisees sit on Moses' seat; therefore do whatever they teach you and follow it; but do not do as they do, for they do not practice what they teach. They tie up heavy burdens, hard to bear, and lay them on the shoulders of others; but they themselves are unwilling to lift a finger to move them. . . . The greatest among you will be your servant. All who exalt themselves will be humbled, and all who humble themselves will be exalted.
>
> "But woe to you, scribes and Pharisees, hypocrites! For you lock people out of the kingdom of heaven. For you do not go in yourselves and when others are going in, you stop them. Woe to you, scribes and Pharisees, hypocrites! For you cross sea and land to make a single convert, and you make the new convert twice as much a child of hell as yourselves. . . .
>
> "Woe to you, scribes and Pharisees, hypocrites! For you tithe mint, dill, and cumin, and have neglected the weightier matters of the law: justice and mercy and faith. It is these you ought to have practiced, without neglecting the others. You blind guides! You strain out a gnat but swallow a camel!
>
> "Woe to you scribes and Pharisees, hypocrites! For you clean the outside of the cup and of the plate, but inside they are full of greed and self-indulgence. You blind Pharisee! First clean the inside of the cup, so that the outside also may become clean. (Mt 23:1–4, 11–15, 23–26)

These quotes from the gospel of Matthew are among the milder ones! Jesus goes on to accuse them of filth, lawlessness, self-righteousness, building on the tombs of the prophets, and decorating the graves of the righteous, and yet they would be accused of their murders. He calls them snakes, a brood of vipers who torture those who tell the truth to them and run them out of the synagogues and towns (Mt 23:29–36). These words, of course, did not endear Jesus to the leaders and led more immediately to their rage and intent to kill him. Only the people appreciated his telling the truth to those in power and telling the truth about them, whether the power they wielded was political, economic, and/or religious.

Today in our churches, have we reached the point where Jesus is enraged at the practices that enforce and sustain traditions from the last sixteen hundred or more years and are a far cry from the gospel—his words and ways of being with people? And what about these traditions that have become more important than Jesus's words and practices?

Why are people excluded from the Eucharist because of failures in marriage, or described as "intrinsically disordered," while those who exclude them have done wrong, and are doing equally grave or worse things? Statistics say that more than 50 percent of the people of God are struggling with marriage, divorce, and remarriage; these people are told they are not to receive communion but are still to come to liturgy. The Eucharist is not a reward for being good—it is the food for all the people of God, sinners all—and Jesus fed every person at every meal he was a part of, either as guest or host. On hillsides he takes the food away from his disciples and has them give away their share of the meal first to the crowds—the disciples do not eat first—and they are to collect the leftovers (Mt 14:13–21, 15:32–39). At the last supper, all share the one loaf of bread and one cup of wine, yet all of them would desert him, deny him, and even the leader, Peter, would curse his name. The prayer immediately before the taking of communion is "O Lord, I am not worthy" not "O Lord, she/he/they is/are not worthy."

Why are churches, altars (no longer seen as tables), and all the utensils—plates, cups, linens, etc.—considered more sacred than the human beings (the actual Body of Christ) who touch them? Currently, they have to be made of precious metals like gold, silver, or platinum rather than glass, clay, or any other material. Jesus certainly would not have picked up a "precious chalice" to drink from ever in his life, and what he handed to his friends in sharing his life with them was at best a clay cup. It is written: "Then he took a cup, and after giving thanks he gave it to them, saying, 'Drink from it, all of you; for this is my blood of the covenant, which is poured out for many [all] for the forgiveness of sins,'" (Mt 26:27–28). It's very clearly stated that Jesus "took a loaf of bread, and after blessing it he broke it, gave it to the disciples, and said, 'Take, eat; this is my body'" (Mt 26:26).

There is also no mention that Jesus ever ate or drank at the last supper, and yet the ritual has developed that in many liturgies there is only the bread given (that has no resemblance to bread whatsoever) and that only a few—the designated ministers—may drink from the cup. First the priest, then the deacons, then the ministers of bread and wine (the servants) all partake while the rest of the congregation waits. Even today, no woman may touch the cups or plates, pour the wine, put the bread (hosts) onto the plates, or clean them afterward. The insult to the Body of Christ in their bodies is now ritualized and required to be enforced in the liturgy while everyone watches those who are "worthy."

These insults and exclusions were extended through canon law (recently revised after centuries—all human man-made traditions in which women had no part) so that no woman could read the gospel or preach and proclaim the Good News; yet in all the gospels—and especially in Matthew's—it is the named women at the tomb who proclaim the Easter proclamation that he is risen. Listen to how it is told:

> So they left the tomb quickly with fear and great joy, and ran to tell his disciples. Suddenly Jesus met them and said, "Greetings!" And they came to him, took hold of his feet, and worshipped him. Then Jesus said to them, "Do not be afraid; go and tell my brothers to go to Galilee; there they will see me." (Mt 28:8–10)

They are first given the gospel message to proclaim and are sent forth, but in their obedience to the Word of God, they meet Jesus on their way to the disciples who are in hiding. "Greetings" is most often translated as "Peace be with you"—*the* Easter proclamation. Jesus sends them to the rest of the disciples with the message of forgiveness and reconciliation. With the words "go and tell my brothers"—they already know they are his sisters—they bring the Good News of resurrection, peace, and communion to all the others. These were the women who had followed him from Galilee, provided for him, and both witnessed Jesus's death from a distance and kept watch at the tomb when Jesus was buried (Mt 27:55–56, 61); they are the first to worship the risen Lord.

Yet in the intervening centuries, all women are excluded from any substantial role in worship, as priest, deacon, proclaimer, or preacher; they are also not permitted to hold any office of authority or power—originally only administrative power and now transformed into sacramental authority—as bishop or cardinal (those who "elect" the pope from among their own ranks). This does not even deal with the many ranks and tiers of power instituted in the Church for the leaders—monsignors, vicars, apostolic delegates, chamberlains—to congratulate themselves with external vestments, titles, residences, and traditions, a few in a litany of public (and economic) privileges bestowed upon one another. It is interesting to note that one is "raised" to these positions, not brought low to be servants of the people of God.

Why is anything that has to do with power and authority in the Church cloaked in secrecy, hidden from the members of the Church? Why is anyone from the larger Church threatened with excommunication (also a man-made tradition—Jesus doesn't exclude anyone from his community) if he reveals anything about the process of choosing bishops, making cardinals, or enthroning a pope? These "elections" exclude any actual members of the Body of Christ, and candidates are chosen through infighting, politicking, and power grabs. The primary characteristic of the presence of the Spirit is transparency and the proclaiming of the truth, and yet there is no openness or participation by any of the 98 percent members of the Church.

Yet, in Jesus's words, those who already have the kingdom—the dwelling place of God—among them are children! He sternly chastises his disciples who want to keep the children and their parents away from him: "Let the little children come to me, and do not stop them; for it is to such as these that the kingdom of heaven belongs." And he laid hands on them and went on his way (Mt 19:13–15). Interestingly enough, this is the only time Jesus lays hands on people who weren't sick and in need of healing—and there is never a mention of him laying hands on any of his disciples in an ordination, or a bestowal of power.

Jesus is adamant—it appears in each of the first three gospels in almost the same words—that if you have any power, authority, or rule in his kingdom, then you are not to act like anyone does with power in the nations and kingdoms of the world. He says clearly:

> *"You know that the rulers of the Gentiles lord it over them, and their great ones are tyrants over them. It will not be so among you; but whoever wishes to be great among you must be your servant, and whoever wishes to be first among you must be your slave; just as the Son of Man came not to be served but to serve, and to give his life as a ransom for many." (Mt 20:25–28)*

And these words are spoken after the mother of James and John is sent to Jesus to bestow a favor on her sons—the favor is that they get the seats of honor to his right and to his left in his kingdom. Even after Jesus begins his reign in his Father's kingdom on the Cross, it seems that those who become leaders in the Church still don't get it. While they may speak the language of being servants, they actually act and live as princes in their own inner circles and hardly know the perspective of a servant from below in regard to the rest of the members of the Church.

Leaders among those committed to God's vision, God's dream

for his people on earth, should come from the most unexpected sources—the bottom, not the top of the heap. About halfway through the gospel of Matthew, we find out where the leadership should be found, who they are, and even about their relationship with our Father. This segment of the Word of the Lord also reveals the fourth cornerstone of God's dwelling among us now—the cornerstone of hope that is found in those who know and live the wisdom of God. Listen:

> At that time Jesus said, "I thank you, Father, Lord of heaven and earth, because you have hidden these things from the wise and the intelligent and have revealed them to infants; yes, Father, for such was your gracious will. All things have been handed over to me by my Father; and no one knows the Son except the Father, and no one knows the Father except the Son and anyone to whom the Son chooses to reveal him. (Mt 11:25–27)

It is the children (infants in this translation) who know both the child of God, Jesus, and our Father, not "the clever and wise in the ways of the world outside God's dwelling." The word *child* in all the Scriptures does not refer to age primarily, but to those without power, without self-righteousness, without a place of prestige, honor, or privilege in society. They are found among the poor, the fringe, and the far edge of the community; they are holy because they know the Father that Jesus has taught them to know, they know how to recognize and to obey the power of the Spirit in imitation of Jesus. Leadership in Jesus's community is not found in the obvious places but is hidden in holiness. They are the people who sustain hope so that just by being in their presence one can catch hope. Jesus continues with an invitation:

> "Come to me, all you that are weary and are carrying heavy burdens, and I will give you rest. Take my yoke upon you, and learn from me; for I am gentle and humble in heart, and you will find rest for your souls. For my yoke is easy, and my burden is light." (Mt 11:28–30)

We are invited in close if we are weary from working and bringing this dwelling place and vision of Jesus's Father into reality on earth. This is our work and burden—this is our yoke, the yoke of Jesus. There are three meanings to the word *yoke* and all of them speak of power and authority, and how it is to be used, shared, and practiced. The first is the most commonly understood—two are yoked together. Power is never meant to reside in one person but should be shared. When two horses or oxen are yoked together, it is usually an older and a younger one. When one pulls out, the other pulls back in; when one just drags along, the other provides added energy and strength, and together they can do so much more than any single one could accomplish.

The second meaning is the yoke that was the Cross. Jesus was yoked to the crossbeam, about fifty pounds of wood that he carried across his shoulders, tied to his arms with ropes. It is the yoke of the slave, deliberately fashioned so that every execution would remind the people that they once again lived in bondage—once to the Egyptians and now to the Romans. It is the yoke that is the result of being meek (nonviolent), humble of heart, a peacemaker, and gentle—compassionate and liberating.

The last meaning of the word *yoke* is best imaged by a dance where men and women stand and throw their arms over one another's shoulders and begin to dance in a circle, streaming out in a long line, picking up people along the way, and weaving back again into a circle, dancing to the music, the heartbeat and the rhythm of Resurrection life, which is Jesus's gift to all in God's new dwelling place here on earth—ringed round with the people of God, energized by the Spirit and singing the words of Jesus, worshipping as they live together.

Power and authority must be shared, shifted, changed (like partners) on a regular basis. It isn't appropriated for a lifetime, though it is a lifestyle of a servant, not in word primarily but in deed—the leaders learn from the Body of Christ what is the will and pleasure of God; the lesson does not come from the top down but the bottom up. Perhaps one of the prayers at liturgy describes best what needs to be reversed: in it the pope, bishops, priests, religious, and deacons are prayed for and only then the "rest of the people of God"—and sometimes they are left out altogether! The prayer according to Jesus's vision should be reversed, beginning with the people of God and then moving on lastly to those who are the servants—and maybe sometimes forgetting them altogether, too!

Where we are now is in need of a poem, a prayer, a hope. This excerpt from Seamus Heaney's *The Cure at Troy* comes as a blessing, and as a song.

> *History says don't hope on this side of the grave.*
> *But then, once in a lifetime the longed-for tidal wave of justice*
> *   can rise up, and hope and history rhyme.*
> *So hope for a great sea-change on the far side of revenge.*
> *Believe that a farther shore*
> *Is reachable from here.*
> *Believe in miracles*
> *And cures and healing wells.*

This is the house of peace, justice, forgiveness, and hope—God's dream coming true, Jesus's Word of truth, and the Spirit's doing. All are welcome here.

Chapter 6

THE GOSPEL OF LUKE THEN

God is a God of life. Poverty is death. Therefore we are committed to the poor.

GUSTAVO GUTIÉRREZ

THE GOSPEL OF LUKE IS THE THIRD GOSPEL IN OUR TRADITION. It is the only one written in a period of relative peace and so the issues that develop in the communities of Luke probe deeper into the communities' practice and worship and beyond faithfulness in the face of persecution and death. It is also a time of expansion, with the gospel spreading into other cultures besides Judaism: Roman, Greek, and pagan religions. There are many issues and descriptions of the gospel of Luke; it is called the gospel of prayer, of women, of healing, of mission, and of the Spirit. Luke wrote the Acts of the Apostles first and then his gospel second, again as a teaching or catechetical text. He addresses his gospel to Theophilus, whose name means *beloved,* thought not to be a particular person but anyone who is interested in the teachings of Jesus. Luke said he collected materials from many sources and witnesses, and wanted to pass on the tradition that was handed down to him (Lk 1:1–4).

Perhaps a story or two will focus our attention on some themes that hold the gospel together and draw the believer into depths and intimacy with the Word of Jesus according to Luke. The first is an old Jewish story told by Rabbi Chaim Meir Rovman of Haifa. It takes place in Siberia during a time of great persecution. The Jewish community was beyond poor, trying to survive in desperate conditions, with forced labor, brutal winter weather, and a shortage of everything: food, water, shelter, even clothing. Once upon a time the rabbi was trying to stay warm in his small shack during a few minutes when he could finally just sit quietly. He knew the time would be short-lived and almost immediately there came a knock on the door. He opened the door to an older man and a younger one—father and son from the looks of them. They entered and sat in two rickety chairs before the rabbi, who was seated at a wooden table. There was an awkward silence while one or the other was trying to decide who should begin.

The rabbi waited patiently, looking at them with kindness, and then it was the father who finally spoke first. "Rabbi," he said, "I am ashamed to be here and to have to tell you my problem. This is my son"—he gestured toward the young man next to him—"we live together in a shack about the size of this room, your office. It is so cold, even frigid. We have a stove but it smokes and doesn't heat the room well and there are cracks open between the boards of the room. I stay at home—I am too old and frail to work—and my son goes out to chop wood, dig ditches and latrines, or whatever else the Russians want done. And I need a coat to stay warm since I do not move around much—there is so little space. And we only have one coat between the two of us. I think that it is only just that I get to wear the coat during the short days when it is so bitter cold. Then my son can have it at night since he needs to sleep. What do you think is the right thing to do?"

He finished his say and there was silence—again it was heavy and awkward. The young man began, "Rabbi, it is as my father says. We live in a small space and there is no adequate heat day or night. But I go out early in the dark and work outside until it is dark again. If I don't work the long hours my father would not only be cold, he would starve to death. I need the coat, otherwise I sweat from all my labor and exertion and then I can easily catch cold and get sick. It is only just that I wear the coat outside during the day and then my father can have the coat at night. What do you think is the right thing to do?"

The rabbi didn't know what to say—he was at a loss for words. He knew, too, that this was the situation for many in the camp:

there just wasn't enough of what were necessities of life to go around for all—some had to do without. He hated answering these questions for he knew that both would obey his words, no matter whose favor he ruled in. Finally the rabbi spoke and said, "I need to think and pray over this problem. Please come back in three days and I will have an answer for you." Both men were not expecting this delay, but both accepted the rabbi's proposal and promised that they would return in three days' time.

The three days seemed to last forever for both the father and the son—and the rabbi, too, who was agonizing over what to say, for both of them had good reasons for needing the coat during the day. They were all thinking about it. The father began to look at his son and think, I could not live without him leaving every day to work. His extra work and toil brings in my food and anything we have. He cannot get sick, or I, too, will die. He needs the coat more than I do—I can stay near the stove and rub my hands and remember to get up and walk around the shack, or maybe I can think of something I can do to keep moving and warm. When we go back to the rabbi I will tell him it is decided: my son gets the coat.

At the same time the son was watching his father and seeing how frail and weak he was, needing more food and water, even some clothes that weren't torn and threadbare. And then he thought, My father is old and he has cared for me all my life, bringing me into the world, protecting and raising me. Where would I be if not for him? My duty is to thankfully give him the coat. When we go back to the rabbi I will tell him it is decided: my father gets the coat.

Three days passed and the father and son returned to the rabbi. Once again they sat at the table before the rabbi. The rabbi was looking for a way to begin but before he could say anything it was the father who spoke first. "Rabbi," he said, "it is decided—my son gets the coat during the day." And he carefully laid out his thoughts about how hard his son worked and that he could easily catch cold, that he had to stay strong. He had already lived a long life and much of it good, blessed be the name of the Lord, and his son deserved to live long and hopefully times would change and he would know freedom and the chance to live as a righteous Jew. The father had barely finished speaking when he was almost interrupted by his son. "No, Rabbi, that is not the way it is to be. It is decided: my father is to have the coat during the day. If it were not for my father I would not be here—I would not be alive at all. He has raised me and cared for me, giving me everything and doing without so much. And he is frail and growing old and I must honor him and thankfully let him have the coat for the day." The father and son looked at each other, stunned at each other's reasoning, and turned once again to the rabbi. Together they said, "Rabbi, what do you think we should do?"

The rabbi fumbled with his words. He had thought about this long and hard and was amazed that in three days' time both father and son had come to the opposite decisions they were strongly bound to so few days ago. Now both could do without the coat that the other now needed more than he did. Finally he stood up and told them that he would be back in a moment. In a few moments the rabbi returned. Over his arm was a coat—a heavy coat with a fur hood. He held it out to them both and said, "Now you will both have a coat and the decision is made." The father and son sat there without moving. Finally the son said, "Rabbi, you had a coat all this time. Why didn't you give it to us three days ago?" The rabbi answered them, "You were arguing over how much you needed a coat. I have a coat—this one—and I started asking myself how much I needed my coat and if I could do without it. But now that each of you says let the other have it, I, too, can say, You can have my coat! Thank you, both of you. Now go home and be warm together and I will be warm knowing that you care so for each other."

It is an incredible story but not an easy one to hear, and our reactions can be varied. What would each of us do in this situation? What constitutes need for ourselves and for others? And how much are we willing to let go of to share with others?

Luke's gospel deals with the poor and the rich and the gap in material possessions between them. Money, economics, wealth, and poverty are realities that rub against one another and impact how everyone lives together. More clearly, Luke's gospel is Good News to and for the poor and so the question immediately arises: who are the poor and what constitutes being poor? The demand to love one another in community asks how love is expressed in terms of sheer human need and what must we share in justice, long before we reach the point of asking what we will give as charity, or sharing generously with the other members of our family, the Body of Christ.

This issue forms the communities of Luke and there are two versions, or practices, of living in community in Luke's gospel. There is the community that lives in Jerusalem, which happens to be the poorest community of the Churches, and how they live together; and there is the Church on the road, or the community in mission, that lives a more prophetic style of the gospel for drawing others into the community—they are sent forth by the more stable community to preach the gospel and they rely on the hospitality of others as they travel. These images of community life reveal the practicality of the Good News to the poor. The lifestyle of sharing and holding all things in common, the practice of the virtue of poverty, and the practical economics of caring for a wide spectrum of people who model belief so that others can see them form the foundation of the gospel. In the Acts of the Apostles and other early descriptions of the Church (such as the *Didache,* a first-century document), the Christian communities were described in startling terms: see how those Christians love one another—there are no poor among them! This reality was part of the impetus and driving spirit that drew people to the Church in great numbers.

About halfway through Luke's gospel, Jesus is gathering followers about him (beyond the more intimate group of the twelve men and a number of women who are his inner circle), and he tells them how they are to travel and live. Jesus has already tried to teach them that suffering, rejection, and even death are a part of following in his footsteps, but they are more interested in their place and rank among the group of disciples. Jesus takes a young child—someone with no power as is usually perceived in society—and is clear about how they are to operate if they are to be his forerunners, his disciples, his teachers, and his leaders:

> *An argument arose among them as to which one of them was the greatest. But Jesus, aware of their inner thoughts, took a little child and put it by his side, and said to them, "Whoever welcomes this child in my name welcomes me, and whoever welcomes me welcomes the one who sent me; for the least among all of you is the greatest." (Lk 9:46–48)*

Authority, power, and influence in Jesus's communities are not to reflect how power is used in other organizations and groups. The word that is repeated over and over again is *welcome*—the sense of hospitality that is a rich and primary tradition from Judaism. In Genesis, Abraham graciously welcomes the three strangers who come to his tent, and so he welcomes the Holy Ones in their persons and presence. In exchange, he is given the good news of a child that he and Sarah will have in their old age. The tradition at this time demanded that all strangers were more than guests—they were blood kin for three days—to be treated as graciously as possible, with food, drink, shelter, and welcome. Jesus is closely associating himself with his followers and declaring that whoever welcomes them into their homes and relationships will be welcoming him and welcoming God the Father who sends him as he sends them out to bring hope and the welcoming presence of God to all. This is the first real indicator of the universality of the gospel.

In choosing a child, Jesus is breaking all of his contemporaries' low opinions and associations with children. Children had no power or status, no rights, and basically had to obey anyone older, stronger, or more demanding. They were like servants or slaves who belong to the group of extended family as well as neighbors or even other figures in the town and surrounding area. Now Jesus is declaring that this is a prerequisite for having any real power to teach or preach the gospel and to invite others into the company of the children of God with Jesus. For Jesus, power and prestige are about downward mobility, freely and joyfully accepted—and that is what draws you closest to the side of Jesus.

Just paragraphs later, Jesus will remind them that, like him, they are not to spend the majority of their time, efforts, and attitudes in acquiring land, places of security, and possessions, nor in the daily activities of how they are to live. These are a reality but should not consume the bulk of their energies and time. Certain lifestyles demand shifts of priorities.

> As they were going along the road, someone said to him, "I will follow you wherever you go." And Jesus said to him, "Foxes have holes, and birds of the air have nests; but the Son of Man has nowhere to lay his head." To another he said, "Follow me." But he said, "Lord, first let me go and bury my father." But Jesus said to him, "Let the dead bury their own dead; but as for you, go and proclaim the kingdom of God." Another said, I will follow you, Lord; but let me first say farewell to those at my home." Jesus said to him, "No one who puts a hand to the plow and looks back is fit for the kingdom of God." (Lk 9:57–62)

Jesus's words are not so much to be taken literally, but are couched in the style of exhortation and immediacy of what is needed if one is going to live like Jesus and not only believe in his words and practices but also to seek to draw others into following him in his company. There are some who will live the gospel more prophetically, as a living sign of the presence of the Kingdom of God here in the world, waiting to be welcomed. Those who follow in his footsteps of going out publicly and seeking others to join them must have more public expressions of their role in the community.

In a long opening paragraph in the next chapter, Jesus chooses seventy of his many followers (the number of nations at that time) and sends them off in twos to go ahead of him into all the towns he intends to visit. When sending them, he reminds them of the many who are waiting for the gospel and the Good News to the poor, of the Kingdom of God already in their presence, and that they must pray as they labor for others to join them in being those who announce and share their Good News with others: "The harvest is plentiful, but the laborers are few; therefore ask the Lord of the harvest to send out laborers into his harvest" (Lk 10:2). He is careful to remind them who they work for and that the focus of their travels is on the harvest—on others who are waiting for their words and hope—implying that it is an honor for them to be doing Jesus's work in the world.

It is worth reading the exhortation to them as he sends them off. In reality it is a description of a way of life: a community on the road, as missionaries and preachers, even prophets of the Church, sent out by the Church at home. They will go forth, gather, and return, bringing with them those whom they have drawn into the net of the kingdom. It is like spokes of a wheel going out, but sourced in the larger reality, the hub and core of the community.

> *"Go on your way. See, I am sending you out like lambs into the midst of wolves. Carry no purse, no bag, no sandals; and greet no one on the road. Whatever house you enter, first say, 'Peace to this house!' And if anyone is there who shares in peace, your peace will rest on that person; but if not, it will return to you. Remain in the same house, eating and drinking whatever they provide, for the laborer deserves to be paid. Do not move about from house to house. Whenever you enter a town and its people welcome you, eat what is set before you; cure the sick who are there, and say to them: 'The kingdom of God has come near to you.'" (Lk 10:3–9)*

This is the lifestyle of the prophets and itinerant preachers. It can be a lifelong commitment, or just for a period of time, but it is always done in pairs and within a larger group that is sent forth from the home community. They go forth and return home to tell of their journeys and the response that they have received—whether it was positive or whether they were rejected. What is important is that the gospel is preached, and the kingdom's reality is pointed out, and it is pointed out first in their way of traveling and living on the road together. Previously it was taught often that all these disciples sent out were men; but it is more probable that they were husbands and wives or friends, and not necessarily just men.

What is more intriguing are the specifics of their traveling. They are initially warned to be lambs among wolves, a dramatic difference of how they are to be perceived and seen. With the mention of lambs, there is the sense of vulnerability and defenselessness without protection, armor, or weapons. They are grazers, eating no meat, staying in an area for a period of time, and then drawn back into the larger flock by the shepherds. This idea is extended with the commands that they are to travel light! No purse, no bag, not even sandals—they are to go barefoot! There is to be no money on their persons and no extra changes of clothing; they go as they are and then they are to rely on the good graces and hospitality of those they encounter in the towns and villages they are sent to. It is not a random "hit the road" trip to see what happens along the way; it is purposeful and specific. They are scouts and they announce who and what is coming behind them—the Word of God in Jesus. They're just a hint of what is to come. They are, at their roots, without violence or harm. They have no staffs either for protection or for attacking, and without sandals they would even have difficulty running from those who would be hostile to them. It is a way of walking that is free, uncluttered, and without hindrance, and it seems to be temporary, not a lifelong way of living. They are ambassadors of the larger community seeking others to join them.

This is one of the ways of being Church: living simply to draw others into the community, relying on the hospitality of those who are waiting for the Peace of the gospel to be brought to them and those who are already open to its reality. But in addition, these who go "before the face of the Lord," like John the Baptist, also rely on their home community for their livelihood and what they need to travel, as well as to take care of whom and what they leave behind and will return to. It is a Church of welcome and of sharing graciously, and the Word of the gospel is central to all that is done in daily life as in sojourns out from home. This is the prophetic, or missionary, Church that reveals by its style the immediate presence of the kingdom but remains connected to the Church that is more stable and growing that takes care of all the poor among them, while still remaining aware of so many who are in need and waiting for the gospel.

The other symbol of Jesus's teaching that is rampant in Luke's gospel is food: of meals shared and Jesus's indiscriminate eating practices that became the basis of the ritual worship and the sacrament of the Eucharist—the breaking of the bread, the sharing of the cup, and the chewing of the Word as food and nourishment of both body and soul. Everything of import that Jesus says and does happens in the context of a meal or a feeding story—some intimate dinners and many crowded picnics and sprawling daylong experiences of sharing and being fed not just food, but hope, healing, inclusion, and strength for a way of living that encompasses all areas of life. Jean Anthelme Brillat-Savarin said, "Tell me what you eat and I'll tell you what you are." This is literally what happens in Luke's version of the gospel.

These symbols and expressions of Jesus's words and ways of being in the world take place in multicultural settings, drawing people together from caste groups, nationalistic and racial groups, and among those who would not usually religiously or culturally eat and share food and intimacy. In this regard, Jesus is scandalous in his behavior and practice of hospitality, inclusion, and no-strings-attached approach to whom one eats with, is nourished with, and worships God with. The basis of worship and ritual shifts from the formal structures of Temple sacrifice and ritual killings of animals to meals with friends and family—believers and followers from all places and groups—and takes place around a table and is interspersed before and after with conversation, teaching, stories, prayers, and emotion. Luke's Jesus is into wining and dining as a sure sign of the presence of the Kingdom of God present in the world, and changing what it means to be religious and human. Jesus stays as food, Word, and Spirit within the community in Luke's gospel.

These are, in some senses, new traditions being born, though all are rooted in earlier Jewish practices. But Jesus's Spirit and prophetic calls to conversion are wedded with the needs of the poorest and the most vulnerable. For Luke's Christians, one cannot be holy by practicing rituals; one can only become holy by practicing compassion and sharing all that one has with others, as God has shared all of God in Jesus and the Spirit with all of us, without discrimination or stipulations.

The most obvious of Jesus's preaching comes immediately after his baptism, after he returns to his hometown of Nazareth in the power of the Spirit. On a Sabbath, as was his custom, he stands up to do the reading and declares why he was baptized and why *anyone* is baptized into the community of his disciples. It is his first sermon, his proclamation that all is going to be new—that what has been awaited is here but has been developed with grace, power, and the Spirit of God so strongly that it's barely recognizable when it appears. It is sometimes called the Jubilee announcement, or his inaugural address. When Jesus stands before his family, friends, and neighbors he grew up with, he is handed the scroll of the prophet Isaiah and it all begins here.

> *He unrolled the scroll and found the place where it was written: "The Spirit of the Lord is upon me, because he has anointed me to bring good news to the poor. He has sent me to proclaim release to the captives and recovery of sight to the blind, to let the oppressed go free, to proclaim the year of the Lord's favor." And he rolled up the scroll, gave it back to the attendant, and sat down. The eyes of all in the synagogue were fixed on him. Then he began to say to them, "Today this scripture has been fulfilled in your hearing."* (Lk 4:17–21)

The impact of Jesus's words, quoting partially (a line or two is omitted and another is inserted) from the book of the prophet Isaiah that he appropriates to himself, would have been stunning and caused consternation, anger, and surprise in everyone present. He is clear about what he is here to do: to set in motion a new way of being, a strict adherence to a set of priorities that are very specific and demanding and that cannot be done by one alone, but only in a community of believers—a people dedicated to changing forever the face of the human race and how we are to live together on earth. There are five priorities that follow one upon the other:

1. *Preach Good News to the poor.*
2. *Release the captives (all prisoners).*
3. *Give sight to those who have been blind.*
4. *Set all the oppressed free.*
5. *Proclaim a year of favor from the Lord.*

Pragmatically, these five works and projects would change forever what it means to be religious, to believe in the God of life and love, and how to live with others. In a word, these realities define *justice*—basic necessities that all human beings deserve because they are human persons created and beloved of God. This is where it begins, in a community where the poor, those lacking and without, those most vulnerable and deemed expendable in society, are cared for first and honored as the presence of God among them.

Then what follows is the release of all prisoners. Many of those in prison, jailed, and captive to economic and political/nationalistic bondage are poor and also know violence, rejection, blame, and punishment either for what they have actually done in society or for what society decides they have done to undermine what is dominant in a group. Theologically this is Jesus's teaching on forgiveness, reconciliation, restitution, and restoration to the community—no matter what has been done or how often. This is holding people accountable with hope and a possibility for a future.

The third reason for baptism in Jesus's community is what is inserted into the text and not found in Isaiah's original. It is recovery of sight to the blind. The blind in all the gospels are self-righteous and hard-hearted, resistant to the Word of God in Jesus, and intent on silencing the Good News and the prophet who preaches it. This is the hinge between the first and last two projects, and many say the most difficult to accomplish because there is nothing more difficult and dangerous than religious people who believe that others are the problem and must be changed, converted, and made like them—or else. What is necessary is to admit one's own culpability and evil, as well as collusion with evil, to accept the truth that one participates in and contributes to the woes of the human community, and to recognize that the world is hard—for everyone.

Jesus moves on to letting the oppressed go free, or, as it is often expressed, liberating the oppressed. The words ring of politics, nation-states, power, and authority to those who find themselves slaves. At that time, being a slave meant being a second- or third-class citizen, crucial to maintaining the status quo and the vast gap between rich and poor and slave and free. These are people who are poor and suffer violence from others without any power to respond, and often have no hope of a real life beyond basic survival. They are seen as enemies, problems, and people to be disposed of; society blamed them for their predicament. In reality, they are the victims of structural injustice and evil that is perpetuated for the privilege of a few.

Lastly Jesus announces that he is here to declare that this year will be a year of the Lord's favor. All in the synagogue would have known exactly what he was speaking about: originally every seventh year in the Jewish nation was the Sabbath year. Later it was moved to every seven times seven years—the forty-ninth and fiftieth year—and called the Jubilee year. The Jubilee year had very specific practices that all Jewish believers and the community set into motion to restore and rebuild the people so that they would always be a "light to the nations," or the chosen people of God. They worked to ensure their society would never be like what they had experienced as slaves in Egypt.

The Jubilee year involved several sections of different practices. In the religious practice, first all debts within the Jewish community were canceled. Second: all prisoners and slaves were released back into the community to begin their lives again. (At the time, there were many indentured servants and families who were forced to sell their children into slavery in order to hold onto their land.

They were so poor, this was the only way to ensure their survival.) Third: all immigrants and illegal aliens were set free to remain in the land of Israel and become residents or were given enough money and seed to return to their own lands and start their lives anew. Fourth: all the land of Israel was received back into the collective and then divided equally among everyone so that no land was held in perpetuity and all people had a chance at owning and belonging to the promised land. Fifth: the land lay fallow and nothing was planted or harvested in that year. This practice not only allowed the land to rest but also reminded the people that it belonged first to God and that it was shared with them. During this year, everyone was also to share the previous year's harvest with one another so that no one went hungry.

The Jubilee year was part of the law of Israel, and was also called the year of the Lord's favor because it was of God's doing and will— and it was practiced intermittently at best because it was onerous to those in power in Israel. Jesus was well aware of this, and that that particular year was not a traditional Jubilee year, or even a Sabbath year: indeed, that year was nowhere near either. But it would have become apparent quickly to those listening that Jesus was opening the door to a new way of living, where every year is a Jubilee and Sabbath year for those who follow him. These would be characteristic marks of his community. And in the early Church, this was practiced for all to see, marvel over, and be drawn into.

Initially, all were loud in praise of Jesus and his proclamation, but this acceptance quickly turned into anger, cynicism, distaste, and even rage. Jesus, surprisingly enough, seemed to know that this would be the reaction to his words of hope for so many long excluded from God's presence and relationship. He baits the disbelievers, telling them the truth about their utter lack of obedience to God and their disdain for God, the prophets, and the Word of God in the Scriptures; he reminded them of stories where God moved outside of Israel with Elijah and Elisha because he found no faith among them. This infuriates them; in the very beginning of Luke's gospel, his own townspeople, neighbors, and family rise against him and drive him out of the synagogue, intending to throw him over a cliff and stone him to death. The start of Jesus's new family of friends that is open to so many long declared unwanted and unworthy begins with both wild hope and expectations and realistic reminders of what this radical upheaval can cause in those who hear the words of Jesus. The rest of the gospel will reiterate this sentiment often, always with the demand and challenge to decide where one's solidarity is found, where justice and compassion truly lie—with Jesus and the poor, or with the wealthy, rich, and violent of the earth, no matter what religion they claim to practice and belong to. Jesus's God is the God of the poor, of justice, and of compassion.

Some of Jesus's most famous words in Luke are often found to be the hardest to put into practice, obey, and take to heart; these words are found in what is called the Sermon on the Plain (chapter 6). And it is said that the rest of the gospel of Luke tells stories and acts out in gestures, rituals, relationships, and confrontations the meaning of what is preached in that sermon. Other than what is spoken in the sermon, the location and how Jesus preaches it speak volumes about how to be a disciple in Luke's communities. It is often missed when it is read or listened to.

> He came down with them and stood on a level place, with a great crowd of his disciples and a great multitude of people from all Judea, Jerusalem, and the coast of Tyre and Sidon. They had come to hear him and to be healed of their diseases; and those who were troubled with unclean spirits were cured. And all in the crowd were trying to touch him, for power came out from him and healed all of them.
>
> Then he looked up at his disciples and said: Blessed are you who are poor, for yours is the kingdom of God. Blessed are you who are hungry now, for you will be filled. Blessed are you who weep now, for you will laugh. Blessed are you when people hate you, and when they exclude you, revile you, and defame you on account of the Son of Man. Rejoice in that day and leap for joy, for surely your reward is great in heaven; for that is what their ancestors did to the prophets.

But woe to you who are rich, for you have received your consolation.
Woe to you who are full now, for you will be hungry. Woe to you who
are laughing now, for you will mourn and weep. Woe to you when all
speak well of you, for that is what their ancestors did to the false prophets.
(Lk 6:17–26)

These words were shocking—they still are to all who hear them!
It is a total reversal of what is the common wisdom of the nations
and even of most religious groups. It is standing with those who are
not making it in society and are not dominant in economics, politics, religion, or culture anywhere in the world. It is encouraging
to the majority of the human race who find themselves with their
lives in jeopardy and their backs to the wall. Yet Jesus is saying,
Hang in there! You're on the right path. I am with you, and you will
know the presence and the power of God. And he stands against
those who live for today, with their eyes intent on now, their own
people and possessions, and think that they are acting like human
beings, but they are not: they are false, and flawed in their heart, attitudes, and actions, and how they live today that contributes to the
destruction of others will be their own experience one day. Luke's
version of the blessings also includes the woes and sets up the situation of many in the community of Luke—the rich and poor who
want to follow Jesus.

The remainder of the sermon is about loving one's enemies, giving to all who beg from you, blessing all who curse you, and praying
for and doing good to those who hate you. It talks about generosity of spirit, of justice and charity for all. This law was incumbent
upon all Jews. For Jesus, his law will stretch the human spirit; one's
actions begin with those farthest from one's own kin, those seen as
enemies, and then works its way back into friends, fellow believers, and family. Again upside down looking at reality—and inside
out—odd wisdom that contradicts what is accepted and practiced
in society. This is the Kingdom of heaven and of God according to
Jesus in Luke's gospel.

Jesus journeys to Jerusalem three times in Luke's account—a

literary way of having Jesus live through the Jewish seasons liturgically and live on the road, always returning to Jerusalem. It affords him encounters with a wide range of people: widows from small towns, centurions, sick and deformed people in synagogues, uninvited guests at banquets in the houses of the wealthy, those driven insane by the pressures of living in a society built on violence and military occupation (the Gerasene Demoniac), huge crowds of people in despair after the brutal killing of John the Baptist, Samaritans (hated heretics of the Jewish community), people struggling with addictions/obsessions and physical ailments, and people who are slowly starving to death as slaves in their own country. He visits cities that resist his Word and want him to just go away and not return.

In Luke's gospel the punch and force of Jesus's words are found in his parables, many of which are found only in Luke. Many still have to do with food and people who normally wouldn't eat together; when they do—drawn by Jesus's presence—there is confusion, conflict, preaching, and storytelling, and new relationships and invitations to intimacy and life with others that no one would have ever dreamed of growing close with. These stories often use food as the jumping-off point and are told at dinner parties. One of the most famous and unnerving is the parable of the rich man and Lazarus—or Dives and Lazarus. This is how Jesus tells it:

> "There was a rich man who was dressed in purple and fine linen and who feasted sumptuously every day. And at his gate lay a poor man named Lazarus, covered with sores, who longed to satisfy his hunger with what fell from the rich man's table; even the dogs would come and lick his sores. The poor man died and was carried away by the angels to be with Abraham. The rich man also died and was buried. In Hades, where he was being tormented, he looked up and saw Abraham far away with Lazarus by his side. He called out, 'Father Abraham, have mercy on me, and send Lazarus to dip the tip of his finger in water and cool my tongue; for I am in agony in these flames.' But Abraham said, 'Child, remember that during your life-

time you received your good things, and Lazarus in like manner evil things; but now he is comforted here, and you are in agony. Besides all this, between you and us a great chasm has been fixed, so that those who might want to pass from here to you cannot do so, and no one can cross from there to us.' He said, 'Then, father, I beg you to send him to my father's house—for I have five brothers—that he may warn them, so that they will not also come into this place of torment.' Abraham replied, 'They have Moses and the prophets; they should listen to them.' He said, 'No, father Abraham; but if someone goes to them from the dead, they will repent.' He said to him, 'If they do not listen to Moses and the prophets, neither will they be convinced even if someone rises from the dead.'" (Lk 16:19–31)

The story begins with the setup, simple and direct. Dives is described, and one can almost picture the purple and linen, the laden table, and the dogs feasting. Outside is Lazarus, so poor and derelict that the dogs are licking his sores. He wants only to grovel and eat what even the dogs might not want. It is a scene of lavish extravagance as the norm for one and miserable starvation, humiliation, and destitution for the other. Unfortunately it is not unlike much of the human race's experience of the few living with excessive wealth and the majority lacking even what they need for survival— and both are close enough to know of the other's circumstances and predicament, with just a fence or a wall or a gate between them. From there, the story moves quickly. Lazarus dies; soon after Dives also passes away, and the judgment is a done deed. Lazarus now resides and dwells in the bosom of Abraham as the Spiritual so aptly rejoices and sings, and Dives is tormented in the agony of flames, knowing desperate want of water.

Interestingly enough there is no discussion of the judgment; the fates of Dives and Lazarus are simply accepted as reality. What is interesting, though, is the conversation between Dives, who was obviously rich and religious, and Abraham, who was the father of Jewish faithfulness and hospitality, and who now holds Lazarus in a welcome embrace. Dives begs for Abraham to send Lazarus to him with a drop of water on his finger for Dives to taste. He does not—will not—even address Lazarus. Instead he goes sideways through Abraham. And the theological or religious discussion is held with Lazarus as a listener—and he is the reason for the theology—but he does not participate. Dives's request is denied, and he's stuck in an impossible situation. There is a fixed divide now between the two, and neither can cross or pass over. It is a done deal, which again is not refuted but accepted. Now Dives is thinking of his family and those he loves, and we learn that he has five brothers on earth and maybe he can save them from what he now knows is reality.

Again he does not ask Lazarus or acknowledge his presence personally but instead asks Abraham to send Lazarus—as one would ask for a slave, a servant, or a missionary preacher to be sent—to his father's house on earth to tell his brothers to change so that they won't end up where he is. Again his request is denied. Dives is reminded that his brothers, like him, were believers and they had Moses (inferring the law) and the prophets (who came when the law was disregarded and ignored); and if they didn't listen to them, why would they listen to anyone else—even one who has come back from the dead. They are too bound up in their own small worlds and without any regard for others, let alone compassion or connection.

During these exchanges, Dives refers to Abraham as "father," and Abraham keeps referring to Dives as "child"—the relationship is still a reality but time has intervened and some things can be righted or changed and others no longer can be shifted. Small bits of meaning add depth to the story. There is Dives, who along with his five brothers constitutes a family of six. What if he treated Lazarus as his family, as his seventh brother? Seven is a number that constitutes wholeness, completeness, universality. Instead, Dives denied Lazarus welcome on earth—indeed, he denied him life itself on earth. He not only refused to eat with him but even refused to give him scraps from his table. Dives was inhuman and never *lived,* and so he never actually worshipped God or practiced a religion. Basically Dives means wealth, while Lazarus is one who has been raised to new life—or come back from the dead. It is the name that symbolizes everyone who is baptized and is a follower of Jesus, the Risen One.

This is a parable about two ways of living in this world, of being a human being—one isolated (even with a family, kin, connections, society, etc.) and one who lives with others, in relation to the entire human race. One of the defining realities of which group a person belongs to is who you eat with or who you refuse to welcome to your table. The gospel declares that we are a universal family that shares all things in common, but most especially the basic necessities of life, and that in sharing there can be a wealth of welcome, communion, and hospitality that embraces all others. A parable is a huge question that demands a response: What if this is reality? What do you need to do so that this won't be your fate? What must happen now, here on this side of the fixed divide, so that there is an alternative of hope and all things can be transformed—so that the kingdom can come and all are welcome in it? Once again, Jesus's words confront daily reality for the world at large, but more specifically for those in his own community who knew this story in their own families and villages.

Toward the end of Luke's gospel, just before Jesus goes to Jerusalem to die, one final story emphasizes the truth Jesus is trying to convey. Again, it is a memorable story because of the character in it: Zacchaeus, the tree climber. This story is believed to be the model for the catechumen for the communities of Luke; it was the pattern for coming to follow Jesus in public and the ritual practice of what was required before one was baptized, which was followed by a celebration of being in the new family of Jesus by sitting down at table in the kingdom here on earth, with one's new status as a child of God and a brother or sister of Jesus and all the followers of Jesus. Listen:

> He entered Jericho and was passing through it. A man was there named
> Zacchaeus; he was a chief tax collector and was rich. He was trying to see

who Jesus was, but on account of the crowd he could not, because he was short in stature. So he ran ahead and climbed a sycamore tree to see him, because he was going to pass that way. When Jesus came to the place, he looked up and said to him, "Zacchaeus, hurry and come down; for I must stay at your house today." So he hurried down and was happy to welcome him. All who saw it began to grumble and said, "He has gone to be the guest of one who is a sinner." Zacchaeus stood there and said to the Lord, "Look, half of my possessions, Lord, I will give to the poor; and if I have defrauded anyone of anything, I will pay back four times as much." Then Jesus said to him, "Today salvation has come to his house, because he too is a son of Abraham. For the Son of Man came to seek out and to save the lost." (Lk 19:1–10)

The story is charming and, like many parables, veers off in unexpected directions that turn the story on the listeners. We see a good deal of who Zacchaeus is and what is important to him; we find out he's a wealthy man who has made his riches off his neighbors. Tax collectors and those in charge of larger communities were the only ones who knew the tax amounts required by Rome. Tax collectors were believed to have collected monies over and above that amount, which they pocketed for themselves. They were hated and despised for stealing from their own people and living in collusion with Rome. Zacchaeus is short, both physically and of stature in the community, but he's also curious about Jesus. Obviously he's heard about him and wants to see for himself. He's interested enough to run on ahead and climb a tree; no doubt he was dressed very formally as befits his place in society. And so he's up in a tree when Jesus comes by. Jesus stops and looks up at Zacchaeus; then he unceremoniously invites himself to his house for dinner. Shocking behavior for both of them! One thinks of Jesus smiling and enjoying the scene, and we are told that Zacchaeus is thoroughly delighted as he gets down from his perch.

Then the reactions begin in the crowd, even probably among Jesus's disciples. What does Jesus think he is doing, approaching someone who is so publicly without shame for his position gained by thievery and deceit? They grumble—or in older translations, murmur. You can hear the murmur moving through the crowd; the same word is used when the Israelites *murmur* against Moses as they are being led to freedom out of Egypt but are stalled in the desert. Zacchaeus, however, holds his ground and declares in public—around all those witnesses—what he is going to do. Declaring himself this way makes his statement a public commitment that will seal his fate in this world, from here on out. First he says that he will be incredibly generous! He will give half of his worth, possessions, holdings, to the poor. And then he will do justice as needed: he will pay back, according to the law, anyone he has treated unjustly with fourfold restitution. Now it is Jesus's turn to be thoroughly delighted and pleased with Zacchaeus! He publicly declares that Zacchaeus is now not only a son of Abraham, a good practicing Jew, but a beloved son of God, and he is welcomed into his own embrace and kin.

The story brings together many of Jesus's words: he looks up at Zacchaeus in the same manner as when he preached the Sermon on the Plain—the blessings and woes to his own disciples come earlier. He practices the art of welcoming and invitation to share in the banquet—another word for the kingdom of heaven, the Good News of the gospel to the poor. He goes out and does not wait for others to come to him, as he has tried to teach his disciples. He welcomes everyone and anyone—enemy, Samaritan, heretic, sinner, or laggard—with openness and does not allow murmuring, cursing, or judgment on who is worthy to sit at the table and eat with him—with them, too, if they want to stay his disciples. This is the heart of being a follower of Jesus, a Christian in the community where the poor are welcomed with dignity and whatever is shared with them is shared with God as worship that is acceptable.

Zacchaeus's standing before Jesus, his disciples, and all the crowd is what was the acceptable practice for being welcomed into the sacraments of baptism, confirmation, and Eucharist. First each person, regardless of rank in society, gives half of what they owned to the poor and then did justice as needed—paying fourfold restitution to anyone they had defrauded. Then the rejoicing over the lost sheep, the lost coin, and the lost son or daughter can begin! Zacchaeus welcomed Jesus into his household and Jesus, delighted with Zacchaeus, welcomes him into his company of disciples and the children of God. In Jesus's community and in Luke's Churches, this was the beginning of calling God "our Father"—a very pragmatic shifting of wealth, where the poor were made kin, and friends and the wealthy shared their excess and became brothers and sisters with Jesus by the Spirit's driving power. And all sat down to feast together—a glimpse for all to see of what the banquet of the Lord, the Kingdom of God, looks like here on earth, now.

Jesus will celebrate a meal with his friends, part of the ritual of Sabbath and Passover, and go to his death. The story will be largely the same as found in the previous gospels. Ritual and worship now are intimately bound to what is done with and for the bodies of other human beings—and that is the essential of any worship.

However, in Luke's gospel, at Jesus's death on the Cross, a Roman centurion is the one to proclaim who Jesus is: "When the centurion saw what had taken place, he praised God and said, 'Certainly this man was innocent.'" (Lk 23:47). The reality of Jesus's words has seeped into the Roman Empire's own levels of power and is transforming even those of the military, the dominant economic culture, and those who occupy other countries. The gospel will end with the Risen Jesus and his friends, many of them eating together on the first evening of the beginning of their new lives as Christians.

Two remarkable realities have been declared. In the words of Leo Tolstoy: "Men pray to the Almighty to relieve poverty. But poverty comes not from God's laws—it is blasphemy of the worst kind to say that. Poverty comes from man's injustice to his fellow man" (*A Confession*). For Luke, the privileged place of revelation and nearness to God is with the poor: this is God's Good News. The second reality is that worship and practice of life are intimately connected: in eating together and sharing bread, wine, and story, God is found most surely and honored—but this ritual that honors the Body of Christ must be extended into the lives and bodies of all human beings. The table and the storytelling in worship must reflect the actual sharing of life together, or the worship is empty and the fixed divide grows more solid, rather than becoming a thin membrane that can be passed through here on earth—and the banquet of God's welcome is the open door into the endless possibilities of tomorrow.

Chapter 7

THE GOSPEL OF LUKE NOW

There is, in a word, nothing comfortable about the Bible until we manage to get so used to it that we make it comfortable for ourselves. But then we are perhaps too used to it and too at home in it. Let us not be too sure we know the Bible . . . just because we have learned not to have problems with it. Have we perhaps learned . . . not to really pay attention to it? Have we ceased to question the book and be questioned by it?

THOMAS MERTON, *Opening the Bible*

SOMETIMES THE BEST PLACE TO BEGIN IS AT THE END: LUKE'S gospel ends with the telling of the Resurrection. In Luke's gospel, there are really three stories—one in the early-morning hours before dawn; one during the day on a road from Jerusalem to Emmaus; and a final story back in Jerusalem where everyone is gathering in the evening. For Luke, the Resurrection was happening simultaneously in different places, but it drew everyone back together again after Jesus's death and their initial impetus to scatter in despair and grief.

Luke's gospel shifts the focus of the community from the Temple, destroyed more than twenty years previously, to the dwelling place of God on earth now, in the Body of Christ risen from the dead. The presence of the Risen Lord is stronger and more pervasive in the world, in Resurrection life, than he ever was during his lifetime. And that Body of Christ is the men and women who are his Body now in the world, in the communities of Luke's time and all other times—the Spirit is spreading throughout the Greek and

Roman world now—sixty or more years after the events of Jesus's life. Ritual and worship are now intimately bound to what is done with and for the bodies of other human beings, and that is the essential purpose of worship. The internal life of the community, the worship life of the community, and life on the road as prophets, missionaries, and preachers are all rooted in these three stories of the Resurrection: revelation, recognition, and witness.

The story begins early in the morning, before dawn, with women going to the tomb intending to anoint Jesus's body for burial. Once inside the tomb they see men in dazzling white garments who question them:

> *"Why do you look for the living among the dead? He is not here, but has risen. Remember how he told you, while he was still in Galilee, that the Son of Man must be handed over to sinners, and be crucified, and on the third day rise again." Then they remembered his words, and returning from the tomb, they told all this to the eleven and to all the rest. (Lk 24:5b–9)*

The women tell the story and they are not believed; in fact it is worded so that they are even derided by the men. New life unbounded and unbelievable has been set in motion, but the reaction is to ignore, belittle, and reject it. The morning story of wild hopes stirred up is left to peter out—Peter goes and checks out the tomb but returns and nothing else happens.

The story switches to a road outside of the city, where two of Jesus's disciples are going to Emmaus—there's a sense that they are leaving Jerusalem behind, and with it, all their hopes—and they try to put the horrors of the last days and all that happened behind them; they are in despair. It is all over. When Jesus begins to walk with them, they are so steeped in grief that they do not recognize him. He begins to question them gently, goading them into talking about what has happened. One of them, Cleopas, describes the events of Jesus's life and who they believe him to be—before the Resurrection. It is a short creed (or statement) of faith. It sums up who Jesus was or could have been to those who hoped for one to bring release from their bondage to the Romans, and freedom to their hearts and minds and spirits. Listen:

". . . about Jesus of Nazareth, who was a prophet mighty in deed and word before God and all the people, and how our chief priests and leaders handed him over to be condemned to death and crucified him. But we had hoped that he was the one to redeem Israel. Yes, and besides all this, it is now the third day since these things took place. Moreover, some women of our group astounded us. They were at the tomb early this morning, and when they did not find his body there, they came back and told us that they had indeed seen a vision of angels who said that he was alive. Some of those who were with us went to the tomb and found it just as the women had said; but they did not see him." (Lk 24:19b−24)

Jesus always sent off his disciples two by two and now two of them are going home, leaving behind them their dreams and the life they had embraced in following Jesus. The two are most probably husband and wife. Indeed Cleopas's wife—Mary of Cleopas—was probably one of the women at the tomb in the morning following Jesus's death. They cannot see him and no longer believe—their expectations have been shattered; they have seen the collusion between their own religious leaders and the Romans, the brutality of crucifixion, and the finality of death. They are talking about it all, but there is no sense, no meaning, to any of it.

They continue, speaking of Jesus as a prophet. The etymology of the Hebrew word for prophet—*Navi*—has three moments, or expressions, to it: to cry out, to gush forward or flow, and to be hollow. This is what a prophet does: cries out the truth specifically about God and the true way to worship and the coming of justice and peace and the care of the poor. For a prophet and for God, the three facets of *Navi* are pieces of a seamless garment. The words gush forth, often accompanied by deeds that flow from these words, which seek to find an empty place in those who hear the word and let awareness take root. And for them, Jesus was one of the mighty ones, like the ones of their ancestors: Isaiah, Jeremiah, and Amos, among others.

And so Cleopas continues and speaks of the morning's events, ending the amazing tale with "him they didn't see"—just as now, they can't see him, either. Jesus shifts from the one who questions to the one who teaches, preaches, and reveals; he chides them, too. He tells them that they are so slow to believe all the words of the prophets who sought to prepare the way so that they could recognize him when he came. Jesus goes through all the portions of the Scriptures, interpreting them in light of his own words, deeds, and life. The core issue is the Cross, suffering, and death—the usual fate of the prophets who must always be remembered and taken into account when preaching and seeking to live out the Word of God.

As Jesus speaks, the road and journey begin to come to an end, but Cleopas and his wife don't want him to go and beg him to stay and come in and eat. And he does. This middle piece of the stories comes to a point of revelation now.

> So he went in to stay with them. When he was at table with them, he took bread, blessed and broke it, and gave it to them. Then their eyes were opened, and they recognized him; and he vanished from their sight. They said to each other, "Were not our hearts burning within us while he was talking to us on the road, while he was opening the scriptures to us?" That same hour they got up and returned to Jerusalem; and they found the eleven and their companions gathered together. They were saying, "The Lord has risen indeed, and he has appeared to Simon!" Then they told what had happened on the road, and how he had been made known to them in the breaking of the bread. (Lk 24:29b–35)

They spend hours listening to him open the Scriptures and apply their meaning to him, to his words and deeds, life and death (the road is about seven miles and very rocky and difficult). Jesus captures their souls, their minds, and their hearts, and they don't want to let go of him. When they finally sit at table, Jesus does what had, even in his lifetime, become a characteristic symbol or gesture for him: he takes bread, blesses and breaks it, and passes it around—and in that instant they see; it is a moment of awareness, insight, and the beginning of faith. And he's gone in the same instant! What is called the celebration of the Eucharist is over in an instant; it took three or four hours, if not more, of listening to and absorbing the Word of the Lord in the Scriptures to facilitate and trigger the moment of recognition in the breaking of the bread. And the effect of the listening and the seeing is not that they eat but that they look at each other and realize that he has been with them all along, and his presence and his words brought them back to life and stirred the flame in their hearts. They get up and run back to Jerusalem. The Word has given them the courage and the meaning they need to face life with all its terrible possibilities and amazing graces.

They are met by the eleven other disciples with the words of life and the news that even Simon has seen him (but not Peter because he betrayed Jesus and still has to repent and be converted to being a believer again). Then they in turn spill out their story. This is where the reading is most often terminated with the line "And how they came to recognize him in the breaking of the bread." And yet that is not the focus of the story: the focus of the story is Jesus opening their minds to the Scriptures, breaking the Word with them so that they are fed hope and insight, meaning and courage— so that they can reach the point where they can see him, if only for a moment, in the ritual of the bread. It is the journeying together, and the sharing of the Scriptures in light of their experiences in life, and their coping with the grief and the horror of the Cross and death, through which they are brought to faith. Any religious experience rooted in the Word of the Lord culminates in the ritual of the breaking of bread, and the important thing is not so much to eat (since Jesus disappears in that instant and they are left to look at each other and decide what to do) but to return and to gather with others and share what they have come to know. The gathering must have been noisy and exuberant, with everyone talking at once.

But this is not the high point or culmination of the Resurrection story that began with an empty tomb, then continued along the road where strangers drew near to one another over shared hopes in the Word of God, and finally sat at table with one another, recognizing Jesus and one another in the breaking of the bread. What comes next—as the disciples are talking—is the focus of Luke's meaning: the power of the resurrected presence of Jesus with his followers.

While they were talking about this, Jesus himself stood among them and said to them, "Peace be with you." They were startled and terrified, and thought that they were seeing a ghost. He said to them, "Why are you frightened, and why do doubts arise in your hearts? Look at my hands and my feet; see that it is I myself. Touch me and see; for a ghost does not have flesh and bones as you see that I have." And when he had said this, he showed them his hands and his feet. While in their joy they were disbelieving and still wondering, he said to them, "Have you anything here to eat?" They gave him a piece of broiled fish, and he took it and ate in their presence.

Then he said to them, "These are my words that I spoke to you while I was still with you—that everything written about me in the law of Moses, the prophets, and the psalms must be fulfilled." Then he opened their minds to understand the scriptures, and he said to them, "Thus it is written that the Messiah is to suffer and to rise from the dead on the third day, and that repentance and forgiveness of sins is to be proclaimed in his name to all nations, beginning from Jerusalem. You are my witnesses of these things." (Lk 24:36–48)

The very telling of the words and the account of being with Jesus as he opened their minds to the Scriptures summons the person and the presence of the Risen Lord in their midst! This is the moment of communal and public revelation and recognition. In Luke's account, three times they are told to "Remember what Jesus told you when he was with you" (the gospel): first to the women in the morning at the tomb; next to the two disciples on the road during hours of instruction; and finally now, when he gathers with all of them and twice tells them to remember his words and once again opens their minds to the Scriptures. He reveals to them what has been referred to as the hierarchy of the Scriptures, or the parts of the Word of the Lord that are more steeped in Jesus's words: the first five books of the Bible, the prophets, and the psalms—and what is the foundational well of Jesus's own words, the gospels of Mark, Matthew, Luke, and John. This is the heart of the matter, and when the community gathers to share their faith in the Crucified and Risen Lord, the words shared summon his presence among them—that is lasting, engaging, and tangible—he eats with them, whereas he did not eat when he broke the bread with the two on the edge of Emmaus.

While eating, Jesus is intent on showing them his hands and his feet—twice he points his body out to them, seeking to make them realize that it is he who is alive and with them. He commands them to look at him, get a grip on their fears, and deal with his presence. This is Jesus, but it is Jesus in glory, and in body, and he is alive and in the world still, though now through his Word, his presence, and when they gather and share the Word and their lives, and in the breaking of the bread. Jesus eats, as prophets did when they were invited in as guests. He is still the prophet and he will now send them forth as prophets onto the roads of the world, to do what he has done: open others' minds to the Scriptures, break bread with them, and gather them into the community of faith, hope, and those who live as Jesus did, liberating the poor and bringing them Good News. He says that he "will give them the gift of the Father— the Spirit—they will be clothed with power from on high." They will be cloaked in power—his own presence and words and deeds— and now they are to go forth together to do what he has done with them. He blesses and leaves them in joy to await the Spirit. This Spirit will be the first given to those who believe so that they will share with others on their journey.

The closing of Luke's gospel seeks to draw together many of the principles and practices that are central to Jesus's own life and worship. These stories are about how to worship, but also about how to live; one must reflect the other. It is a cyclic rhythm that forms the community and spreads the hope and the Good News to the poor and to everyone.

Throughout the gospel, Jesus sees himself as the servant of God and of the poor; he sees himself as the one who models for his disciples how to be servants in the world, as their worship of God. At his last meal with them before he dies, he reminds them (they are arguing even then) to look at how he is with them and how they are to be with one another and with the rest of the community. His words in Luke echo those of the other gospels, but differ in that they emphasize even more his own being a servant who waits on them at table: "The leader is the one who serves. For who is greater, the one who is at the table or the one who serves? Is it not the one at the table? But I am among you as one who serves" (Lk 22:26c–27). This reference is crucial, because those who sit at table in the community—as in God's dwelling place on earth now—are the poor as well as all those welcomed and invited in to eat and to be treated as honored guests.

There are two stories about being a servant that put all this into perspective and extend this image to a way of living with others and being prophetic by reversing roles with the poor and upending the structures of power and prestige. The first is a bit disconcerting. Listen:

> "Who among you would say to your slave who has just come in from plowing or tending sheep in the field, 'Come here at once and take your place at the table'? Would you not rather say to him, 'Prepare supper for me, put on your apron and serve me while I eat and drink; later you may eat and drink'? Do you thank the slave for doing what was commanded? So you also, when you have done all that you were ordered to do, say, 'We are worthless salves; we have done only what we ought to have done!'" (Lk 17:7–10)

Jesus has been exhorting his followers that they must be careful in the way they live and what they do, and not to put themselves at the center of anything. He has been talking about faith, and how little they have. But even in small doses, faith can do amazing things, and they must learn to focus on Jesus's words and being faithful to them rather than on their work—it is faith that opens spaces in the existing reality, but it is focus on the Word of the Lord in Jesus that sets these things in motion. This little parable is in response to their plea that Jesus increase their faith. It's about the nature of servants. The servants (men and women) work in the fields with sheep, herding, gathering, caring for their needs, and protecting them from harm, as do those who sow seeds and bring the crop to harvest. This is what he sends them out to do as mission: to create a new society where the poor are free and all are welcomed.

And then you come in from the fields and the roads to serve at table (which has always meant as well to serve at Eucharist—the liturgy of serving others the bread and wine). And afterward the servants eat. They do what servants are called and expected to do—obey—and then they eat after the one at table is served. The ones served at the table of the Lord are the poor and those who are hungry, starving even, for food, justice, peace, hope, and the Word of God. And so it is to be with all of them: others come first, and when it is all said and done, you're just useless servants, having done no more than what you were required to do. This is humility and the truth in Jesus's company. What Jesus is saying in one line is: the more you serve, and the more you obey, the more your faith increases. The more we serve the poor, the oppressed, the imprisoned, those in need, and the more we obey their needs and the Word of the Lord, the more our faith increases—not exactly what most of us would want to be told. It starts with just doing your duty, being a servant, and obeying the needs of others and the Word of God.

The second story comes earlier in the gospel and balances this story in a surprising way. Jesus is warning his disciples to be alert, watchful, and attentive; to uncover the kingdom, God's presence with us in the Word, in the poor, and in the world.

"Be dressed for action and have your lamps lit; be like those who are waiting for their master to return from the wedding banquet, so that they may open

the door for him as soon as he comes and knocks. Blessed are those slaves
whom the master finds alert when he comes; truly I tell you, he will fasten
his belt and have them sit down to eat, and he will come and serve them. If
he comes during the middle of the night, or near dawn, and finds them so,
blessed are those slaves." (Lk 12:35–38)

The saying comes in the midst of warnings of what will transpire
if you aren't waiting and are found wanting, or worse if you scandal-
ize others or spend your life worrying about your own comfort and
life rather than serving God and obeying Jesus's Word to be Good
News to the poor, set the captives free, open the eyes of the blind,
free the oppressed, and make sure this year and every year reflects
the favor of God and the communion of all people. But it would have
been a shock to his followers then—and should be a shock now—to
hear Jesus telling them that he, the master, will turn tables on them,
put on his apron, and wait on them! In reality, God waits on us all the
time, and in Jesus's presence upon the earth God waits on us, fulfill-
ing our needs and drawing us together so that we can live more fully
as human beings, sharing what has been shared with us by God.

But what does it mean to be the servant of God—the servant
of the poor? This is what is at the heart of these sayings and images. What does it mean to be prophets, sent out into the world,
with the power of the Spirit, fed on the Word and Bread together
as witnesses to the life, death, and Resurrection of Jesus? Eduardo
Galeano, a prolific writer from Uruguay, wrote a book called *Open
Veins of Latin America;* as soon as it was published, it was banned in
his home country, as well as in others controlled by dictatorships.
In response, he stated in public, "They do not allow what I wrote to
be seen, because I write what I see." Individuals and the communities of the Church must first see, and then speak, write, and protest
what they see in the world around them and then stand with those
who are poor.

Archbishop Oscar Romero was interviewed in the United States
about the Church in Latin America, North America, and universally. He spoke of the Church at times when it truly acted and spoke

as the Body of Christ in the world, seeking to serve those most in need and in the most danger. He noted that when it did this in history, it also knew the rejection and suffering that its Founder knew. But he was also careful to be clear that more often than not the Church did not act like the Body of Christ but instead betrayed and disfigured the Body of Christ in the people because it accommodated itself to nations and groups, and lived in a position of being served while living in collusion with the great ones of the earth. When he was asked to speak of what it looks like when the Church is faithful, this is a portion of what he replied:

> *The Church betrays its love for God and its fidelity to the Gospel if it ceases to be "the voice of those who have no voice," defending the rights of the poor, animating all who are yearning for a just liberation, orientating, empowering and humanizing all who are legitimately struggling to gain a just society that prepares the way for the true reign of God in history. This requires the Church to place itself among the poor with whom it should stand firmly, taking the same risks as the poor, their destiny of persecution, ready to give the greatest testimony of love by defending and promoting those whom Jesus loved with preference.*
>
> *The preference for the poor, I repeat, does not signify an unjust discrimination of class but an invitation to all regardless of class to accept and take up the cause of the poor as if accepting and taking up one's own cause, and the cause of the poor is the same as that of Christ. "That what you do to the least of My brothers and sisters you do to me."* [1]

This merging and interlocking of life, worship, and the imperative of aligning oneself with the poor and their destiny—in community—is the trifold foundation of Jesus's life and the lives of those who follow him in Luke's gospel. What does it look like in worship? This quote from John Chrysostom, a preacher in the fourth century, will help to clarify:

> *Do you wish to honor the body of Christ? Do not ignore him when he is naked. Do not pay him homage in the temple clad in silk only then to neglect*

him outside where he suffers cold nakedness. He who said "This is my body"
is the same One who said: "You saw me hungry and you gave me no food,"
and "Whatever you did to the least of my brothers and sisters you did also
to me." What good is it if the Eucharistic table is overloaded with golden
chalices when he is dying of hunger? Start by satisfying his hunger, and then
with what is left you may adorn the altar as well.

This is the same man who said that all the extra bread in your
cupboard belongs on the table of the poor; that the extra shoes in
your closet belong on the feet of the beggar and the one on the
street; and the extra cloak hanging on a hook in your house must be
on the back of the one who is cold and in need of shelter. He said,
"It is a better thing to feed the hungry than it is to raise the dead."
He was loved by the poor of Constantinople, and they wept when
he was exiled from the city after his words bothered so many of the
officials both in the government and in the Church.

The issue has to be dealt with as individuals in the Church, as
Churches/parishes, and in the Church universal. All need to integrate personal spirituality, public worship, and lifestyle in one
piece—and in many different ways—to express the primary teaching of Jesus: the reason he came into the world, was baptized,
and eventually was killed. Jesus shared the power of the Spirit
that came upon him to preach Good News to the poor. It has
sometimes been called the Sword of the Spirit cutting through
personal delusion and selfishness, public structures and dominant
cultures, prevalent values, and even what has become encrusted
as religious teachings, rites, and ways of living like those that rule
in society. It is sometimes couched in terms of whether or not to
do charity or to do justice. A succinct way of looking at this issue
was heard on TV, spoken by the journalist and commentator Bill
Moyers. He said:

Charity depends on the vicissitudes of whim and personal wealth; justice
depends on commitment instead of circumstance. Faith-based charity pro-
vides crumbs from the table; faith-based justice offers a place at the table.

I've heard a story in both the Jewish and the Islamic traditions that puts it bluntly and reminds us, like the early Christians, of what we already know but are reluctant to actually put into practice. It seems that once upon a time Moses was going up the mountain to see God—in both traditions Moses is still going up the mountain to ask God questions and to bring back answers that are needed in this day and age. Moses was admiring the mountain and its blossoming, and wondering what God had to tell him this time around—and how the people would react to it—which was always the hardest part of these journeys back and forth. Facing God was hard enough—God always seemed to be able to shock him—but facing the people, that was even harder. At the base of the mountain, Moses met a beggar. The beggar recognized him and said, "Moses, are you going up to see God?" He answered yes, he was—what could he do for him? The man answered that he knew that God was aware of his situation and that he barely had enough to survive; he could often handle it, but his wife and children, his elderly parents and grandparents—it was agony for him to watch them so hungry, listless, and dispirited. Could he ask God what he could do so that he could change things in his life? Of course, Moses said . . . of course.

Moses continued up the mountain and met a man and his wife, who were making a pilgrimage/vacation. They, too, recognized him immediately and said, "Moses, are you going up the mountain to see God?"

"Yes," he told them, "what can I do for you?"

"Well," they both said, "we've been on pilgrimage and are so aware that God has blessed us and never stops blessing us. What are we to do? We build churches and we have our own private chapel and we give gifts for the altar—what can we do since we keep getting more and more money?" So Moses said, "Of course, I will ask for you," and he continued up the mountain.

At the top of the mountain, he waited and God came again. They spoke at length, with God asking how things were going from Moses's point of view, since God already knew what was going on from his vantage point. He encouraged Moses to keep at it, to keep speaking on behalf of God in the world and reminding people that they were to be holy as their God is holy. As Moses was getting ready to leave, he remembered both petitioners and told God about them. There was a long silence afterward. Moses was surprised and wondered, Aren't all these questions easy for God to answer? Finally God answered: "Moses, my servant—what can I tell you? In the case of the beggar and his family and the rich couple, you did not do and say what you and they already knew—what is just is equitable—the excess of the rich couple belongs already to the family of the beggar. How can I tell you—or them—to do more, when you and they don't even do what you're supposed to be doing already? All those prayers, worship, pilgrimages, building churches—what does any of that mean to me, or to the poor? Go back down there and tell them all the truth—both the poor and the rich—that the gap between their way of living angers me and that both of them need to change. Tell the rich ones to 'give it up' and connect with the poor. And tell all the poor that it is their right to live with hope and they are to struggle for justice. Moses, I've sent so many prophets, so many preachers, told them so many stories—I even sent my beloved servant and child—when will they listen?" And so Moses went down the mountain knowing that this time, like all the others, it was not going to be easy telling his people what God had said.

Jesus's behavior scandalized everyone in Israel—his family, his community in Nazareth, the religious leaders, the scribes, the Pharisees and other sects within Judaism, the wealthy, and those in collusion with the Roman occupying forces. First he spent time with all the poor, hungry, outcasts, lepers, sinners, Gentiles, runaway slaves, anyone undesirably unclean religiously; and worse still—he ate with them, laughed, told stories, and encouraged them to live in such a way that they believed that God loved them all. It was a hard message to put across to his own people, and just as hard to get through to his followers.

The stories that perhaps best illustrate this are like the story of the man who comes to Jesus asking him to tell his brother to share his harvest and inheritance with him. And Jesus responds to him with a parable about the rich fool. This is what he says to everyone to hear. Listen:

> *"Take care! Be on your guard against all kinds of greed; for one's life does not consist in the abundance of possessions." Then he told them a parable: "The land of a rich man produced abundantly. And he thought to himself, 'What should I do, for I have no place to store my crops?' Then he said, 'I will do this: I will pull down my barns and build larger ones, and there I will store all my grain and my goods. And I will say to my soul, "Soul, you have ample goods laid up for many years: relax, eat, drink and be merry."' But God said to him, 'You fool! This very night your life is being demanded of you. And the things you have prepared, whose will they be?' So it is with those who store up treasures for themselves but are not rich toward God."*
> (Lk 12:15–21)

The parable and lines from it are familiar. We've heard it all before, and yet our culture proclaims loudly that "Greed is good." The answer to all problems is "Go out and shop. Use your credit cards. Stimulate the economy." In previous times, the word *consumption* described a lingering, debilitating disease that infected many and spread. Now consumption is an acceptable form of living. The business of saving is for oneself and the future, though economic conditions lately have destroyed that cushion for many in the middle and lower classes. The people listening to Jesus's story would have been appalled at the man building more barns—as a Jew with wealth it was part of the community's understanding that he should share that wealth and excess with his own people, especially the poor in the land. Almsgiving was considered a fire that burned away sin and made atonement for injustices.

In the early Church, after baptism, sins were forgiven by going to the Eucharist and by prayer, fasting, and almsgiving. The joke was that everyone knew the Christians: they were all skinny and poor. In reality, they shared, and so in the words of others, "there were no poor among them." That can hardly be said of our churches today. In the United States, the Catholic Church is the richest religious group and has been for more than the last fifteen years; yet in what it gives to the poor it is dead last in the list of all other Christian denominations who give to others. This is an indictment of Catholics (and many other Christians, too): that they are the most wealthy, selfish, mean-spirited, ungenerous, and self-righteous folk in the country.

In many places I and others visit to preach and teach, we are told, "Oh, we are the best parish in the diocese. We have the best liturgies and community spirit. We have all these outreach groups and everyone is welcome." And yet there are two very telling realities that disprove this claim. When asked if they take up a collection for the poor at all the worship services (liturgies, penances, adoration hours, pilgrimages, religious orders masses, and retreats), the response is usually, "Oh, we have a collection at liturgy on Sunday." But when I push, I usually find that it is not for the poor but for maintenance of buildings, new programs and books, lectionaries, sacramentaries, booklets, educational programs for sacraments for children, sound systems, trips to shrines around the world, diocesan assessments, new statues, chalices (since all the Waterford crystal ones or those made of clay or anything else should now be broken up and buried and be replaced only with precious metals), and so on. The poor are shortchanged; perhaps from one mass on a weekend the collection is given to a specific group. And yet we feast on the Word of the Lord, on community and support, on meals, on donuts and coffee after masses, and at banquets in honor of those who work in the parish (servants of the community). Sometimes at these events, the leftovers are taken to the local soup kitchen or house of hospitality, but more often than not, they're just taken home by the people who brought them.

In the last ten years, the question is put to such parishes: how many of your people have lost their homes, their health insurance, their jobs? If we really were communities that shared and took care of one another no one in the parish—or the area—would have lost their shelters or health plans, and people would have pushed their privilege in regard to jobs or shared what they did have with others. It is words mostly, not practice, and it rarely extends past parish boundaries. There are special collections, but the bottom line is: not much is shared, not even much of our excess. In Luke's community, bread, food, meals, worship, and the necessities of life were shared with all. And Luke's Church had to keep asking themselves over and over again: can the rich make it into the Kingdom of God?

There is a simple story someone gave me on a sheet of paper by that prolific person Anonymous called "The Tree." Once upon a time there was a tree on the edge of a city, just as you would begin to walk out into the desert and across the expanse to other cities. It was a huge old tree, magnificent, surrounded by a low fence and some grass. It was a landmark, a meeting place, and a place to rest before you began your journey or as you ended it, before going into the city. The people believed that it had been touched by God and was a gift to them because it was always laden with fruit and flowers. The limbs stretched long, past the low fence, and the roots spread far, too. Everyone who walked past took a piece of fruit or two for the journey or their family, or to share later. The tree had been there for so long, and everyone just thought of it as theirs.

And then one day word went out that someone had bought the land and the tree and it was now private property. No one could believe it—it was theirs, it belonged to everyone. But a high fence went up—eight feet high—and a sign, too, that said PRIVATE PROPERTY. YOU WILL BE FINED FOR STEALING. Well, that didn't last long. The fence was climbed and segments were taken out and the fruit was thrown over by children and tree climbers so that everyone could still get some of the fruit, though they couldn't see the tree except for the very top of it now. There was a confrontation with the owner and the fence rose higher. It's my tree, my fruit, my flowers, my land. Stay off it and don't take any of it.

And then a terrible thing happened. Overnight the tree was dead. There was no fruit, no flowers, the grass dried up around it, the leaves fell, and the bark and trunk were filled with rot. The people stood and held vigil. How could this have happened to their tree? And a prophet, a wise woman, solemnly spoke the truth: "This is the law of giving. It is as predictable as the law of gravity. If you stop giving, bearing fruit ceases and death follows inevitably. Not just with trees but with all things." And so it is—the truth.

The other story in Luke's gospel is about a rich young man, but it is best if his character is seen as everyone who must choose again and again whether they are going to do more than simply say that they believe in Jesus, if they will actually begin to follow him in a community of believers known for their sharing, justice, and generosity. The story begins with the aforementioned young man having a theological conversation with Jesus and asking, What do I have to do to inherit eternal life? The question is couched in very specific terms: what do I have to do? Jesus is quick to respond with the basic laws of honoring one's parents, no killing, lying, stealing, cheating, coveting, and so on. The man tells Jesus that he's done all that and has obeyed all those laws since he was young. Now that in itself is a major statement—could we say as much?—but then Jesus replies with a summons of what to do next and an invitation to the man to join him more closely.

> When Jesus heard this, he said to him, "There is still one more thing lacking. Sell all that you own and distribute the money to the poor, and you will have treasure in heaven; then come, follow me." But when he heard this, he became sad; for he was very rich. Jesus looked at him and said, "How hard it is for those who have wealth to enter the kingdom of God! Indeed, it is easier for a camel to go through the eye of a needle than for someone who is rich to enter the kingdom of God." (Lk 18:22–25)

This story is also known as the Un-disciple, The Thirteenth Disciple, or The One Who Got Away. Jesus invites and is rejected. The man turns deliberately and consciously, sadly and definitively, away from Jesus and becoming his follower. Jesus, the Wisdom and the Word of God, is standing before him and being very specific in what is lacking in him, and in all of us. Just one thing is needed to start off everything else: go sell your excess, and give it to the poor—that's treasure in heaven and in the dwelling place of God here on earth—and come, and follow me. It is like a sword thrust. Once you obey the basic laws that order society, then it is time to move on to what makes one more human, and in this case, like Jesus, like God. This is the first step in becoming a believer, a servant, and one who is intimate with Jesus. And it is something that *must* be done; it's not an option. All we know of the one who leaves is that he's sad, wealthy, has many possessions, and he said no to Jesus. His choice is quick—things are more important than people, more important than friendship or intimacy with God, and more important than being given joy and a community to dwell with and do the work of God. He goes back to his small world.

He and all of us are told that if we give to the poor then we have treasure in heaven—we are already in the kingdom, the dream, and the relationship that God offers to us in Jesus. This is the first beatitude, the first step: Blessed are the poor, for the Kingdom of God is theirs—now, here! We can say yes, or we can refuse and walk away—or, as many of us do, we can say nothing at all, still call ourselves followers and believers in Jesus, and not share our excess with anyone except as we wish. And then we try to live a double life, the bulk of our time and energy in our tight prison of society and its values, standards, possessions, insecurity, greed, and selfishness, while still trying to claim we are Christians because we pray, go to church on Sundays, and go on pilgrimages and retreats; but we will not change—we will not befriend the poor—and so we will never know God in Jesus much at all. Jesus's life, eternal life now, begins with sharing and becomes a lifestyle shared with others, held accountable by others, standing in solidarity with the poor.

As members of the first-world countries, living within the dominant economic structures of globalization and American culture, these words and commands of Jesus are shocking and dismaying; we most respond that such rules are only for maybe a few—and so curtail what it might be to know Jesus intimately, closely, and deeply, as one of his friends.

As long ago as 1989, Richard Shaull wrote the following words describing the predicament of Christians in the first world standing before Jesus like that young man and being invited more deeply into Jesus's company:

The development and expansion of our Western capitalist system, legitimated in great part by the Christian church, has brought about tremendous economic and technological development, awakened aspirations for material well-being among people throughout the world, and raised the standard of living of millions. But this same system is also one of imperial exploitation and domination of third world nations. It is rapidly using up natural resources and polluting air, land and sea to a catastrophic degree. With all this development, one billion human beings are living in desperate poverty.[2]

In the rest of the article, he speaks of experiences in base communities in Latin America, where the poor study the Scriptures and come to an awareness fueled by the Holy Spirit that they must share what they have, work together for their needs, struggle to change their society, and rely on the Word of the Lord to remain faithful, nonviolent, and work as peacemakers in situations of repression, oppression, civil war, political persecution, and even martyrdom. It was a transforming experience for Shaull and his wife, as it has been for many others who have spent time in the many countries of South America, Africa, and Southeast Asia learning from the poor—that indeed the poor are the privileged place of revelation in the world today.

Someone in Peru once told me there are three conversions—first to the Word of God in Scriptures, in the gospels, and in the prophets; then to the Word of God spoken and lived in the bodies and communities of the poor; and lastly to standing with the poor in the work for justice and the Peace of Christ in the world—with no harm to any, including the earth, sharing and being prophetic by one's presence, words, and deeds. Over the years I have learned there are profound levels of wisdom in those three calls to conversion.

Americans and Europeans, or anyone living in capitalistic,

first-world countries, often forget that we are privileged, part of the dominant structures of the world, and living at the top of the heap. Today, with the rapid expansion of globalization and the destruction of the earth's resources, 2.5 billion people live in poverty, in destitution, on the roads, as immigrants, and barely walking the edge of survival.

We must first be converted to the knowledge of how the world lives around us and not to live in fear and insecurity, obsessed with our own personal and familial standard of living. Then we must look to our relationships with God and Church to make sure that they are deeply connected to the world at large, and that our religion is not devised as an insular wall of protection that is mostly God and me, God and my family, or God and my group. We have to let the Word of the Lord radically impinge on our lifestyles, prayers, ways of worship, and the priorities of our churches and the people we live with alongside our families. We have to see if we are lacking a group of people with whom to study the Word of the Lord weekly, prior to our worship on Sunday, and read the Sunday Gospel for conversion of life as individuals, as families, and as small churches within the larger Church, so that we can live more and more authentic lives of integrity. And then, together, we begin to do the corporal works of mercy and work together for justice.

We have to make sure that these ideas of Good News to the poor, listening to the poor, and solidarity with the poor are not just ideas to integrate into a spirituality or theology, or to be able to talk about, but that they actually begin to reconfigure and reconstitute our lives so that we change our lifestyles and are displaced from commerce and politics and religion "as usual"; and with others we become more truthful and prophetic in calling our own churches, parishes, dioceses, and structures to live the gospel and serve the poor of the world.

For Americans, that can mean questioning whether or not our primary religion and worship is actually the gospels—the Word of the Lord and God's kingdom, God's dream and dwelling place among us now, here on earth, with no borders or boundaries—or whether our primary allegiance is to the country of the United States. The lines are very blurry—evidenced by such realities as the flag of the United States and the flag of the Vatican alongside the Cross of Christ in our churches—to more devastating realities of direct betrayal of Jesus's words in the gospel when we back the wars of the United States, the taxation system that favors the wealthy, and policies such as the criminalization of immigration, the legality of the death penalty and abortion, and the ignoring of the continuing needs for those who bear their children for the basic necessities of life beyond survival. It is not enough to make sure that children are born; it is also demanded that they have a chance at life—ever more abundant life instead of a life of oppression, the imprisonment of poverty, and despair.

We must look at the use of the prison system as a place to warehouse the poor, the destruction of farms, and the degradation of the earth's resources like air, land, and water. There are so many other issues, like the lack of universal broad-based health care, the need for low-income housing, sustainable living wages, the growing gap between the wealthy and those on the edge, the need for jobs and bailing out ordinary folks to keep them in their homes rather than bailing out corporations that have just recently been given the legal status (as persons!) that once only human beings shared. And the position of the United States in regard to other countries directly contradicts Jesus's words—war is obsolete: no killing, love your enemies, do good to those who hate you, bless those who curse you, and pray for those who abuse you (Lk 6:27–28). These commands (not optional) are for starters: the gospel tells us how to stand and work for justice with the poor but without the arsenal and array of practices employed by the violent structures of domination, or those used by the majority of people in the world who do not obey or adhere to the Word of the Lord in Jesus.

All of this starts at home in our local churches, but it must impact other levels of administrative structures, leadership, and the universal Church. This is the reality of most of the world, and its throw-backs and remnants are found in our own cities, states, and nation. When Jesus spoke at his hometown synagogue in Nazareth, the parishioners were enraged and "were filled with wrath, and they rose up and put him out of the city" (Lk 4:28–29). The Spirit of the Lord that came upon Jesus and upon his followers as the gift of God to accompany them in the world comes upon us to continue this journey and to make the meal of the breaking of the bread and the telling of the story reality in the world today. And in the words of Helen Graham, a Maryknoll sister and theologian in Asia, we must also remember that a Church that takes such a task seriously is bound to follow the same path as Jesus: "It is a Church that will know the suffering of the cross for its message can be rejected and resisted only by the powerful of the world."[3] For the world today knows poverty, and the majority of the human race is waiting for Good News of sharing, liberation, freedom, and hope.

Every Eucharist must question us as Jesus questioned the man who sought what he had to do to gain eternal life. To put it in liturgical terms and to remind us of what that might be like, here are some words by Paul Bernier, SSS, in his book *Bread Broken and Shared*:

> *A true Eucharist is never a passive, comforting moment alone with God, something which allows us to escape the cares and concerns of everyday life. Eucharist is where all these cares and concerns come to a focus, and where we are asked to measure them against the standard lived by Jesus when he proclaimed for all to hear that the bread that he would give would provide life for the entire world. But it will do so only if, finding ourselves with a basket of bread, we have peered deeply enough into the heart of Christ to know what to do with it.*

To sum this all up—the connection between the Word of the Lord, the worship of God, the Good News to the poor, being ser-vants of God and the poor, and walking the way with others in life now—we end with these very simple and memorable words of Ida Bethune:

> *Who offers food, offers self. This is true of my giving a sandwich to a person at the door, or of my entertaining friends in the kitchen or the dining room. It is also true of banquets, where the servers are the ambassadors and representatives of the host who gives the food. It is true of farmers who raise food, of butchers who dress meats, of bakers who make bread, of grandmothers who put up preserves, of anyone who peels, cooks, or prepares food for others. It is also true of every Christian who offers the bread and wine at the sacrifice of the Mass.*

And it is equally true of my Nana's words: There will be no going to bed without your supper. Not in this house. The least we can do is eat together. And no one is getting up from this table until everyone is talking to one another again and there is no ill will. Come, children. Let's eat.

Chapter 8

THE GOSPEL OF JOHN THEN

*I still believe that standing up for the truth is the greatest thing in
the world. This is the end of life. The end of life is not to be happy.
The end of life is not to achieve pleasure and avoid pain. The end of
life is to do the will of God, come what may.*

MARTIN LUTHER KING JR.

THE GOSPEL OF JOHN, THE FOURTH GOSPEL, IS RADICALLY
different than the other three. The previous three are called the
"synoptic" gospels, from the Greek meaning "seen together." They
share many of the same angles of vision, interpretations of Jesus's
ministry of healing and forgiveness, and the bringing of the Kingdom of God upon the earth in history and in the presence of Jesus.
They concentrate on the preaching of Jesus—the Good News to
the poor—and the call to discipleship, the following of Jesus's way
in a community of believers. The difference between the first three
gospels and the gospel of John can perhaps be summed up in one
line: "I am the way, the truth, and the life" (Jn 14:6). John's gospel
is focused intently on the person of Jesus as the revelation of God;
as the Word of God Made Flesh in a human being; and as the Word
of God in history on earth, in the Scriptures, in the bread and wine
of the Eucharist, and in the Body of Christ—the beloved friends of
God that are his presence now on earth.

John's gospel is dense with meaning and revelation. It is layered
and complex, interwoven with a set of words and symbols in myriad
combinations. Someone once said that there are thirty-nine major
words/symbols in the gospel that are continually rearranged and
offset with one another, drawing the listener and the seeker into

ever more levels of understanding and truth. As with the other gospels, those who hear it are already believers seeking deeper meaning concealed in the mystery of the Word Made Flesh among us. Even the structure of the text is circular and chiastic (from the Greek meaning "parallelism"). The first chapters are connected intrinsically to the last and the first lines to the last lines. And this parallelism is found within each of the chapters—often with the center lines acting as major statements of belief that begin with the words "I AM"; this structure is found in chapters 1 through 20, while the Prologue and the last chapter, 21, are added to the core of the text like parentheses.

There have been many ways to read this gospel in the last twenty centuries—often with seven major moments seen as signs that reveal who Jesus is and what is happening in the gospel. Ninety percent or more of the text is original, meaning that it does not appear in the other gospels. (One of the main stories that appears in all the texts is what is referred to as "the driving of the money changers out of the Temple"—a story that obviously is thus based on somewhat of a historical occurrence.) In many ways John's gospel is a result or product of the community's sixty to seventy years of belief in the person of Jesus as the Risen Lord vibrantly alive in the community and active in the world. This very thought is found in the gospel itself, in the portion that is called the last discourse, or the last will and testament—the long section at the last meal of Jesus with his friends. Twice he says something to this effect:

> "I have said these things to you while I am still with you. But the Advocate, the Holy Spirit, whom the Father will send in my name, will teach you everything and remind you of all that I have said to you." (Jn 14:25–26)

And again Jesus speaks to them:

> "I still have many things to say to you, but you cannot bear them now. When the Spirit of truth comes, he will guide you into all the truth; for he will not speak on his own, but will speak whatever he hears, and he will

declare to you the things that are to come. He will glorify me, because he
will take what is mine and declare it to you. All that the Father has is mine.
For this reason I said that he will take what is mine and declare it to you."
(Jn 16:12–15)

From just these two passages, a number of the recurring themes
and emphases are highlighted. The gospel of John is revealing an
image of God that is Trinitarian—threefold—the Fathering God,
Jesus the Truth of God Made Flesh among us as the Word (the
beloved child), and the Spirit of Truth, the abiding presence of
the Risen Jesus still speaking. God is first a community, and those
made in the image of God are to reflect that communitarian life
together as revelation to others, primarily in living and practice
rather than in creed, dogma, or doctrine.

The next focus is on the Truth. This is not partial truth or
understanding that individuals or groups seek to profess or know;
it is The Truth, the all-encompassing reality of the universe, of life,
and the source and foundation of all meaning for human beings.
To use another word, it is the Wisdom that is God and all reality
seen from God's perspective. This Truth and Wisdom of God is an
abiding presence in a person, the Word Made Flesh—Jesus—who
is somehow the grace, the glory, the truth, the light, the freedom,
the love, and the power of God. This is the essence of what the
Prologue of the gospel seeks to express (Jn 1:1–18). Taken in conjunction with the Jewish revelation, it is equivalent to a new telling
of the Genesis story—the beginnings of all things. And so John's
portrait of Jesus transcends time, space, and place, and yet is found
in a human being that was born (incarnated) in a very specific time
and place. This person was always God, is God still, and will be
God throughout all time and beyond.

Another revelation is that Jesus is the power of God made visible and living in interaction with others. It is power beyond any
seen, displayed, or practiced upon the earth in history. This power
is rooted in being beloved children of God with Jesus, and, even
more than that, becoming beloved friends of God with Jesus, in the

power of the Spirit. Because of the grace, truth, and power of the holy in Jesus and his Spirit, we are made and called to be human like Jesus, and to be intimate with God in Jesus. This is the revelation of John's gospel. It can be summed up in the last line of the Prologue: "No one has ever seen God. It is God the only Son, who is close to the Father's heart, who has made him known" (Jn 1:18).

There are innumerable other facets of John's gospel, but the last one we will concentrate on is the development of what it means to be called "friend" by God. John's gospel is often called the Gospel of the Beloved Disciples—those drawn more closely and intimately into the relationship with God that is boundless and unbelievably powerful, demanding, and somehow mysteriously and gracefully dwelling with God, in God, and living through God's power. The heart of this new way of being human is found again in Jesus's long discourse before he leaves his friends to go and die so that we might know something of everlasting life even here and now, in the midst of death. The words still echo as invitation to all.

> "This is my commandment, that you love one another as I have loved you. No one has greater love than this, to lay down one's life for one's friends. You are my friends if you do what I command you. I do not call you servants any longer, because the servant does not know what the master is doing; but I have called you friends, because I have made known to you everything that I have heard from my Father. You did not choose me but I chose you. And I appointed you to go and bear fruit, fruit that will last, so that the Father will give you whatever you ask him in my name. I am giving you these commands so that you may love one another." (Jn 15:12–17)

John's gospel offers a quantum leap in the way we can know God, abide in God, and live sourced with the power of God found in the Word—both as the person of Jesus and in the Word found in the gospel. It is the story of God that is to be told and then will come true in the lives of all who believe. As the Word became flesh to dwell among us, now through the power of this Word, our flesh is to become the Word of God speaking and living the Truth of God.

Perhaps a story within a story from the Buddhist tradition (from the Jataka tales) can draw us into looking at John's gospel as wisdom, revelation, and truthfulness that we are to incarnate into our own flesh and community. This is the way I heard it told years ago in Japan. Once upon a time there was a huge monastery of monks—over six hundred of them. It was late one night and many were up arguing about the truth of the teachings of the Buddha, who was asleep in his small hut in a back garden. The tenor of the arguments and disagreements grew louder and eventually woke Buddha, who got up and went to see what was going on in the middle of the night. They were startled to see Buddha standing in the doorway of the great hall and were instantly silent. Buddha looked around—he was wide awake now—and said, "You know, in the days gone by, the old wise ones would say that no crime, no hatred, no deed that harmed could be hidden for long, or kept secret. No one who is enlightened or is wise ever does something that can harm or cause destruction. Let me tell you a story from long ago—and then maybe you will be ready to go to bed!

"Once upon a time there was a wise old teacher who decided that his many students were due for a test. He knew where they all stood on what he taught and what they believed, but the test was to let them see where they stood singularly and with one another. He gathered them all together, with the students that had been together the longest, and said to them, 'You have studied long and hard and learned much—almost all that I have to teach you of the noble ancients. But have you noticed I, too, have grown old. My hair is white, my back is stooped, and I have great difficulty walking now. Sometimes I feel like a turtle and at other times—like a snail,' he said, smiling ruefully. Some of the older students responded quickly, 'Yes, master, we have noticed and we have wondered and talked among ourselves what will become of us when you die.'

"The teacher looked at them and said, 'It is time for you to take responsibility for this monastery and the school and the students, the gardens and upkeep. I can no longer do this. You must find ways to raise the money and then organize yourselves so that my legacy continues and you begin to pass on all that you have learned with me.' There was silence for a moment and then the group came to life with zest, wanting to take over and lift this burden from their old teacher's shoulders. But soon reality crashed down on them and they realized they knew very little about making money. They knew how to rake the garden in circles and do the ancient rituals and to sit and meditate and chant the sutras, even to follow the disciplines of eating and sleeping and behaving with moderation and attentiveness—but they were woefully lacking in such things as making a living! Almost together they cried out, 'What are we to do?'

"The teacher looked at them and said, 'Look around at all the people who come here to light incense and pray to the Buddha and to give offerings. Have you noticed their clothing and the transport they arrive in—or their many servants unloading their offerings? Don't you think we have been in their midst long enough that it's time for them to share more of what they possess with us?' A few of the students were a bit shocked—was their old teacher slipping? But the teacher wasn't finished: 'Here is what I want all of you to start doing. Start noticing, and watching, seeing clearly. Put your skills of being aware and attentive to good use. See where they keep their purses and when the moment is ripe, take it from them—lift some of their burden so that we can put it to good use. But, you must not get caught—no one must see. Then bring what you have found and taken to me and I will begin to teach you how to put it all to better use. However, if anyone sees you, I will not take anything from you, no matter how valuable. We must do this in secret.'

"There was a long and awkward silence in the room and no one moved or spoke. The teacher looked at them and spoke again: 'Look, I would never ask you to do this if it wasn't absolutely neces-sary, and I'd never ask you to do what I myself would not do.' Still there was silence and all kept their eyes away from their teacher's gaze. 'Look at me,' he said. 'The school must continue. The mon-astery must be maintained. The teachings must be passed on, or all that I have taught you and all that you have learned will be for nothing. And we will make their burden lighter, and certainly we can put their riches to better uses than they can—why, we can even give more to the poor and the elderly and those who come begging at our gates.'

"A student lifted his eyes and said, 'We'll do it. And we will do it well, reflecting on what you have taught us.' And soon all of them rose up and said they would do it. They were a little afraid, but there was excitement and tension in the air—they would learn if they could do this. 'OK,' the teacher said, 'now is the time to go. It's dark and it will be easier in the city and on the roads. You can work alone or in twos, or even in groups if you think that you can work better together. I will wait for you all to return and see who has done well. Go now.' And they slipped out, growing silent again, intent on their work. Soon the room was empty except for one student who stood alone before the teacher.

"The old man approached the young woman student. He looked at her and her face was bent down, her eyes on the floor. He spoke and said, 'Why aren't you going? They all left. They all want to help out their old teacher. Don't you?' And softly but surely she answered, 'I can't. Please don't ask me again.' The teacher moved closer. 'Why won't you go and do what I suggested?' Again came the reply: 'I can't. The wise ones have taught that anything we do will be uncovered. There is no place on earth where we are not seen. All will be revealed. Even if you don't get caught now, one day it will be made known. And even if no one does know now, I will know! I cannot claim to believe in the truth of all you have taught and do this thing and especially in secret. I cannot.'

"To her astonishment the teacher reached out and grabbed her and hugged her, laughing delightedly. 'Yes! Yes! Yes! You got it— you understand. You know. You are my disciple and you have be-friended my words and teachings!' The young woman didn't know what else to say than 'Yes—I listened and I had to obey. I love you and your words.' By the morning sun the rest of the students had all returned. Some were clumsy and couldn't do it. Some had sec-ond thoughts. Some stole and came back triumphant only to be chastised and taken aback. Some had gone and done other things. Others just didn't return. But when they all returned they saw the old teacher leaning on the young woman's shoulder and his face shining—suddenly they realized it was a test! They heard the words they would not forget from the young woman teacher: 'Wherever I am, I am seen. Wherever I am, I know the truth. Wherever I am, the world watches and knows.'"

With that the Buddha ended his tale and looked around at them and said, "That young woman was my best friend so many years ago. Now, all of you, go to bed and sleep and dream and remember the power of words, the power of truth, the power of practice, and the power of friendship."

In many ways this story reflects John's gospel, and wondrously that young student is the presence of God among us in Jesus, befriending us and seeking to make us the friends of God. The core of Jesus's teaching can be summed up in two oft-quoted passages.

> *"For God so loved the world that he gave his only Son, so that everyone who believes in him may not perish but may have eternal life. Indeed, God did not send the Son into the world to condemn the world, but in order that the world might be saved through him." (Jn 3:16–17)*

The second passage reinforces this statement and extends it out universally, serving as a foundation for all that Jesus says, does, and calls others to imitate in obeying him: "I came that they may have life, and have it ever-more abundantly" (Jn 10:10b).

A third passage, not often referred to, extends Jesus's Word, presence, and power to those who hear and believe in him: "If you continue in my word, you are truly my disciples; and you will know the truth, and the truth will make you free" (Jn 8:31–32). The first of these statements comes in a teaching dialogue with one of the members of the Pharisees, named Nicodemus, who comes to Jesus by night, afraid, but seeks to understand his wisdom. And the other two statements are spoken in the midst of heated and ugly arguments with religious authorities seeking to kill Jesus. Most of the gospel is narrated within the context of looming violence couched in religious language that inevitably erupts into the calculated conspiracy to murder Jesus—the Truth that sets one free but also lays bare the truth of all human beings.

This power of the Word and who speaks it is alive and passed on to and into all human beings. The great Jewish writer Martin Buber once told his people that a Hasidic rabbi once said every time he would reach the words "And God spoke" in a text that he would be overcome with awe, terror, and ecstasy as though the fire that created the Word on tablets of stone was once again being spoken into the air of the universe. But he continued to say that any man or woman who speaks in truth or receives the Word in truth has the power, with that one word, to uplift the whole world and to purge the whole world from evil.[1]

John's gospel has more words than all the other gospels; it honors them and seeks to make the hearers become words of God enfleshed and living in the world today. The story that initiates this in all believers and reveals much of what is the foundation of John's theology is found early in the gospel in chapter 4—it constitutes the first two-thirds of that chapter. The story of the woman at the well, or the Samaritan woman, is about every person who questions Jesus and the words he speaks; in turn, these questioners go through a process of being questioned by Jesus themselves. This questioning culminates in a point of making a decision on where they stand with Jesus, and whether or not they will follow him. It is the first step—that of being baptized and coming to believe in Jesus—in a long process of being initiated into the community of believers, the community of beloved disciples. The process is never ending and must continue with the new believer being drawn more deeply into the mysteries of who Jesus is as the Word Made Flesh, through the Word of the gospel and the Word in the community that continues in the power of the Spirit to convert, transform, and transfigure the person and community into being the presence of God in their flesh in the world. The portion of the text is found in

John 4:4–26 and 39–42. It also serves as a model for other portions
of the gospel, which draw a believer closer to the person of Jesus
and reveal more of his personal nature and actions. Together with
Jesus, the reader can build the community of beloved disciples. The
first of many people to believe in Jesus after his death and Resurrection were many of the Samaritans; and so the woman of Samaria
serves not only as every one of them who came to believe in Jesus
but also as everyone in John's community who eventually came to
the community seeking the Word of the Lord and entrance into
the community.

During this segment of John's gospel, many of the laws, traditions, and customs of the Jewish community are broken or even
just ignored, beginning with the choice of a woman as the model
for one who comes to belief and then reaches out to draw others
toward Jesus the Word Made Flesh among us. Again, this portion of the gospel is scribed and narrated long after the death and
Resurrection of Jesus, and the Christian community has separated
from the Jewish community and is developing into its own religion
with its own set of practices and beliefs—reflecting more the reality
of the early Church than the reality at the time of Jesus. But this is a
text that would have shocked and been seen as radically developing
out of Judaism and into something altogether new for Christians
(with this development born of the Spirit of Truth in the community). Listen to the first segment because it is the setup for the entire story and lays the foundation for the practice of believing in
Jesus and hearing the rest of the gospel.

> But he had to go through Samaria. So he came to a Samaritan city called
> Sychar, near the plot of ground that Jacob had given to his son Joseph. Ja-
> cob's well was there, and Jesus, tired out by his journey, was sitting by the
> well. It was about noon. A Samaritan woman came to draw water, and
> Jesus said to her, "Give me a drink." (His disciples had gone to the city to
> buy food.) The Samaritan woman said to him, "How is it that you, a Jew,
> ask a drink of me, a woman of Samaria?" (Jews do not share things in com-
> mon with Samaritans.) (Jn 4:4–9)

As a story and teaching dialogue, this passage is the setup or jumping-off place for all that follows. Jesus has left Judea for Galilee but has to pass through Samaria—outside Israel—first. Now he is the stranger, the outsider, and in this situation, the enemy and one to be avoided and shunned. The Samaritans and Jews believed different traditions of the earlier testaments and worshipped in different places, and yet both considered themselves to be Jewish and waiting for the Messiah to come. But politically, socially, economically, and religiously the two groups were at odds with each other, and there was deep hostility and disdain between them—the Jews considered the Samaritans heretics who had betrayed the beliefs of their forebears for convenience and survival. The two groups had nothing to do with each other, if at all possible.

John's gospel sets it up as a one-on-one encounter, with the disciples off in the city to get provisions. This passage takes place at noon, the hottest time of the day in desert countries, when thirst is most acute and the need for water is intense. Jesus is at the well, but unable to access the water and in need of assistance. The scene is ripe with rich symbology: the wells, water, desert, the sense of need, and encounters with strangers and enemies. (John's gospel is also set up on a twenty-four-hour, one-day time frame—enough material to write another book on!) Jesus initiates the conversation and is blunt about his demands—he doesn't politely make a request. This is often missed completely when the passage is read as text but is unmistakable when it is spoken aloud: it is jarring, off-putting, and unexpected. The conversation that ensues is reactive initially but soon begins to develop. The following text operates on a number of levels: that of a man wanting/needing water and a woman with the ability to give it to him from a well in her territory; and then that of a man who has water, which he refers to as living water, that he wants to give her. She is reluctant at first to take anything from him but discovers she wants it and expresses her desire for him to give it to her. Listen to both levels.

Jesus answered her, "If you knew the gift of God, and who it is that is saying to you, 'Give me a drink,' you would have asked him, and he would have given you living water." The woman said to him, "Sir, you have no bucket, and the well is deep. Where do you get that living water? Are you greater than our ancestor Jacob, who gave us the well, and with his sons and his flocks drank from it?" Jesus said to her, "Everyone who drinks of this water will be thirsty again, but those who drink of the water that I will give them will never be thirsty. The water that I will give will become in them a spring of water gushing up to eternal life." The woman said to him, "Sir, give me this water, so that I may never be thirsty or have to keep coming here to draw water." (Jn 4:10–15)

There are five lines of dialogue, and a wealth of theology is given in a process that moves with great leaps of perception, want, and misconception with each answer back and forth. They begin with hostility, facing off against each other while Jesus asks her for water! She reacts to him as a Jew, as an outsider, and as an enemy, knowing that most Jews make it a point not to speak with or have dealings with Samaritans, let alone one who is a woman.

Jesus is again the first to make a huge leap by basically saying: if you only knew who I was—God's gift to the world in love—you'd be asking me for water and I'd gladly give it to you—my living water— for that is why I am here. She hears part of it—if you only knew who I was, God's gift—and again has mixed feelings and reactions. Most of us don't take kindly to being told that the person in front of us is God's gift to us! But she also catches a word that would be a symbol for both believing Jews and Samaritans: living water. Living water is literally what is in the well that Jesus is sitting next to and she is standing next to—even this arrangement is the setup for the teacher, who has wisdom, and the student, who wants to learn that wisdom. Living water is deep-source water that seeks a way up and out of the ground. If it is blocked, it will turn and retreat deeper into the ground and come back up again around whatever is blocking it. It is fresh water and "living" in the sense that it both moves and seeks freedom and expression, and that it gives life (especially in a desert) and is a necessity for all human beings. Jacob's well is in the West Bank, in the town of Nablus, and is the primary water source for the entire region—over four thousand years old—it is a spring of living water.

But living water is also a theological concept shared by all Jews and Samaritans; it is another word for the Torah, the Scriptures—the Word of God, the revelation of God to the people of God. And with that word, the woman is intrigued and drawn in—she understands that the man before her is not just a Jew. This man is a rabbi, a teacher, perhaps a wise one, and she is thirsty for knowledge and wisdom of her tradition.

What follows reflects both levels of the discussion but often crisscrosses each scenario as they speak to each other and Jesus seeks to give the woman his gift of living water. She points out to him that he has no bucket—no access to the water—and that she does; she also points out that her tradition—that of Jacob and Joseph (rather than Abraham)—gave her people this well and its rich sources of belief. She's interested, but skeptical that Jesus is greater than those masters of faith in the past. Jesus calmly tells her that his living water—his Word and revelation and knowledge of God—is far deeper than anything in her tradition. His Word does more than quench thirst: it converts the hearers into living water so that they become a fountain in the desert of the noonday heat; they become an ever-renewing source of life, even stronger than death!

Immediately, of course, she wants that water! But her reasons for wanting it reveal that she is only half-hearing Jesus and is actually understanding very little of his words, only enough to know that she wants his Word and wisdom. She wants it to make her life easier, and on a more pragmatic level, so that she won't have to keep drawing water from the well and lugging it back to her village. Yet in that moment, she is drawn in: Jesus has drawn her to his Word and his side, and the conversation that follows teaches her more, especially in relation to her previous beliefs and failures of faithfulness and practice—not just for her personally but for everyone who comes to the waters of baptism and initiation, and to the living waters of the gospel—the Word of God in Jesus.

When she asks for the waters, she is told to go and bring her husband—she is not married at that moment but had been married five times previously and was with another man still. This has nothing to do with the structure of marriage in either of the communities, but it is a theological symbol rooted in the words of the prophets of Israel: Israel is the unfaithful half of the marriage and God is the one who returns again and again, drawing the people back into relationship. Israel represents the people of Samaria—and all people, whether Jewish at the time of Jesus, or Greek, or now Americans, Europeans, Asians, etc.—who claim to believe and yet fail to practice that belief and live with many gods, idols that must be served nationally, economically, politically, and even socially, along with the worship of the God of Truth.

Historically the people of Samaria made deals and pacts with the five nations that had conquered them since the destruction of the northern kingdom of Judea; at the time of Jesus, they have another arrangement with the Romans. They worship the conqueror's gods as their own and yet still profess to believe in their own tradition and await the Messiah of their ancient promises. They will sleep with the Romans, so to speak, but they will not marry them. In a sense, this is the second step in being initiated into the community of the Word of God—conversion and turning from one's old failures and way of life.

They move on to issues of worship—where, how, when, and who it is they are actually staking their lives on and siding with in matters of authority and power. She begins to believe that Jesus is a prophet. Prophets are intent on just three aspects of one thing: what constitutes true worship of God, the care of the poor, and the coming of justice—all one piece to a prophet and to God. Jesus becomes very clear about who is to be worshipped and how worshippers are to live, and that where one worships isn't the issue: it's actually worshipping with one's life rather than the ritual and the place.

Jesus said to her, "Woman, believe me, the hour is coming when you will worship the Father neither on this mountain nor in Jerusalem. You worship what you do not know; we worship what we know, for salvation is from the Jews. But the hour is coming, and is now here, when the true worshippers will worship the Father in spirit and truth, for the Father seeks such as these to worship him. God is spirit, and those who worship him must worship in spirit and truth." (Jn 4:21–24)

With these words the entire cult and structure of religious traditions (of both Judaism and Samaritanism—and all other religions) are put in perspective. The rituals of worship serve the actual expression of the worshipper and encompass all of life, in spirit and in truth (or in the Spirit of God and the Truth of God—the practice of living like Jesus). This in itself is staggering and shocking, and undercuts all the emphasis of any religion, including Christianity, on the outward manifestation of what is believed in creed and celebrated in the cult and worship in structured places. But what Jesus says strikes a chord of want and truth in the woman, and she moves along with him, suggesting that she, too, believes that there is one who is coming in the fulfillment of all the prophets and ancient teachings. In reply to her statement of belief, Jesus tells her point-blank who he is and that she is standing before the long-awaited one. He responds, "I AM HE, THE ONE WHO IS SPEAKING TO YOU" (Jn 4:26).

With these words, the heart of John's gospel is unleashed and proclaimed. This is I AM, all of the expressions of the traditions of Judaism in the person of Jesus. He is speaking with her as God spoke with Moses or the prophets—in the old traditions if you see, hear, and speak with God, you die, and yet, here she is, alive and well! This is a fleshing out of John's introduction that Jesus is THE WORD OF GOD—the fullness of revelation in a human being's flesh and blood and bone, dwelling among us and gifting us with light, with freedom and grace, and, above all, with living water— love and friendship that makes us into fountains in a desert to gush up and out, and quench the deepest thirsts to be human and like God.

At this moment, the disciples return and are a bit put out by her presence and the obvious reality that she is not simply speaking with Jesus but that they have become friends, both as man/woman and as Jew/Samaritan. As the disciples themselves talk with Jesus, they don't say anything. She soon goes back to her village but leaves her water jar at the well. With that simple gesture, she proclaims she is a believer, that she has drunk of the living water and is now about to be a wellspring for others, seeking to share what she has been given as a gift. But when she begins to speak to her own people, we hear that once again she has both perceived some of Jesus's words and reality and missed much of what Jesus has told and revealed to her. One can only understand and gain so much wisdom individually. She tells her story and invites them to the water.

> Many Samaritans from that city believed in him because of the woman's testimony, "He told me everything I have ever done." So when the Samaritans came to him, they asked him to stay with them; and he stayed with them two more days. And many more believed because of his word. They said to the woman, "It is no longer because of what you said that we believe, for we have heard for ourselves, and we know that this is truly the Savior of the world." (Jn 4:39–42)

She has left her water jar behind her just as the disciples left their boats behind them; she follows Jesus by telling the story of her encounter with him and describing who she has come to believe he is: the Messiah. She is a follower, using the words "Come and see," which were earlier used by Jesus in the first chapter and then by Philip to Nathaniel. The community grows with this invitation: "Come and see." The people of her village initially believe in Jesus because of her testimony. This is the group of people who Jesus will pray for in his last words when he prays for all those who "believe in me through their testimony" (Jn 17:20). But even in her preaching she is lacking and has taken Jesus's word to mean that he is the Messiah. She has been told that he is the Word of God Made Flesh, the Logos of the Prologue of the gospel, but she must be drawn back

again and again to the living water with the community to understand what that means and the depth she has been brought into
with Jesus's gift. Again she has both heard the Word and not heard
it, and needs to continue to drink of the water.

Now the community that she originally invited to come and see
and hear Jesus for themselves returns to gift her again. This follows the structure of John's community, and there will be the constant reminder that one follows the Word with others—that one
becomes a member of the community of the beloved disciples (with
the emphasis on the plural—with others). They beg Jesus to stay
on and he obliges for two more days. Again Jesus's actions are both
word and symbol and action. John's gospel is about initiation into
the mystery of the Incarnation, death, and Resurrection of Jesus,
and the abiding of the Spirit that together worships God the Father. This is characterized by the three days of mystery that is the
foundation of all those who believe. And once you have seen and
heard and become a fountain of living water gushing up in the desert, you must be sourced in a community that hears the Word and
celebrates it ritually in worship and lives it publicly together. The
woman of Samaria, as with each and every believer, now learns the
next description of who Jesus as the Word of God Made Flesh is:
in truth he is the Savior of the World. He is beyond Messiah for
the Jewish nation. He is the fulfillment, and more, of all that has
been spoken before to the people of God. This is just the beginning. There is always more to hear, more living water to drink, and
more to know of who Jesus is. The norm is to learn together as a
community.

Later Jesus will cry out at one of the festivals in public these
words:

> "Let anyone who is thirsty come to me, and let the one who believes in me
> drink. As the scripture has said, 'Out of the believer's heart shall flow riv-
> ers of living water.'" Now he said this about the Spirit, which believers in
> him were to receive; for as yet there was no Spirit, because Jesus was not yet
> glorified. (Jn 7:37–39)

When one needs water to feed body, mind, heart, and soul, the living water is there. As individuals and as community, the group that follows Jesus lives on the waters of the Scripture—the Word of God in the gospel and the Word of God heard in community and shared so that all are held accountable to be sources of life, ever more abundant life for all the world in the power and the truth of the Spirit. All worship must serve to actually become words of God in Truth for the life of others. For John's community, it is not so much what you believe as what you put into practice in your life with others so that all are drawn to the waters of abundant life and Truth.

But amazingly this is only the first step. Anyone who believes is invited further still into the mystery of Jesus's relationship with God in the power and Truth of the Spirit. At his last meal with his disciples, Jesus will serve them, reversing the roles that are common between master and servant and God and human beings. Jesus will wash their feet, showing them how they are to serve others and stand and kneel with Jesus as his messengers. But during the meal he invites them deeper and deeper into his relationship with God as Father, telling them of the gift of the Spirit of Truth, and that he wants us to be friends—with him, with God, with one another—this is what is meant by the community of the Beloved Disciples. He tries over and over again to share with them what this could mean.

> "If you love me, you will keep my commandments. And I will ask the Father, and he will give you another Advocate, to be with you forever. This is the Spirit of truth, whom the world cannot receive, because it neither sees him nor knows him. You know him, because he abides with you, and he will be in you." (Jn 14:15–17)

We often short-circuit the power of Jesus's words by concentrating on them for ourselves as individuals. They are meant for the individual in community with others because they are sourced in commonality of belief and presence. The Spirit of Truth—the presence of the Word of God, in Jesus risen from the dead—abides primarily, most truthfully, and powerfully in the Body of Christ—all those who believe in the Word. Jesus is adamant that they will know sorrow and suffering or rejection and persecution in their lives, just as he did, if they obey his Word; he is also adamant that the gift of the Spirit will be his own presence with them to rely on, stand with, and source them with courage and hope and the power of love.

Chapter 17 is entirely devoted to Jesus speaking to the Father in the Spirit about his friends—all those with whom he has sought to share his relationship, wisdom, and power, and all those who will know that intimacy and intensity through the preaching of the Word and the sharing of Living Water in the Scriptures and their living them out—as they become true words of God for and with others. The chapter and prayer ends with the vision of what all human beings are to become through the Word of God in Jesus lived out in the world.

> *"I ask not only on behalf of these, but also on behalf of those who will believe in me through their word, that they may all be one. As you, Father, are in me and I am in you, may they also be one in us, so that the world may believe that you have sent me. The glory that you have given me I have given them, so that they may be one, as we are one, I in them and you in me, that they may become completely one, so that the world may know that you have sent me and have loved them even as you have loved me." (Jn 17:20–23)*

Any knowledge and wisdom of God is and must be expressed in communion with all others and with the world in abundant life and love—love as God loves us, in Jesus, in Spirit and in Truth. Universal communion is revelatory of communion with God and is to mirror the communion of God in God. We are invited in and with the power of the Word, the Living Water, and the Spirit, the Truth of God, we are empowered to abide and dwell in God—here and now, with all others. This absolute living-out of communion is essential and core to the practice of expressing that one believes in the Word Made Flesh.

John's gospel is the gospel of the Community of the Beloved Disciples, and one of the last and most lingering—and strongest—images. Where do we find that community? Where is it visible? Where do those who believe in the Word of God Made Flesh put their bodies—wordlessly and completely? Listen to see and learn where they are found.

> *Meanwhile, standing near the cross of Jesus were his mother, and his mother's sister, Mary, the wife of Clopas, and Mary Magdalene. When Jesus saw his mother and the disciple whom he loved standing beside her, he said to his mother, "Woman, here is your son." Then he said to the disciple, "Here is your mother." And from that hour the disciple took her into his own home.*
>
> *After this, when Jesus knew that all was now finished, he said (in order to fulfill the scripture), "I am thirsty." A jar full of sour wine was standing there. So they put a sponge full of the wine on a branch of hyssop and held it to his mouth. When Jesus had received the wine, he said, "It is finished." Then he bowed his head and gave up his spirit. (Jn 19:25b–30)*

They are found at the foot of the Cross as Jesus dies, attentive to him, their presence testimony and their bodies in solidarity and communion with him. They are always found at the foot of the Cross, where innocence is destroyed; where violence attacks; where there is collusion between the powers of the earth—religion, politics, nationalism, and economics. The community of John's beloved friends of God is one of resistance with flesh and blood that fiercely denies that any power that is not based in life for all and love beyond rationality, like God loves us, is no power at all. It is a community defined by the presence of suffering and solidarity with it. It isn't defined by marriage, or blood ties, or kinship; its intimacy is defined by need, by the breaking of boundaries and borders to include all.

The disciple whom Jesus loved is never named, for everyone

who drinks of the living water and knows God's thirst for us is that beloved disciple. The gospel is heard from that vantage point—as one who has become mother to the Word, bringing it forth into the world and as beloved friend intimate and dear to the heart of God—as dear as Jesus is to God's own heart and held in the same Spirit of Truth. There are four at the foot of Jesus's Cross—two named women, both Mary or Miriam: the name means "sea of bitterness and sorrow," witness to injustice and unnecessary suffering, pain, isolation, torture, and death. The others are the unnamed mother and the beloved disciple, also unnamed. They can be relatives, friends, and anyone who puts their body where the words of their mouth claim to be and believe. It is an awkward community of intimacy and of grieving, seemingly with no power, but it is a community of the flesh of human beings standing together and becoming words of truth and love; they will rise again to draw others into hope, freedom, and what it means now to be human, born of God and the Spirit, words of Truth and bodies that are created to love as God loves.

This is a short and pieced-together introduction to John's gospel and the shocking new way of being human beings in the world: men and women friends of God. Jesus's words in John are repeated often: "As the Father has loved me, so I have loved you; abide in my love. If you keep my commandments, you will abide in my love, just as I have kept my Father's commandments and abide in his love. I have said these things to you so that my joy may be in you, and that your joy may be complete" (Jn 15:9–11). The reason for being created, born, and alive is simply to know joy completely together and so to know God. This is the basis of John's gospel.

There is a simple and remarkable story floating around on the Internet that I have been sent by a number people in various forms. It opens a door to the possibilities of what John's gospel might mean if it is put into practice every day here and now. Once upon a time there was a woman who was diagnosed with a terminal disease and told she had only a couple of months, maybe even just weeks, to live. Immediately she ceased any treatment and began to give away her possessions, make her will, and tell people what she had often wanted to say but didn't—asking forgiveness and speaking of love. She planned her funeral and the service in detail: the music and readings, who she would like to sing and speak, and gifts she would like to have given to those who came. Everything was dealt with including what she wanted to be buried in. Finally, she stipulated that she wanted to be buried with a silver fork—a large one—in her hand.

The rabbi or the priest or whoever is telling the story was shocked—why the fork? She smiled and said it was the most important piece of the whole service and what she wanted people to know and remember and take to heart. She was enjoying the minister's puzzlement. She laughed and said, "You have to understand. I come from a large, sprawling family that used to get together religiously for meals, and even when we were out eating at someone's house or at a restaurant, we'd finish the appetizers and then soup and the main courses and there would come a pause. There would be much storytelling, laughter, even tears sometimes, music and singing, and someone would lean over and conspiratorially whisper, 'Keep your fork!' I'd smile, knowing that probably the best was still to come—dessert, extra, unexpected. So I'd love to say it to someone else: 'Keep your fork.' Now when I die I want everyone to see me in my coffin with my fork in hand so they can know—it's still time to 'Keep your fork.'"

And at her funeral she was buried in a gorgeous cape with fork in hand. And everyone who walked by was struck by the fork! "What's with the fork?" And so as part of the service the story was told to everyone. Whatever was to follow she believed that there was more to come—the best was still to come. And everyone who left went home with the sight and thought of that fork.

This was a funeral, and a woman facing her own mortality, and her friends and family facing her loss and the unknown. But the story is illustrative of the gospel of John. No matter how much you hear the Word of God or drink of the living water, there is more to come. Hang on to the Word, keep your cup, your fork, and, of course, it's not really joy and sustenance unless it's done together— lived together with life and food and freedom ever more abundantly for all.

Chapter 9

THE GOSPEL OF JOHN NOW

Preach the truth as if we had a million voices, for it is silence that kills the world.

CATHERINE OF SIENA

A gospel that doesn't unsettle, a word of God that doesn't get under anyone's skin, a word of God that doesn't touch the real sin of the society in which it is being proclaimed, what gospel is that?

OSCAR ROMERO, MARTYR, MARCH 24, 1980

SOMETIMES THE PLACE TO BEGIN IS WHERE EVERYTHING FAILS or seems to be ending. For John's gospel (and for all the gospels) this place, this moment, is the Cross and the execution of Jesus as a criminal, a danger to society, its structures, its values, and its methods of enforcing its authority and power in the world. In John's gospel this event is a political statement of confrontation between opposing forces and powers in the world. It is stark, pragmatic, violent—a warning to all who would be drawn to this teaching and his company. What surrounds the single instant of Jesus's death is reality and a reminder that goodness is destroyed, truth is ignored, and evil and violence often triumph in life. Listen:

> So they took Jesus; and carrying the cross by himself, he went out to what is called The Place of the Skull, which in Hebrew is called Golgotha. There they crucified him, and with him two others, one on either side, with Jesus between them.

Pilate also had an inscription written and put on the cross. It read, "Jesus of Nazareth, the King of the Jews." Many of the Jews read this inscription, because the place where Jesus was crucified was near the city; and it was written in Hebrew, in Latin, and in Greek. Then the chief priests of the Jews said to Pilate, "Do not write, 'The King of the Jews,' but, 'This man said, I am the King of the Jews.'" Pilate answered, "What I have written I have written." When the soldiers had crucified Jesus, they took his clothes and divided them into four parts, one for each soldier. They also took his tunic; now the tunic was seamless, woven in one piece from the top. So they said to one another, "Let us not tear it, but cast lots for it to see who will get it." This was to fulfill what the scripture says, "They divided my clothes among themselves, and for my clothing they cast lots." And that is what the soldiers did. (Jn 19:16–25)

Pilate is intent on getting in the last word and wants to taunt the Jewish leaders who dragged him into their petty internal religious squabbles (as he perceives it). He is furious that they used him to make sure that Jesus was executed—legally, though unjustly. Pilate, the Roman personification of power in the occupied territory of Palestine, detests everything about the land he is assigned to govern and control. And so he has a sign made that reads: "Jesus of Nazareth, the King of the Jews." It is meant as an insult, filled with disdain and bile. The sign is in three languages—the known spoken languages of the world at the time of Jesus—making it a universal pronouncement. Pilate has unwittingly declared that Jesus is not a mere upstart in an insignificant tribal nation but that he somehow belongs to the world.

The soldiers divide Jesus's clothes among them—the spoils of war, an odious work assigned to them by the government. Each gets a piece. But Jesus's tunic is a seamless garment, so they do not tear it but cast lots for it, gambling for the prize, in other words. There are four corners to the world, four seasons to the year, four stages in a lifetime—again even his clothes are taken to the ends of the earth, and yet his tunic, closest to his body, is seamless and not torn asunder. There is continuity and unity in the Body of Christ's clothing.

It is said that these are characteristics of the followers and friends of Jesus—the Body of Christ in the world today.

Jesus spoke of a kingdom, a realm, a reign, and made it clear that his version of a kingdom was unlike any seen in the world before. And Jesus steadfastly refuses to accept any title of kingship or example of historical kings in regard to his own person. He was reluctant even to use the title of Messiah, or the Anointed One, of the promises and hopes of the Jewish nation. The connotations of these titles harkened back to David and were linked to the overthrow of the Roman domination, who were abhorred as oppressors. All of this is prelude to Jesus's execution—the trial that is presided over by Pilate, who is not interested in religion but in politics and power. He doesn't care about who Jesus is within the context of a religious group but whether or not this Jesus is dangerous to the reign of Rome. The dialogue between Jesus and Pilate is also the basis for Christians in the Roman Empire more than sixty to seventy years after the death and resurrection of Jesus. The Jewish leaders have handed him over to Pilate. Now he is Pilate's problem.

> Then Pilate entered the headquarters again, summoned Jesus, and asked him, "Are you the King of the Jews?" Jesus answered, "Do you ask this on your own, or did others tell you about me?" Pilate replied, "I am not a Jew, am I? Your own nation and the chief priests have handed you over to me. What have you done?" Jesus answered, "My kingdom is not from this world. If my kingdom were from this world, my followers would be fighting to keep me from being handed over to the Jews. But as it is, my kingdom is not from here." Pilate asked him, "So you are a king?" Jesus answered, "You say that I am a king. For this I was born, and for this I came into the world, to testify to the truth. Everyone who belongs to the truth listens to my voice." Pilate asked him, "What is truth?"
>
> After he had said this, he went out to the Jews again and told them, "I find no case against him." (Jn 18:33–38)

First it is crucial to note that Jesus never says that he is a king, only that others refer to him as one, and he never actually answers any of Pilate's questions. He is intent on speaking the truth of who he is and why he now stands before Pilate, who will condemn him to death whether there is reason to kill him under Roman law or not. Jesus's initial response is pivotal: "My kingdom is not from this world," which has often been mistranslated and then misunderstood and misused as "my kingdom is not of this world." One preposition makes all the difference in the world! These words in Greek—*ek tou kosmou toutou*—are the basis of how Jesus and Christians ever since see themselves in relation to politics, the power of nations, and how power is used in the world at large. Jesus is intent on making sure that Pilate—and everyone else—knows that his kingdom and the power and authority sourced in his words, his life, and his person come from very different sources than any nation or kingdom in this world. He continues: "But as it is, my kingdom is not from here." And this disconnect from the "world" is a source of consternation throughout the history of Christians in relation to the rest of society.

But Jesus reveals the source and foundation of his power—the Truth. The reason for everything in Jesus's life is to testify to the Truth, and to call others to listen to his voice to respond in following him and testifying to the Truth with their own lives. These words, put succinctly before Pilate, were spoken just the evening before with his friends at table, when Jesus warned them—all who follow him—that they will know persecution and murderous hate from others in society, other nations, and even among religious leaders. Listen to some of the last exhortations that Jesus shares with his friends, which was already examined prior but warrants another look:

> *"This is my commandment, that you love one another as I have loved you. No one has greater love than this, to lay down one's life for one's friends. You are my friends if you do what I command you. I do not call you servants any longer, because the servant does not know what the master is doing; but I have called you friends, because I have made known to you everything that I have heard from my Father. You did not choose me but I chose you. And*

*I appointed you to go and bear fruit, fruit that will last, so that the Father
will give you whatever you ask him in my name. I am giving you these commands so that you may love one another." (Jn 15:12–17)*

This is where Jesus's power and authority come from—and what
he shares with his friends—from the Father whom he obeys and
serves as they are to serve, too. And his kingdom, his power and
reign, his abiding and dwelling with human beings on earth is love:
the power to love one another as he has loved us, as the Father has
loved him. This kind of power stands in opposition to all other
powers on the earth, in all of history. Pilate cannot hear that: he is
quick to retort that he isn't a Jew and is not interested in anything
that has to do with their religion—Pilate's religion is Rome. But
then Jesus continues with sharp and hard words of reality:

*"If the world hates you, be aware that it hated me before it hated you. If you
belonged to the world, the world would love you as its own. Because you do
not belong to the world, but I have chosen you out of the world—therefore
the world hates you." (Jn 15:18–19)*

The words *hate* and *world* and *belong* need to be looked at and understood as Jesus meant them, not as they have often been interpreted. The words in Greek are *ho kosmos,* and they do not mean "the
world" but "the system." Walter Wink and many other scholars and
theologians posit that this *ho kosmos* is not the world as we think of
it—the universe, the earth, the world we live in, and so on—but
has the meaning of the structural systems that dominate worlds:
nations, states, economic systems, armies, kingdoms, governments,
laws, social strata, castes, even religious hierarchies, dogmas, doctrines, and traditions. In these words to his friends, Jesus is teaching them that love (agape, meaning love that is the love of God for
us; love that is shared with enemies, neighbors, friends; love that is
intent on holding and binding the community together, restoring it
through forgiveness, reconciliation, repair of the world, and mercy;
and love expressed even in laying down one's life for one's friends)

is in opposition to the *systems* of history, not the world at large. And these systems often provoke rage, hate, persecution, and even torture and death because they cannot control it, stop it, or obliterate it. This is Jesus's Truth: other forms of power cannot abide love that human beings steep their lives, their practices, and their hope in—with Jesus, crucified and risen from the dead. This kind of love, this kind of kingdom, this kind of leader—this Jesus, in other words—is revolutionary beyond any concept of change yet known. Jesus's truth is found in the Word Made Flesh and dwelling among us, and it is that Truth, practiced toward all with compassion, that will, in Jesus's words, "set us free!": "If you continue in my word, you are truly my disciples; and you will know the truth, and the truth will make you free" (Jn 8:31–32).

Are we, who claim to be Jesus's followers today, continuing in his Word? Do those who know his truth, and are free in the world to speak the truth, stand together against "the system"? The system is self-contained and self-perpetuating, enforced to maintain stability at any cost, and often runs roughshod over the majority of people. Its values are sustained by force, threats, lies, bribery, armies, weapons, economics, greed, and a virulent capitalism that sees profits as essential, overriding people's basic needs and even contributing to the destruction of the world's and the earth's resources. And "the system" is perfectly capable of hatred that is organized, efficient, legal, and sanctioned often by whatever religion is the designated one of that system. And if this is true today, where do we stand? At the foot of the Cross, in the small group of one single woman, one married woman, one widow, and one unnamed Beloved Disciple? Do we stand with anyone who listens to the Word and dwells in the truth?

What does it mean to stand in solidarity with the Crucified Jesus and to love like God loves Jesus and Jesus loves us? What does it mean to be in communion with God and all those whom God embraces as beloved? This is what John Coleman says it might mean. Listen:

People who threaten the existing power system in a society are crimi-
nals. . . . So I am putting the human Jesus in the same cell with King,
Gandhi, Rosa Parks, Dietrich Bonhoeffer, Father Daniel Berrigan, and
Nelson Mandela. Toss in your own prisoner of choice. . . . Such is Jesus'
brand of criminality, which teaches us that if we are to live as he would
have us live, we ought to stand in solidarity with those whom society re-
jects, to call them sisters and brothers, to use whatever blessings we have that
they might know the embrace of Christ, and to find in them the presence
of Christ waiting to teach and nourish us. We should fully expect that our
solidarity with society's rejects would brand us as subversives and rejects. As
disciples of Jesus, we'll destabilize our society and face persecution or at least
make those around us uncomfortable because we won't mindlessly adopt the
norms of our culture.[1]

What is important to remember is that one doesn't do this
alone—to stand alone is to stand as a prophet, but to stand in agape,
in love at the foot of the Cross in solidarity with Jesus, is to stand in
community. There are communities like this in the world. They
have leaders for periods of time; those who initiate the movement
for justice and peace and then stand there—wherever people
find themselves excluded, treated unjustly, persecuted, and without
their rights as human beings. Some of those who have died were
mentioned above; there were many others just in the past decades:
Dorothy Day and Peter Maurin of the Catholic Worker Movement; Pope John XXIII; the women of Bread and Roses and the
women who worked for decades for the right to vote; Cesar Chavez
and Dolores Huerta (still alive) who worked with the farmworkers;
Helen Prejean (still alive), a prophet gathering communities to
work against the death penalty; the groups who in solidarity live on
borders where war rages, with the people, as a human wall of protection. There is Jean Vanier's communities of L'Arche who live
together: those who are disabled and those who are able-bodied—
one group taking care of heart and soul and the other taking care of
heart and physical needs in small communities that are always, in a

sense, "washing one another's feet," obeying Jesus's words and practice of worship at his last meal with his friends (Jn 13).

There are the communities of Sant'Egidio found living among the poor of Rome, Naples, Genoa; Antwerp in Belgium; in La Boca in Buenos Aires, and El Salvador; in the Ivory Coast and Mozambique—with more communities sprouting up yearly. They live with the poor but over time have learned through experience what they call "the poverty that is the mother of all poverties—the absence of peace—to have war as the one desperate companion of one's life." And so they work for peace in countries torn to shreds by war and its aftermath. For over sixteen years they worked in Mozambique, finally forging a lasting peace that ended the civil war. They are committed to friendship across borders, and along borders, sharing the Cross and helping to carry the cross of whole peoples. This is the way one of their members, Mario Marazziti, once described them in a talk in London years ago.

> Today, in the left-hand aisle of the church of Sant'Egidio, you can see a wooden cross. We found it some time ago, thrown away by the roadside. One can hardly call it a cross because it lacks the transversal branch, the arms. Today only the central body, the trunk, of the cross remains. It even conveys the expression of suffering. We call it "the Christ without arms," "the powerless Christ," "the Christ of weakness." For us it symbolizes the call to transform the world through the weakness of the cross, without resorting to powerful means. . . .
>
> It is in this way that the Church can become what Pope John XXIII called "the village fountain." . . . It can become a place where the people of the village can stop by for clean water, for water that comes from afar, and brings with it tastes, echoes, tensions and passions of distant worlds. The village fountain is perhaps, as in some Byzantine places, the holy fountain where one can buy images of the mother of God and where all come, all the citizens, the sick, the rich and the poor alike, pilgrims and traders, to be cured of their diseases, of their closures and their egoisms. . . . We, in the Community of Sant'Egidio, like to be in harmony with this village fountain and we are content to be able to spend ourselves for this end.[2]

These are communities of people who use love and that power of solidarity together to approach the Cross—the world and all the sufferings of people—in imaginative, constructive, and life-giving ways, moving in to abide and dwell with people for the long term and short term in their struggle for human dignity and the right to live ever more abundantly. They are more than visionaries who have learned through practice and experience that you cannot undo harm using the same thought processes and ways of approaching people that were used in the past; often, these practices were in part responsible for making situations intolerable and unbearable. They know in their flesh that the Spirit of Truth found in the Word of God (the gospels) and in the person of Jesus crucified and risen from the dead present everywhere in the world, in the Body of Christ, is always offering new suggestions, untried ways of living, and life-giving ideas and practices for making peace a reality in the midst of war and destruction; for bringing solace, justice, and human rights to those who find themselves treated as scapegoats and pariahs in a nation or a society's conditions. They know intimately Martin Luther King Jr.'s words about love and power in a sermon he gave on August 16, 1967, just months before he was murdered: "Power without love is reckless and abusive, and love without power is sentimental and anemic." This is the power of love in the community of Jesus—not only power to do something but power with others, shared and shifted and risked.

The Spirit of Truth is alive and strong in these communities seeking to undo the harm done to others, to alter the bases of economic injustice, and to make sure that all have a chance at life. While in South Africa, I saw a sign in a community center—a ten-by-twelve concrete-block building with one door and one window—that read: "There was no paradigm, no precedent, nothing. We had to CARVE it, and so perhaps we were more willing to listen." (These are the words of Trevor Manuel, the first black minister of finance in South Africa.) Are we listening to the gospel of John? Are we listening to the Truth in the Word of God Made

Flesh among us? Are we listening with others to the Spirit, still hoping and intent on teaching us all we need to know now?

There are communities like Thich Nhat Hanh's Plum Village in France, Buddhists who welcome people from every land and religion to live together; Taizé, also in France, is an international community of Christians that provides a base and hospitality for thousands of young people from countries described as "third and fourth world," as well as those from industrialized and technologically elite nations, to pray, study, and dream together and later return to their countries for dialogue, conflict negotiation, shared projects, and communal living at the service of others, with others. They share the discipline of their religious tradition as a structure that creates harmony and grows people who are dedicated to the well-being of others with joy and compassion. These disciples, who chant, meditate, and read the Scriptures and sutras, provide a collective awakening and awareness of not only the problems and the pain of the world but also the possibilities of transformation and construction of new realities. They live in the world in which we find ourselves now but are sourced from the world of the human family and faith—they are the continuation of the Buddha and the continuation of the Risen Lord's Spirit in the world today. This is how Thich Nhat Hanh of Plum Village describes our present predicament and our future.

> Violence, corruption, abuse of power, and self-destruction are happening all around us, even in the community of leaders, both spiritual and social. We all know that the laws of our country don't have enough strength to manage corruption, superstition, and cruelty. Only faith, determination, awakening, and a big dream can create an energy strong enough to help our society rise above and go to the shore of peace and hope.
>
> Yet everything, even the Buddha, is always changing and evolving. Thanks to our practice of looking deeply, we realize that the sufferings of our time are different from those of the time of Siddhartha, and so the methods of practice should also be different. That is why the Buddha inside of us also should evolve in many ways, so that the Buddha can be relevant to our time.[3]

For Catholics and Christians, the question needs to be asked: where are these communities of the Beloved Disciples, not organizations or movements but gatherings of flesh-and-blood folk who put their bodies alongside those who are today's victims of the system? Hugo Assmann, a Latin American theologian, put the issue out there forthrightly: "To live the commandment of love involves a political position, whether one likes it or not. Today one cannot follow the Gospel without political activity. It is impossible that one live responsibly without being concerned with the organization of society."

For American Catholics—and all Christians who proclaim the gospel of Jesus—there is one large and sprawling group that believers must stand with in solidarity and community. It is all those people who find themselves in these categories: immigrants, migrants, gypsies, those without a country or a home—most often referred to as "aliens" (as though they were from outer space) or "illegals," criminals destroying our country, taking our jobs, and causing all manner of ills in our society and nation. The name-calling and hatred directed at so many millions of people (12 to 20 million out of 313 million in the United States) is found in the mouths of those descended from people who—unless they are descendants of Native Americans—came primarily as aliens, illegals, and criminals from their countries of origin. It seems there is a very short memory span when it comes to blaming others for contemporary problems. A photographer named Sebastião Salgado, who documents migrants and refugees, lets his pictures of actual human beings speak for themselves. His latest books, *Migrations: Humanity in Transition* and *The Children: Refugees and Migrants,* are as shocking as any depiction of the Crucifixion. This is how the book was described in a March 2004 review in *U.S. Catholic*:

> Salgado brings the viewer into the world of the exiled and landless, the poor and the dispossessed who are driven from their homes by famine, war, and economic chaos or forced to leave behind family and homeland in search of work, safety, or some promise of security and peace. Here are

the faces of those we only see as alien, the faces of those with no place to put their heads.

But where are the Churches, the Bodies of Christ, to stand with these people who are the crucified body of Christ today, right next door to us? The gospel is not about making statements, though they can be helpful in calling people to attention and to joining with others to work for the rights of those who do not work the system. The gospel is about people in every parish being welcoming, hospitable, and generous, sharing food, clothing, shelter, language classes, advocacy, health care, and access to the legal systems; it's about accompanying their neighbors, and beloved brothers and sisters, as they seek asylum, a life without fear of arrest and deportation, status as legal citizens. At the same time, other members of the Churches should work to change laws and provide a safe haven, a sanctuary for the millions just here in our own country now.

The Truth of the Word of God Made Flesh in Jesus links his last words to his friends and his death by crucifixion to what constitutes worship in the community of the Beloved Disciples. In the gospel of John, there is no breaking of the bread and sharing of the cup at the last meal with his friends. Instead, Jesus takes off his outer garment and takes up a pitcher of water and kneels before each of his disciples, including the one who would set the betrayal by all of them in motion, and washes their feet. Then he rises from his kneeling position and sits at table with them and shares that what he has done is what they must do—this is the model for life, for service, and for worship of God. It is a ritual of subservience and a rite of bodily mercy. It models relationships within the community where those with the most power (love) surrender to the care of the most acute needs of the community in public. They are appalled as we should be while reading this part of the gospel—for we have ignored this account of the Eucharist altogether, except as a rite performed only on Holy Thursday, before the last rituals of Holy Week begin, and this ritual often excludes anyone who is the Body of Christ, the actual Church, all women, anyone who is not a priest or a deacon from the experience. Yet for John, and for Jesus, this act of service is the foundation of all the words and for dying for his friends.

Even in Jewish and Roman society, no servant was required to wash his owner, master, or mistresses' feet, and yet here is Jesus, kneeling before each disciple, humbling himself before them, honoring them, and providing them an actual service that was a daily need. Peter balks, and is chided, but finally submits to letting Jesus wash his feet. None of them understood or could accept what was happening, or that this was to be their form of worship, daily. With Jesus's death and resurrection, the Spirit teaches them the Truth. And when he is finished washing their feet, Jesus tells them that this is what he expects and demands of them: an attitude of service, humble respect, honor for all in the household, and care for the needs of those most in danger, in imitation of their Master, who humbled himself even unto death. This is Jesus's worship of the Father, and it is supposed to be ours—all the other liturgical practices are to serve this liturgy and this way of living.

That night is called Holy Thursday, and when it is celebrated and enacted in Holy Week, it is often called the Feast of Friends, but it is also the night of betrayal by all of Jesus's friends. The night and the ritual sum up the ecstasy and agony of life, the misery and the glory of being a community and belonging together to God. We must wash one another's feet—do this in remembrance of Jesus's life of love and sacrifice as our worship. We are told to do this: wash feet, baptize, drink of living water—the Word—forgive, reconcile, heal, serve, honor, make peace, do justice, be merciful, and care for the bodies of the poor and the crushed, to give solace and aid, and to see God in all, but especially in those most in need of touch, the basic needs of survival and life ever more abundantly. And we are to do it on our knees before others—not in a church or building before God. This is worship in Spirit and Truth, and the only kind of worship God wants: the kind of worship that brings life ever more abundantly to the poor and uncovers and spreads the kingdom of love in the world. We are told to do the Eucharist (which means "give thanks to God") on our knees with others, before others—the other Body of Christ. Anything done in church—"the place we go forth from," in the words of Martin Luther King Jr.—is to make us actually be the servants of the people of the world and the beloved friends of God.

Very early in the gospel, in chapter 2, are two stories that deal with the vital and intimate connection between worship and life in the community. They are the stories of the wedding feast of Cana and the cleansing of the Temple. This last story is the only story that is told in all four gospels—in the other three gospels toward the very end of Jesus's life because it is the last straw, so to speak, that leads to Jesus being rejected by his own people and to his execution by the Romans. But in John's gospel it is the first public action of Jesus, setting up the opposition to the "system" of Temple, cult, sacrifice, and its connections to the structures of religion economically, socially, and in regard to the law, in collusion with Rome. The "system" accommodated Rome's presence in exchange for continuation of the religious leaders' control over the life and worship of the people. The first story is not about a wedding per se but echoes the wedding feasts of Isaiah and the prophets that described the coming of the kingdom of freedom, feasting, no poor, and justice that all would know when the hope of the people would arrive.

Isaiah cries out and invites the people. Listen!

> *Ho, everyone who thirsts, come to the waters; and you that have no money, come, buy and eat! Come, buy wine and milk without money and without price. Why do you spend your money for that which is not bread, and your labor for that which does not satisfy? Listen carefully to me, and eat what is good, and delight yourselves in rich food. Incline your ear, and come to me; listen, so that you may live. (Is 55:1–3)*

This is the beginning of Jesus's teaching, of Jesus's way of living, Jesus's way of worshipping, and his method of drawing a community around him that will become witnesses to all the earth of his love and truth. The liturgy and worship of his community is a festival, a meal, a feast where everyone, but especially the poor and those unable to provide for themselves, are invited and drawn in and welcomed as honored guests. It is water made wine by the Word of God—the waters of baptism; the wine of love/life handed over daily until one dies; the wine that makes life ever more abundant and is the Word of the gospel, the Word Made Flesh dwelling among us. When obeyed, this wine has the power to transform all reality. The work and power of the Spirit is found with those in the back rooms with the servants who obey the Word—they're the ones who know where the good wine comes from after the first wine has run out. This wedding feast is what the kingdom looks like here on earth, now, among Jesus's friends and family.

There is rejoicing, the strengthening of relationships, the provision of the poor, and the honoring of all those present—no one is shunned. No one is humiliated. And those who have positions of power in this worship and the community are the servants doing the hard labor of filling water jars that could hold twelve to twenty gallons of water and pouring it out and serving it to the guests. They are unknown and unnamed, not singled out or in the places of authority. Those places are reserved for the bride and groom, also unnamed, and all people of God and their guests celebrating God's wedding of Jesus's flesh with our own, and the power of the Word and Spirit to create a new community stronger than any family blood lines or marriage. The celebration begins with the mother of Jesus—in John's gospel part of the community of Beloved Disciples at the foot of the Cross—and all who announce the needs of the community that need to be attended to and served immediately.

The words of the Church, the community of the Beloved Disciples, proclaim in the only words necessary: "Do whatever he tells you" (Jn 2:5). This is the beginning of the preaching of Jesus. The Church—the believers in Jesus—must be well known in all the back rooms and servants' quarters, in all the places where service and the works of justice and mercy are practiced. They must live and work for reconciliation, peace, and to keep the community together in spite of scarcity and problems that arise. This is what it means to be a deacon, a servant, one who serves at table, whether it is in daily life or at the table where the Body of Christ feasts and worships together.

It is a story that describes the sacraments and liturgy of the community. The water jars are filled (baptismal references of the living water that is the Word of the Lord) and are turned into wine by the service and obedience of those who follow Jesus. The wine is brought to the head steward (the leader of the small community). All are amazed—the head waiter, the groom, and, when they drink of it, the guests. The wine is born of service in response to the larger needs of the whole community. And this is the first sign of revelation and glory! This is the first sign of what Jesus's people look like, what their worship is like, what their lives are to be like—and what their God is like! It begins here and they move on to Capernaum with his mother, his brothers, and his disciples, and they remained there a few days. It is the beginning of the unveiling and the bringing forth of Good News and the letting loose of the power of the Spirit into the world (Jn 2:1—12).

What follows is intimately connected to this story of the wedding feast. From the beginning of John's gospel, Jesus is on a collision course with the leaders of the Temple, the priesthood, the structures of institutionalized worship, the way the law is interpreted and practiced, and any group that is in collusion with the powers and "systems" of the world that hinder the honor of God, the care of the poor, and the coming of justice. Listen to the story and let it shock you as the experience did to anyone there, or who heard it told.

The Passover of the Jews was near, and Jesus went up to Jerusalem. In the temple he found people selling cattle, sheep, and doves, and the money changers seated at their tables. Making a whip of cords, he drove all of them out of the temple, both the sheep and the cattle. He also poured out the coins of the money changers and overturned their tables. He told those who were selling the doves, "Take these things out of here! Stop making my Father's house a marketplace!" His disciples remembered that it was written, "Zeal for your house will consume me." The Jews then said to him, "What sign can you show us for doing this?" (Jn 2:13–18)

Passover is near. This is the feast of drawing the people out of slavery and into freedom, and Jesus is beginning to tear down the old ways and tear people away from what enslaves them and destroy what is evil and unjust, beginning in the Temple, his Father's house. This story is about home, about Church, about us and how we use power, money, and the systems of the world, and how we mix those practices with religion and worship. In the Temple precincts, he comes upon people selling, buying, and changing coins—business that allows and continues the existing outside injustices and, worse, allows the practice of worship to serve the "system." Jesus is forceful and angry, and moves with power and preciseness, driving them out, and declaring his relationship with God as the basis for what he is doing—cleansing the Temple so that what the religious system does doesn't hinder people from actually worshipping God. The passage he quotes is from Jeremiah 7: "Zeal for your house consumes me!" It is sacrifice language, and what he does, how he lives, and the words he speaks are always the Truth, which will kill and destroy him in the end. Jesus begins with purging and purifying religious practices. And everyone, especially those engaged in religious practices and running the Temple, is enraged and demands answers—where do you get the power and authority to do this?

The story continues. Listen:

Jesus answered them, "Destroy this temple, and in three days I will raise it up." The Jews then said, "This temple has been under construction for forty-six years, and you will raise it up in three days?" But he was speaking of the temple of his body. After he was raised from the dead, his disciples remembered that he had said this; and they believed the scripture and the word that Jesus had spoken. (Jn 2:19–22)

Jesus's answer is as convoluted, strange, and misunderstood as any absurdity that can be put into words without faith in God, in mystery, and in God's ways of mercy, forgiveness, justice, and love. This is one of the blatant moments in the gospels where one must be a believer to begin to fathom its meaning and depth of power. They are talking about the actual building of the Temple that has been in various stages of construction for forty-six years, while Jesus is talking about his own body. To try to compare the two as equal is fundamentalism par excellence. Everything in John's gospel is in essence about Incarnation—the Word of God becoming flesh and dwelling among us—and the Resurrection, the raising of Jesus from the dead in the power of the Spirit by the Father so that Jesus lives more powerfully now than he did when he was on earth. Jesus is proclaiming that what will happen to his body will also happen to his Body—the community—in individuals and collectively. Those who follow him will be cleansed, purified by the zeal of God in the Word of God, who is intent on making us all holy, which means that much in us must be destroyed and transformed. We must listen to and embody the Truth of Jesus's Word and be his servants in the world. We are all called to commit ourselves to the Truth—all that Jesus speaks and does and is is the Truth—and to die and rise with him liturgically or in religious rituals of baptism and worship, but we must actually die to all that hinders our belonging to God and being true witnesses in our lives together.

This gospel is written decades after the actual destruction of the Temple; Judaism is shifting painfully from worship in the Temple to a religion of the Torah and law, the home and the synagogue structures. In the meanwhile, the Christian community is shifting away from the Judean religious experience of the Pharisaic rabbis and the priesthood AD post–70. Now the Christians center around the Body of Christ; not a Temple or a structure, but the Body of Christ that is the community of believers and the Body of Christ crucified in the poor, the broken, the outcast, and all those who reflect and mirror the person of Jesus in the world.

The last paragraph of chapter 2 is full of sadness and truth about the people around Jesus, his own disciples, and still all of us today. It forces us to look at our own worship, our own churches, and our own rituals, and whether or not we need drastic purification, destruction, and transformation in what we consider worship, as opposed to what Jesus considers true worship of his Father in the power of the Spirit, with him.

> When he was in Jerusalem during the Passover festival, many believed in his name because they saw the signs that he was doing. But Jesus on his part would not entrust himself to them, because he knew all people and needed no one to testify about anyone; for he himself knew what was in everyone. (Jn 2:23–25)

This is John's Jesus, who knows the heart of every individual, his own believers, and those who would be leaders after him. This, of course, includes all of us and those in positions of religious power and authority in the Body of Christ today. Basically, we rarely look at the reality of Jesus's words—that we are not holy, or consumed with zeal for our Father's household, the Body of Christ still being crucified and battered and treated unjustly. We are divided and absorbed with language and correctness of how rituals are to be performed. We are more concerned over who does what in the rite and who is not allowed to touch "sacred vessels" than we are with whether or not the poor are being fed, and we are being challenged to make the Word of God incarnate in our lives, practices, and public works. Nothing we do in church, worship, or liturgy is worship in Spirit and Truth, unless it mirrors the larger universal reality of love for all, beginning with our enemies and the poorest among us, the outcast and condemned, those we judge brutally and exclude from the table and the feast and our living in solidarity with them as they know rejection and crucifixion.

Based on Jesus's words and teaching in the Scriptures, our worship is not building based. Our worship is not sacrificial. Our worship is not based on the traditional practices that have developed over the last twenty centuries when the Church was a nation-state, or when the power of Rome became Western Christianity. Our worship is not based on the priesthood of men. Our worship is not based on rigid adherence to practices that exclude the majority of the community from partaking in the feast because they are judged unworthy. Our worship is not based on specific words in a language Jesus never spoke, or word-for-word transliterations of a small piece of the rich and universal tradition about how the first followers of Jesus worshipped before the Church became the "Holy Roman Empire" and institutionalized only one way of doing worship, ignoring all the prayers and liturgies and rites of many churches, embolden by the Spirit and inspired by the Spirit to worship in Truth—with their service, their feet washing, their songs and hymns and prayers.

Our worship is with the human body of Jesus, who made his dwelling (the Greek word *eschenosen,* which means "tented") among us. The Body of Christ—all human beings—is the locus of our worship, all temples of the Holy Spirit, the dwelling place of God. What was lavished on temples, churches, and buildings is what is to be lavished on the poor, the hungry, the immigrant, the imprisoned, the thirsty, the homeless, the tortured, the displaced, the leper, and those considered "unworthy." All are to be welcomed at our table, regardless of what society or institutionalized religious structures insist. Our God is concerned with whether or not we live and stand in solidarity at the foot of all the crosses, live in love, and offer the gift of hope and freedom to all those bent, broken, and flayed alive by the "system." Our churches are witnesses to Jesus the Word of God—not in what we do on Sunday in ritual but what we do daily in the world.

One must wonder what Jesus would do if he went into our churches today or went into the Vatican, the cathedrals, and the basilicas after walking the streets of our cities, along the borders of our countries, and in the fields and factories of capitalistic society. There is an old story told about Dom Hélder Câmara, who was the archbishop of Recife, Brazil, for years. He would preach the same sermon every Good Friday in his cathedral church. The church is small and now it is dwarfed by towering office buildings where nearly a million people go to work daily. This is the way I heard he told the story and preached.

Once upon a time there was a man who worked in one of the office buildings down the street from this cathedral. Every day at noon, on his lunch hour, he would hurry down in the elevator and make his way here. He would climb the steps, weaving around the people selling food and those begging for it, those resting on the steps or sleeping on the heating grates, and enter the church. He would go immediately to a small chapel in a corner and kneel down. The only thing in the chapel was a crucifix about six feet tall, but it rested against the wall rather than being hung high—so the feet of Jesus and the body (the corpus) were close to anyone who knelt before it. The man would pray, his lips moving silently in the beginning, but as he continued he would whisper and then pray out loud: Lord, Jesus Christ, have mercy on me, a sinner. Lord, Jesus Christ, I did this to you. I crucified you. My sins tortured you. Lord, have mercy on me, a sinner. He would kneel there for around forty-five minutes. And then he would rise off his knees and quickly leave. As he went down the side aisles he would reverently touch the many statues of Mary and the saints, kissing some of their feet or lighting a candle to one or another of them. And then he would emerge into the bright light of outside.

It would take him a minute to adjust his eyes and then he would hurry down the stairs—he only had a few minutes to grab some food from a vendor and get back to his office. He had to be on time or be docked his pay. And it was always an obstacle course. The steps were old and chipped and crowded with too many people. Most had their hands outstretched begging and were either silently staring at him or loudly demanding something from him. He was adept at ignoring them all and slipping past them down the stairs, zigzagging his way to the street. And they always annoyed him and sometimes angered him. He would mutter under his breath—get away from me, don't touch me. You should be ashamed of yourself. You're blocking the way to church. And one day, it was a cold

Good Friday, and he couldn't get to the street. There were so many people crowded together on the heating grates of the cathedral that he would have to backtrack and go around them. That was it—he pushed at them, stepped on a hand, a foot, and continued pushing his way through them. And then he reached the street and ran for his office. He would be late.

At this point Dom Hélder would pause, and there would be deep and uncomfortable silence in the cathedral packed with worshippers for Holy Week services. And he would always end the same way—he would begin to weep and say, That man did not pray. That man did not worship God. That man was offered the Other Eucharist—all those women and children, men, young and old, unemployed and without shelter, old and frail, sick and depressed, and he treated them all so shabbily. That Other Eucharist reached for him and he just ignored them or treated them violently. The Other Eucharist, Jesus the Word Made Flesh dwelling among us reached for him and he passed him by. We must honor God in the Body of Christ—the other Body of Christ—or we do not worship God at all. Let us go now to reverence the Cross of our Lord who tells us again to love one another as I love you, as God loves you, as God expects us to love everyone now. And he would sign himself with the sign of the Cross and turn toward the table to continue the liturgy of Good Friday.

This is John's community of the Beloved Disciples who worship God in Spirit and in Truth and love one another, all others, as our God loves us in Jesus the Word Made Flesh among us. Our communities and parishes must begin to reflect this passion and purpose, this devotion to the Living Water of the Word, to the gospels, and to the Other Body of Christ in our worship. We don't have to live in the same house, but we must live together and stand together with those in our world who have been rejected and excluded from the "system" and know in their flesh the sufferings of Christ. We must be communities of hope that draw them in, with grace and dignity, to share their life and to share what we have been given.

For in John's gospel, when we stand before the king, the crucified flesh of Jesus, the Word risen from the dead, the Living Water, the Body of Christ, we will be looked at and then we will be told: "Give me a drink!" We will be asked what crosses we stood beneath and who we stood in solidarity with—putting our bodies alongside theirs and sharing their suffering as silent witnesses to injustice and violence if we could not ease their pain and give them solace. We will be asked if we worshipped God the Father with the Truth that is Jesus in the power of the Spirit. We will be asked: With whom did you come and who did you bring with you? Are you their friend? If so then I, too, call you friend.

Listen to the words of Diane Nash, an organizer for the Freedom Riders during the civil rights movement.

The movement had a way of reaching inside me and bringing out things that I never knew were there. Like courage, and love for people. It was a real experience to be seeing a group of people who would put their bodies between you and danger. And to love people that you work with enough that you would put your body between them and danger.[4]

John's Jesus calls us friends—this is what it means to be a friend of God, in the community of the Body of Christ, the friends of God. This is the kingdom of home, of feasting, of freedom and love that will not break in the face of any "system" and that touches most passionately our enemies, those lacking abundant life, and in all those God is seeking to befriend us, speaking a Word that is filled with the Spirit and Truth and revealing us as all belonging to the Father who gives birth to us and draws us beyond and into what it means to be human according to the Holy One's Wisdom.

Chapter 10

THE OTHER GOSPELS TO BE WRITTEN NOW

"Hope is like a road in the country; there was never a road, but when many people walk on it, the road comes into existence."

LIN YUTANG, CHINESE WRITER AND INVENTOR, 1895–1976

IN WRITING THIS BOOK AND DELVING INTO THE FOUR GOS-pels over and over again, certain things began to surface. History and the plight of the human family, even the plight of the earth itself, are forcing us to look at everything in the world from angles other than those that were the core of religions and life two thousand years ago. And now, because of developments in religions, society, science, and culture, there are issues that are absolutely central to religion that weren't necessarily so historically. There are issues that need to be highlighted and new ones that Jesus and his contemporaries just did not experience or know. The seeds are in the gospels, but they need to be studied, nurtured, and brought to harvest. As the philosopher Han Feizi once said, "Before they become a tangible reality, all phenomena are seeds. The wise one takes great care of seeds."

This chapter will look at the possibility of new gospels—sourced in seeds of the original four (with sometimes only a few lines, but the seed is there). Some of these address universal issues that have been with us since the beginning of our awareness of time but have festered and developed into aberrations that are now spreading destruction in ways that seep into every area of life, such as war, violence, and injustice.

THE GOSPEL OF PEACE

So the first gospel would be the Gospel of Peace. Jesus's words are found in the gospel of John during his farewell meal with his friends. Listen:

> "I will not leave you orphaned; I am coming to you. In a little while the world will no longer see me, but you will see me; because I live, you also will live. On that day you will know that I am in my Father, and you in me and I in you. They who have my commandments and keep them are those who love me; and those who love me will be loved by my Father, and I will love them and reveal myself to them. . . .
>
> "I have said these things to you while I am still with you. But the Advocate, the Holy Spirit, whom the Father will send in my name, will teach you everything and remind you of all that I have said to you. Peace I leave with you; my peace I give to you. I do not give to you as the world gives. Do not let your hearts be troubled, and do not let them be afraid." (Jn 14:18–21, 25–27)

These lines share many of the characteristics and foci of the Gospel of Peace. It is about presence—the presence of the Lord of Life who lived among us, died with and for us, and rose to deeper and truer life among us—that is shared with us throughout all time and space. The first words of Jesus cited after the Resurrection are always "Peace be with you! Shalom!" It is a blessing, a command, a hoped-for reality, a statement of truth with its fullness yet to come upon us and in us, for all. It is a proclamation of belief and a cry of triumph in spite of horror and death. It is a prayer, God's prayer for all of us: abiding peace that is the result of justice and compassion, forgiveness and mercy. It is a person standing there, here, with us—we are never orphaned or left to our own designs. The company and presence of God in Jesus is with us.

And the presence of the Advocate, the one who stands by us faithfully with counsel, advice, knowledge, and wisdom, abides with us, as well: Jesus's first gift to us as he returns to the Father and entrusts us now with the world and his message and dwelling place—the Kingdom and hope of God for all. This Spirit is a rememberer, an advocate, preacher, prophet, teacher, illustrator, storyteller, poet, singer, prayer, source of power, and all that leads to peace. The gift is given not as the systems of the earth give or as the organizations, nations, and groups of people in power give, but it is universally given with integrity, and it abides, stays, deepens, and lays the base for imagination, creativity, and newness that springs forth in the most unlikely places.

These places are often those stained with blood and destruction, marred by violence and hatred among peoples who were victims yet remained human, graceful, and hopeful in the face of such inhumanity. These are places where life springs forth anew and where resistance breeds mercy and another way of being that is new upon the face of the earth. Oscar Arias Sánchez, after winning the Nobel Prize for Peace in 1987, reiterated these thoughts:

> *Peace is not a matter of prizes or trophies. It is not the product of a victory or command. It has no finishing line, no final deadline, no fixed definition of achievement.*
>
> *Peace is a never-ending process, the work of many decisions by many people in many countries. It is an attitude, a way of life, a way of solving problems and resolving conflicts. It cannot be forced on the smallest nation or enforced by the largest. It cannot ignore our differences or overlook our common interests. It requires us to work and live together.*[1]

And again in the same speech, he writes:

> *Hope is the strongest driving force for a people. Hope which brings about change, which produces new realities, is what opens man's [woman's] road to freedom. Once hope has taken hold, courage must unite with wisdom. That is the only way of avoiding violence, the only way of maintaining the calm one needs to respond peacefully to offenses.*[2]

This gospel would be rooted in the past, and in those who refused to fight or bear arms; in the poets who ruefully told the truth before, during, and after the conflicts and killing, trying to make others hear with the sword of words and the pen of truth, declaring that ink and hope, desire and commitment, are stronger than anything that draws blood and kills—and harder to wield. They would tell stories and quote lines from others like those of Martin of Tours, now the patron of the military in the world: "I am now a soldier of Christ, and it is not permissible for me to fight." Or in the words of Pope Paul VI: "If you believe in peace, it is possible. If it is possible, it is a duty."

I would quote the Japanese poet Basho. I first heard his poetry while sitting on the floor after a shared meal—the group included an elderly Buddhist couple, a priest from the Philippines, and myself. The couple knew no English, I knew only a few words of Japanese, but the Filipino knew both languages. A huge book of photographs of Japan was brought out and opened to a picture: wild grasses on hillsides and one haiku in Japanese calligraphy at the corner of the page. There was much discussion on the exact or best way to translate the three lines. They settled on "Summer grasses . . . all that remains of soldiers after imperial dreams." We were sitting in a corner of old Hiroshima, and they said, "You must remember this. This is the wisdom we must pass on around the world."

Instead of the daily statistics of how many dead there are—of our own soldiers or those of the enemies (or the civilians, who aren't included in the statistics but who far outnumber those doing the killing) recorded daily in newspapers in the United States, Iraq, Afghanistan, the West Bank, Israel, North Korea, the Sudan, Pakistan, India, etc.—there would be top stories of the day in the realm of peacemaking: new accords, pacts, promises, and pictures of those who labored so long and hard to stop the killing and destruction. There would be stories of dissenters, revolutionaries that practice nonviolence, and groups that walk the borders protecting people on both sides. Or in the words of John F. Kennedy: "War will exist until that distant day when the conscientious objector enjoys the same reputation and prestige that the warrior does today." That distant day must be today, or else we will all perish. The words of women like Arundhati Roy will be internalized and taken to heart:

> When we are violent to our enemies, we do violence to ourselves. When we brutalize others, we brutalize ourselves. And eventually we run the risk of becoming our oppressors.

The words of women and the leadership of women must become reality, and those who speak of bearing children for life, not war, must be treasured. To be a warrior is not necessarily a thing to be held up as worthy of dedication anymore—unless the warrior is dedicated to peacemaking and hard tasks of renovation, rebuilding, and restoring what has been so quickly and totally destroyed. Novels like Tim O'Brien's *The Things They Carried* need to be read in every community, high school, and orientation program for the military (people who are willing to give their lives for peace but not to kill in the name of any religion, nation, or corporation). As he describes in "An Immoral Story":

> A true war story is never moral. It does not instruct, nor encourage virtue, nor suggest models of proper human behavior, nor restrain men from doing things men have always done. If a war story seems moral, do not believe it. If at the end of a war story you feel uplifted, or if you feel that some small bit of rectitude has been salvaged from the larger waste, then you have been made the victim of a very old and terrible lie.[3]

There would be lines from the four gospels, taken as foundational, such as "Love your enemies, do good to those who hate you" (Lk 6:27), and stories and practices, encouragement, models of action and recourse. The lives of those who have practiced this exhortation would become parables of today. And part of the gospel would deal with repentance, restoration, restorative justice, and atonement practiced religiously by all religious groups and by all the nations involved in any breach of peace. It would be the focus of all worship and prayer, of acts of repentance, fasting, almsgiving, and justice—fourfold restitution. Collective responsibility for the world and what happens in it would be part of any prayer and theology and exegesis, such as Our Father, on earth as it is in your dream and realm of peace, forgive us our debts as we forgive those in debt to us, give us this day our daily bread. And it would be very clear that this word *our* is universal and pragmatic and to be taken very seriously when dealing with God. Are we the children of God, those who are the peacemakers of the world?

This gospel would be about "a Perfect Spiritual Work," a phrase written about by John Calvi, a Quaker, in *Friends Journal* (August 2010, page 5). He speaks of spiritual works that engage both the individual and the corporate body, and that are great works that appear to be impossible in the beginning. But what holds the work together is that it is vast, critical, necessary, and of immediate importance; it is about what needs to be made right, transformed, and made holy now. And it is work that is steeped in reverence and awe, and treated with extreme care. And it is a daunting task, as well, fraught with conflict and challenge, and it must draw in diverse people who bring their own light to the work. The perfect spiritual work he envisions as the one to tackle now is a mix of getting out of war and holding our own nation and religious communities accountable for recent and present-day wars. By doing this, the work would shift into the work of justice, the economy, and abolishing poverty. This is what he says:

> Imagine this: the United States of America gets out of the business of war. No more undeclared wars that go on for years against tiny countries. No more spending half the budget on wars built on lies. No more of our young soldiers wounded or dead by the thousands. No more weapons manufacture promoted by former members of Congress or Pentagon generals taking overpayments, to kill innocent citizens. No more U.S. torture in our names, using our tax dollars.

> *Holding U.S. leadership accountable for crimes against humanity has never happened. All the U.S. wars in Vietnam, Latin America, and now Iraq and Afghanistan involve crimes as large as any in history resulting in extensive profiteering and no justice or peace.*

War is a religious and moral issue and cannot be relegated to the world of politics, nations, corporations, and leaders with personal agendas who often just want to make their place in history at the expense of millions of other human beings. And it must be the first moral and ethical issue of all religions and churches. No more war. No ifs, ands, or buts, saying this is a "just" war, of which there is no such thing and never has been. No war is to be sanctioned, no arms blessed, and no soldiers trumpeted as heroes and peacemakers. No one is to be killed in the name of any god, and no one is to be sacrificed to prove that one believes in a god (the story of Abraham and Isaac). It is upon this Gospel of Peace that really all the others depend and from which they are derived. Without the practice of this Gospel of Peace, the others are merely making do, as all that the Creator has made and sustains is obliterated; no worship makes any sense at all—war is a slap in the face of God, an insult and a blasphemy. This is the beginning of the new gospels.

THE GOSPEL OF THE POOR

The second would be the Gospel of the Poor, written by those who have known the brunt of the disobedience of humans to the commandment found in nearly all religions: Thou shalt not kill! This gospel is about economics and justice, but even more it is about freedom from oppression and the raising of hope in the midst of seemingly huge and unsolvable problems. Its basis can be found in Jesus's first sermon detailing the reason he came into the world and was baptized and why all of us are baptized and what we are to do with the power of the Spirit given to us. Found in Luke 4, it is the defining sermon of Jesus, delivered in his hometown synagogue in

Nazareth on a Sabbath. The Spirit drove Jesus into the desert to be tempted—tested on how he would make this new dream and vision of human life on earth a reality, one that would serve as foundational to make "your kingdom come, your will be done on earth as it is in heaven" and "to give us today our daily bread" and fulfill the other requests of the Our Father, our public, daily, and private model of prayer that is Jesus's own prayer on earth.

And it would entail listening to the poor of the earth: those described in the sermon in Luke—the poor, the captive and the prisoners, the oppressed and broken, and those caught in the trap of the world, the system that dominates and destroys for the benefit of the few. And it would entail listening to the contemporary prophets: those who have been killed for their words and visions of justice in the recent past and those crying out today for the poor of the earth, often just surviving and trying desperately to make a life for themselves. Martin Luther King Jr. put clearly to the churches and those who profess to be believers where they must put their resources, priorities, finances, words, voice, prayer, and works. These are the words of his son Martin Luther King III:

> [Martin Luther King] said that any religion that is not concerned about the poor and disadvantaged, "the slums that damn them, the economic conditions that strangle them and the social conditions that cripple them[,] is a spiritually moribund religion awaiting burial." In his "Dream" speech, my father paraphrased the prophet Amos, saying, "We will not be satisfied until justice rolls down like waters and righteousness like a mighty stream."[4]

This gospel has much to rely on from the original four gospels because all that Jesus tells stories of and preaches about is this gospel of Good News to the poor. Unfortunately, because the church became the dominant force in society, much of the gospel was reduced to an agenda for personal salvation—primarily to be experienced in the afterlife and individualized in devotion, prayer, and penance, and even sin was reduced to what one did sexually or what affected one's personal relationship with God. What affected one's neighbors was either ignored or lightly proscribed or seen only in regard to an individual rather than corporately, communally, structurally, or systematically, as well. A good deal of what the previous nine chapters of this book looks at as what would have radically shocked Jesus's own hearers and what should be radically still shocking believers today would be in this gospel in new stories, poetry, prayers, parables, and outright commands.

Such exhortations and preparation for adult baptism (the norm) and for the community's yearly preparation for making new Christians at Easter would actually be practiced in Lent—giving half of one's resources to the poor—or at least start with one's excess (the stories of the rich man who turns from the invitation to follow Jesus with his disciples) and doing fourfold restitution in justice to any that you had harmed or treated unjustly. This would be demanded not only of individuals but also of churches, organizations, corporations, and those that called themselves Christian nations (Lk 19:1–10). This gospel would be extending the original four, beginning with the admission of sin, and failure and refusal to put into practice and believe many of the words of Jesus originally. It could begin with words like these by Søren Kierkegaard:

> *The matter is quite simple. The Bible is very easy to understand. But we as Christians are a bunch of scheming swindlers. We pretend to be unable to understand it because we know very well that the minute we understand we are obliged to act accordingly. Take any words in the New Testament and forget everything except pledging yourself to act accordingly. My God, you will say, if I do that my whole life will be ruined.*[5]

Two things that would be emphasized, which were lost in the past centuries from the original Good News to the poor, would be the communal nature of preaching and working for and with the poor—listening to them and struggling with them—and the globalization of poverty. Many of the earth's inhabitants were always poor, but now the rest of the world is aware of this disgrace and participates in the structures and economies that make the problem worse and keep it spreading exponentially. There is poverty, and now there is degradation, human misery and death by slow starvation, not enough clean water, airborne disease, and pollution of the basics of life: air, water, soil, crops, animals, all of earth's resources. Many of the world's poor suffer the same fate as the earth and its resources. Both are seen and treated as expendable, useable, and a commodity to be wiped out without respect in seeking profit. A very short story called "Manpower," collected by Eduardo Galleano, describes the situation more than accurately and is intended to stir up guilt and, optimally, a response that will listen to the reality of those who are poor and work with them for change.

> Mohammed Ashraf doesn't go to school. From sun-up till moonrise, he measures, cuts, shapes, punctures, and sews soccer balls, which then go rolling out from the Pakistani village of Umar Kot toward the stadiums of the world. Mohammed is eleven. He has been at this since he was five. If he knew how to read, and could read English, he would understand the label he sticks on each of his products: "This ball was not made by children."

This Gospel of the Poor would be not only about the experience of the poor but also about penance, remorse, atonement, and restitution for all in the Church. Originally, the early Church was described this way: "See how those Christians love one another—there are no poor among them." This is a far cry from any reality of the Church today, except among the poor themselves, many of whom struggle in communities sharing what they have and seeking to incorporate the gospel into their own lives while they strive for justice and human rights and attempt to transform the structures that have created their worlds of poverty and humiliation. It would focus forgiveness and reconciliation on groups, organizations, churches, and dioceses as they learn to undo some of the harm they have been complicit in as they encouraged or reaped benefits of their own.

Again it would be written by the poor who are already living this forgiveness and reconciliation with the practices of mercy, truth telling, and awareness of their own failures but conscious too of what society has done to them as it continues to lay heavy burdens and crosses on them. This admission of sin and failure is expressed in telling the truth about situations and relationships; it is forgiveness given in graciousness and mutual reconciliation to begin the process of transformation and conversion not only of individual lives but of structures, laws, economic systems, racial injustice, hatred, slavery, trafficking, criminalization of immigration, exiling of migrants, gypsies, and other groups, and so many other elements that constitute being poor and being treated without justice. Jon Sobrino once told the story of what this truth telling and forgiveness looks like in reality. He said, "When Joan Alsina was executed in Barcelona, he said, 'When you are going to shoot me, don't blindfold me. I want you to see that I forgive you' (from "Victims and Perpetrators," translated by Juan Carlos Sarasua). This gospel is intimately connected to the next one.

THE GOSPEL OF THE EARTH

The next gospel is needed because of the disregard of the earth and its resources that has been the result of violence, war, rampant greed, undisciplined and unchecked capitalism, and many attitudes and practices of the major religions' contempt for this earth in lieu of another (often called heaven, of which no one actually knows or has experience at all). It is the Gospel of the Earth or the Gospel of the World. In her poem "Beginners," Denise Levertov writes the opening line: "But we have only begun to love the earth. We have only begun to imagine the fullness of life. How could we tire of hope?—so much is in bud" (dedicated to the memory of Karen Silkwood and Eliot Gralla).[6] Truly we are beginners with this gospel. Much of Church teaching, public prayers, and focus on salvation and the afterlife (heaven, purgatory, hell) has denigrated creation, encouraging people to "hate this world," and this religious hate and disdain has led to abuse and destruction of the planet.

Certainly it has not encouraged appreciation and care for the earth and prudent use of its resources, which will be handed on to future generations. Sometimes it has resulted in direct destruction, using pieces of Scripture to validate that it's all going to be destroyed one day anyway, so what does it matter what we do to it now? It all belongs to us and we can do with it what we please—and we have in great measure done so. As William Sloane Coffin said in one of his sermons decades ago: "While the heavens continue to tell the glory of God, the firmament today also proclaims sonic nefarious human handiwork—smog, acid rain, an immense hole in the ozone layer."[7] We are only beginning to understand the naturalist John Muir's words: "Tug on anything at all and you'll find it connected to everything else in the universe."[8]

A more poetic and equally revelatory way of saying this is found in one of Thich Nhat Hanh's poems:

> When I touch paper deeply, I touch a cloud.
> If we look into the nature of paper, what do we see?
> We first see a cloud.
> Because without the cloud, there would be no rain and the trees would not
>   grow.
> And what else do we see?
> We see the sun, because without the sun, the trees would not grow, and we
>   also see the earth . . .[9]

This gospel would have to begin with teachings on appreciation, on seeing and respecting all of the earth: its creatures and processes. Jesus had this awareness and sensitivity of being connected to everything that is made, and he used images of earth, including weather, flowers, fruit, seeds, trees, crops, birds, animals, waters, fish, signs in the sky, and moments of place in the world in much of his teachings. Even the underlying relationship, both in similarities and differences, are found in his words. And there is no sense that it is solely for our use or misuse, but rather that it gives its own glory to God and we can learn from it—its wisdom and knowledge are all around us. Listen:

He said to his disciples, "Therefore I tell you, do not worry about your life, what you will eat, or about your body, what you will wear. For life is more than food, and the body more than clothing. Consider the ravens: they neither sow nor reap, they have neither storehouse nor barn, and yet God feeds them. Of how much more value are you than the birds!" And can any of you by worrying add a single hour to your span of life? If then you are not able to do so small a thing as that, why do you worry about the rest? Consider the lilies, how they grow; they neither toil or spin; yet I tell you, even Solomon in all his glory was not clothed like one of these . . . (Lk 12:22–27ff)

The images are used in teaching, but the appreciation is clear. And while he speaks of valuing human beings' lives so highly, he still connects them to the value of the other creatures, the birds, the flowers, etc. Do we have even this basic sense of valuing all things? For the Jewish community, the earth—all of creation—was the first book that God ever crafted and wrote for all the people to read. The earth, the seas, the sky, the planets and stars, and all that dwelled in and on and under and above the earth was/is the first book of revelation about God. And the thought was that if you could not read that one and take it to heart, you would never be able to understand any written book of revelation. Have we forgotten to see, to smell, to taste and hear and feel this first revelation that is all around us and yet in danger now of loss forever in extinction? In another story, Jesus describes a man to be a fool when he tears down his barns and builds bigger ones and hoards his crops and does not share or use justly what he has attained (Lk 12:20ff).

This gospel would borrow the wisdom of farmers, agriculturists, scientists, oceanographers, those who study climate change and industrial/chemical/biological effects on air, water, soil. It would work with those who have lived close to the land for generations around the world, including Native Peoples who have long traditions of oral wisdom in regard to biospheres, local ecologies, sources of medicine and healing, crop rotation, and how to live in any number of environments, with an eye not only to supplying what is needed in the present but also to ensuring that it survives into the future. There is wisdom around the world that would be quoted like the words of Hong Zichen: "A deed as great as the Earth is effaced by a single word: pride. A crime as huge as the heavens is effaced by a single word: repentance."[10]

It would even publish a moveable section that would catalog and inform believers of the hard realities of where we stand in the world today and what the results are of our actions—or our inaction and neglect. Statistics like these would be inserted periodically (the gospel wouldn't just be on paper but also online). Note that as of AD 2000 the following is acknowledged and work must be initiated immediately to stop and reverse these realities: 820 species have gone extinct in the last five hundred years, including a quarter of all mammals; one in eight birds; one-third of the amphibians; and two-thirds of all the plants (from the International Union for Conservation of Nature's Red List). And then there would be the listing of all that is endangered, including what is taken off the list in rejoicing and what is added in sadness, to be mourned. It would remind us that this is God's creation and we are all of a piece of it and as it goes, so also goes the human race.

Thomas Aquinas wrote: "Creation is the primary and most perfect revelation of the Divine . . . if we do not understand Creation correctly, we cannot hope to understand God correctly." If this is true, what have we misunderstood about God and what it means to worship the God of creation and earth in all these years of ignoring it, fouling it, denuding it, and dismissing it as something to be used up, a thing with no soul? This gospel would overlap into food, drink, clothing, shelter, sanctuary, transportation, protection from the elements, and all the ways we live our everyday lives.

THE GOSPEL OF SCIENCE AND RELIGION

Closely aligned to this earth gospel is the Gospel of Science and Religion. As history developed, a gap sprang open between the disciplines and languages of science and religion. This has continued to widen and has often become acrimonious and bitter—a war of words, financial resources, and camps that seek to explain reality. The cross-pollination between these two ways of uncovering knowledge, seeking meaning, and living on the earth is now essential. The vastness, the depth and the amazing knowledge that science is learning, must be translated into the language of theologies to enrich the human mind and soul. The knowledge of the universe is expanding at such breakneck speed that it is nearly impossible to catalog, even as the diversity of creation on earth is disappearing or becoming extinct. This gospel would be the one that is most absorbed in the study of mystery, of leaping out into the unknown for many believers. And yet it is essential to a foundation of mystery, mysticism, prayer, and true worship. Albert Einstein once said these words:

> *To know what is impenetrable to us really exists, manifesting itself as the highest wisdom and the most radiant beauty, which our dull faculties can comprehend only in their primitive forms—this knowledge, this feeling, is at the center of true religiousness.*[11]

The relationship between religion and science is one that can yield the deepest and most penetrating knowledge and wisdom for the human community today. To begin with what is actually there, in space, and here in the world and the intelligibility of the universe along with the laws of nature and then to posit notions of God is both fascinating and demanding if we are to speak with truth about God theologically. The experience of being human beings, which is so universal and diverse and as far-flung in some ways as what exists in space, must be taken in tandem and merged. The universe, God, and humans must face so much that is just unknown, speculated about, and derived from existing information, but all exist together and must be seen together in relationship. There will be differences and blind spots on both sides of the table or inconsistent switches of language when trying to speak about elements of science and of theological belief, but there is so much more that must be shared for balance and harmony in both groups. The scientist and popular writer Stephen Jay Gould wrote of this relationship in the past decade: "Science and Religion shouldn't be viewed as opposed to each other but simply distinct from each other: nonoverlapping disciplines that shouldn't be used to explain aspects of the other." The National Academy of Sciences adopted his stance, saying officially a decade ago: "Demanding that they [science and religion] be combined detracts from the glory of each"(*Mending the Gap Between Science and the Humanities,* accessed online, 2003).

On a positive note, theologians need to study this information that astronomers and others are photographing and experimenting with and begin to ask new questions: What does this universe tell us about God? If the universe is so massive, dense, and invisible, what does that tell us about life on earth and what it means to be a human being? The double sources of knowledge and belief need to feed each other.

I will never forget the time I spent two weeks looking at pictures from the Hubble telescope, mesmerized and amazed—even more so when I read an introduction by Carl Sagan where he wrote that there has been so much data coming into telescopes around the worlds that it is a constant race to catch up and identify the consequences for other areas of science. The one thing all were agreed on, though, was that with the information available, they knew that 97.9 percent of the universe was invisible! Sagan's sidebar comment was: "What do we know about anything really?" And my reaction was the same—what do we know about God really? The paleontologist and mystic Pierre Teilhard de Chardin wrote that while he was digging up bones and calculating the ages of the earth, he would sit on a hilltop and without any elements of bread or wine celebrate his mass on the world's altar, offering all of creation to God. We need many mystics, scientists, and theologians to revitalize our liturgy, prayers, and devotions to our everexpanding and more intimate God!

The relationship, dialogue, and cross-pollination between these two huge areas, science and religion, is a great looming adventure into the future for so many areas of theological study. Fourteen billion years of earth's existence have much to share with just about six thousand years of Judeo-Christian religions and other beliefs. Science, technology, and advances in biology, medicine, consciousness, and health must be incorporated into ethics and morality in all levels of life, taking into consideration that much of the statements of ethics and moral decision-making might be based on seriously flawed information or lack of knowledge in regard to biology, the nature of being women and men, and the development of human consciousness.

THE GOSPEL OF ART

Alongside the Gospel of Science and Religion would be the Gospel of Art: all the myriad forms that are used to express many of the above issues and how human beings either learn to absorb and live with these massive experiences or creatively and imaginatively dream up and create new responses and expressions that redeem and transform the realities that reek of death, violence, and inhumanity and put us all in danger of ultimate destruction. This gospel would look at image, metaphor, and narrative and seek to protect the languages of so many peoples and cultures that are becoming extinct at rates equivalent to or worse than extinction in the natural world. These rich evocative realities of music, dance, art, narrative, poetry, drama, photography, film, weaving, pottery, all the tactile arts, and architecture must be invited to become intimate parts of liturgy and prayer. Arthur Schopenhauer wrote so long ago: "Music is the answer to the mystery of life; it is the most profound of all the arts; it expresses the deepest thoughts of life and being; a simple language which nonetheless cannot be translated."

What is ancient or medieval was used at its time in history. Now more contemporary and modern modes of speaking and acting out truth must be welcomed and sought out, as well. Other cultures and peoples know the power and the presence of the holy, and it suffuses their lives and prayer. The ancient shaman Orpingalik wrote centuries ago: "Songs are thoughts, sung with the breath when people are moved by great forces and ordinary speech no longer suffices." This gospel would have chapters written and created by artists in all the many forms of art with responses from those who admire the result, are moved by it, and are brought to new levels of insight, prayer, and devotion to God, the earth, and other human beings. Words like "Phosphorescence! Now there's a word to lift your hat to! To find the phosphorescence, that light within, that's the genius behind poetry," to quote Emily Dickinson, say much about theology, about prayer and liturgy, and about any discourse that has to do with God and humans—ah, to seek and find that phosphorescence in life, thoughts, translations of prayers, rituals, architecture, and even ethics!

Music, painting, drawing, science, the earth and religious devotion, and human longing often all come together in an artist's renderings or musings. Van Gogh wrote: "I have . . . a terrible need . . . shall I say the word? . . . of religion. Then I go out at night and paint the stars." This depth of truth is found in every form of expression. The writer Flannery O'Connor wrote:

> It is what is left over when everything explainable has been explained that makes a story worth writing and reading. The writer's gaze has to extend beyond the surface, beyond mere problems, until it touches that realm of mystery which is the concern of the prophets. . . . If a writer believes that the life of a man is and will remain essentially mysterious, what he sees on the surface, or what he understands, will be of interest to him only as it leads him into the experience of mystery itself.[12]

At this point in history, the approximately seven billion people in the world need vibrant ways to understand one another for the sake of the survival of all. In a sense this gospel is also the Gospel of the Wild Spirit.

Oh what a lyrical, flowing, startling, surprising, singing, crying, gospel this one would be—with as many stories to tell as there are spaces left empty on the page. What a delight, a pleasure to read, to know by heart and express in your own particular gift of art and expression!

A GOSPEL FOR CHURCH TRANSFORMATION

Another gospel must be written for the Church itself—in-house, so to speak. As the Christian religion became the dominant religion, as well as the dominant culture, governing body, economic system, language, even race in the Western world, it adopted specific languages and philosophies to do its theological studies and to design its laws, dogmas, doctrines, creeds, and expressions of worship, public in liturgy and private in prayer and devotions. Its ancient languages and ways of perceiving the world are not universal, though they are dominant still within religious structures. Latin and Greek and, to some extent, Hebrew (Jesus's own language was Aramaic) and Greek philosophy formed the basis of the moral, ethical, canonical, and legal structures of Christianity as it split into Roman and Orthodox Christianity and then again into Roman Catholicism and Protestant traditions.

The time for total reliance on these ancient sources is over. Other sources, old and new, must be drawn in as integral to understanding our belief; it is a necessity for communication and development through the world. If the Catholic (universal) Church is to speak to the world, other languages, philosophies, and forms of knowing must be studied and appreciated and incorporated into its daily experience, especially the languages of the other major religions and of science, technology, the arts, and diverse local languages. First languages to learn would be Arabic, Chinese, Swahili, and the languages of Native Peoples as well as the philosophies of China and other parts of Asia, the anthropologies of Africa and Native Peoples, the understandings of South American cosmologies, such as that found in the image of Our Lady of Guadalupe before Western artists added their own to the tilma and its language of symbols that narrated a whole history and theology in this one picture.

This gospel would stress openness, discussion, dialogue as the gifts of the Spirit of Truth and Integrity, and that the Spirit resides first and most strongly in the people of God gifted at baptism and confirmation with all the wisdom, knowledge, understanding, counsel, courage, faithfulness of devotion, and practice and fear of the Lord and awe that is needed to uncover the hidden Truth of God and make it manifest. The institutional Church's role in this gospel would be to keep encouraging and pushing people to dig deeper into their experience of living the gospel as individuals and in community with both new insights given by the Spirit of Grace and Wisdom as well as those given in the past. In the words of Timothy Radcliffe in a his talk "A Spirituality for the 21st Century" given in Rome on Ash Wednesday, 2010, this sense of a gospel to and for the Church today was introduced as follows:

> Our times are marked by a mixture of a thirst for God, aggression, and suspicion [toward religion] and vast [religious] ignorance . . . spirituality must be theological, ethical, and aesthetic, rooted in the tradition but open to our contemporaries . . . and this requires boldness. We need faithful questioners, people who dare to float a hypothesis, experiment with an idea, venture into a new way of thinking, not knowing where it will lead. Meister Eckhart said that we only attain truth if we make 1,000 errors on the way. If the great tree of the Church does not have these leaves open to the world, then we shall end up with what Karl Rahner called "the heresy of dead doctrine." . . . [He defended the need of a Vatican doctrinal office "to keep us steady as we search" but with a twist.] I believe that its main function should be to stop us succumbing to premature answers. It should keep open

the debate until God grants illumination for the next step on the journey. That will come, he said, only by being rooted in the life of prayer and silence. [The brackets are provided by the reporter's seeking to gather pertinent pieces of the talk.]

This gospel would meet with fierce resistance and refusal to let go as well as condemnatory rhetoric and retaliatory reactions toward those who would seek with prophetic language and actions to call the Church to its own radical conversion and to shift toward a truly universal and greatly diversified lifestyle and practice of worship, prayer, and expressing belief. Perhaps it could be called the Gospel of Truth Incarnate.

Included in this gospel, or in its own gospel, would be the reality of the Incarnation—the mystery of God's becoming flesh and blood in the Word of Jesus, dwelling among us and declaring that all human flesh is holy. This gospel would reverently look at what the Incarnation means for bodies, for sexuality, for gender orientation, for being single, married, divorced, widowed, celibate—all being people of desires, bodily expressions of love, the creation of children, and the many ways of being family.

It would begin with the statement that sexuality and being human compose an intimate blending of body and soul, and it is not to be seen as evil or a problem to be mastered and subdued but as the usual way of being holy in the world for the majority of the human race. We are not souls trapped inside our bodies; perhaps we are more truly bodies expressing our souls, and sexuality is one of the major ways humans declare the love of God and manifest that love using their bodies in the myriad major relationships of friendship and marriage, between men and women, women and women, men and men, child and adult, elder and younger, across cultures and languages. This gospel, of course, would be written by those who live these many expressions of being human, not by those in a small group of people lacking experience of most of these matters. Its name could perhaps be the Gospel of Flesh and Blood.

THE GOSPEL OF
INTERRELIGIOUS DIALOGUE

The next gospel is that of other religions or Interreligious Dialogue. The word *religion* at its roots means to bind or to tie together, and at the moment on the earth there are seven major recognized religions, though there are thousands of denominations, sects, cults, splinters, etc., within each of these dominant religions. There is infighting that is vicious and divisive, but this fractured and splintered adherence within a faith tradition is also projected outside in fundamentalism, the sense that my/our religion is the only true religion, which results in wars, terrorism, wanton destruction of the earth, and whole peoples being attacked and murdered in the name of a particular group's god. These religions are often declared the religion of a nation, state, or group of peoples and overlap into nationalistic and political aggression and domination.

The ancient Asian saying "There is one mountain and many paths up the mountain" puts in a nutshell what must be incorporated into this gospel: tolerance, reasonableness, respect and understanding of others' religious practices and beliefs, and dialogue that serves as a bridge for all members of the human family to cross over—visit—and return to their own traditions enriched and more human. The Metropolitan Philaret of Moscow said just recently, "The walls of division do not rise all the way to heaven." It is time to start climbing over these walls to visit one another, and opening doors within the walls and, eventually, removing them altogether. Or in the words of the Lakota Sioux nations: *Mitakuye Oyasin,* meaning "We are all related."

This Gospel of Interreligious Dialogue would lay the basis for all religions to work together to deal with the problems of the world that all share, each in their own tradition and expression praying for insight into how to honor God, by whatever name, and religiously atoning for failure to practice the commands of God. And any religion that actually is a religion must honor and obey the God of Life. This gospel would look honestly at the pluralism and differences in belief and practice and yet seek to reconcile and commit to universally accepted commonalities that every belief in God calls us to live together. I have heard the phrase in at least four of the major religions, and each claims it as their own: "Whatever name you call God by, God's name is Truth." All religions must reach a starting point of shared agreement, fervent hope, and communal practice that announces to everyone that war is to be outlawed and no killing and harm is the first commandment. And so this Gospel of Interreligious Dialogue brings us back to the first new gospel, that of the Gospel of Peace.

There are some suggestions for still other gospels that seem to cry out for expression immediately and universally, but those written here, gleaned from many people around the world, need to be written about, told orally, and shared communally in public right now. The issues must be openly addressed and absorbed, and new solutions and ways of looking at the issues and responding with grace, integrity, risk, trust, and hope must be initiated now. Other internal issues in the Church must be laid aside and some forgotten and laid to rest altogether. Time, energy, finances, personnel, resources, and research need to be directed at these issues—and an honest acknowledgment must be made that many of the resources of the Church are being wasted and squandered on details and goals that belong to a small minority of either the hierarchy or groups devoted to particular agendas bound to power, influence, and self-aggrandizement.

It is time to ask a few questions in regard to any project, decision-making group, and priority of the Church: Does this promote peace in the world? Will this actually be Good News for the poor? Or in the words of Ambrose of Milan in the early Church: "There is your brother or sister, naked, crying! And you stand confused over the choice of an attractive floor covering!" Does this endeavor engender respect for the earth, the world, and the universe, and open up avenues of communication with science, technology, and other forms of knowledge that can contribute ideas and will enable the human community to live lives that are healthier, more humane, and with more just and equitable distribution of resources while protecting those resources and the earth itself for future generations (down to the seventh generation, as the Native Peoples urge)?

Will this project and statement look to, listen to, and connect with artists and writers, finding in their work the power and expression of the Spirit that does theology first in the world of lived experience and then perhaps in more rational constructs? Will this lead to interreligious dialogue where these issues of abiding peace, human rights and dignity for all peoples, restorative justice, and a climate and atmosphere that will seek to undo some of the harm already done to the earth, air, water, resources, cultures, and daily lives of the majority of peoples be shared and worked with together? Will this serve to draw people together, disarm hostilities, and encourage people to look to the universal Spirit of life and awe that is seeded and found in all things and all men and women? Will this help people to celebrate life, share joy and delight in creation and diversity among peoples, and recognize that the world is the sacrament of the Spirit constantly revealing the goodness of God in infinite ways, faces, places—that, as the Sufis say, there is no place that God is not but are we looking, listening, watching, attending to God's revelation?

Words to end with, words to begin with:

We live limited lives until we "cross over" into the concrete world of another country, another culture, another tradition of worship . . . I have left forever a small world to live with the tensions and the tender mercies of God's larger family." (Joan Puls, Every Bush Is Burning)

The whole purpose of the Bible, it seems to me, is to convince people to set the written word down in order to become living words in the world for God's sake. For me, this willing conversion of ink back to blood is the full substance of truth. (Barbara Brown Taylor, Sojourners)

We are always at the beginning of things, in the fragile moment that holds the power of life. We are always at the morning of the world. (François Cheng in Föllmi, Awakenings: Asian Wisdom)

Words do not have sharp points like arrows or spears, but they shatter the heart into many pieces. (Tibetan saying)

Jesus Christ . . . is not only the Lord of small places like the heart, the soul, the church, he is the cosmic Lord of large spaces like politics. (Leonardo Boff)

The freshness of my eyes is given to me in prayer. (Attributed to the prophet Muhammad)

There is no large and difficult task that can't be divided into little easy tasks. (Buddhist saying)

Our Scriptures have spoken to us and our lives ought to speak back. That's how we love our religions, challenge them, care for them, transform them and help them deliver their promises to the world. (Samir Selmanovic, It's Really All About God)

A person is a person because of the people. (African proverb)

And lastly, in the words of Scripture: Jesus was standing there, and he cried out, "Let anyone who is thirsty come to me, and let the one who believes in me drink. As the scripture has said, 'Out of the believer's heart shall flow rivers of living water.'" (Now he said this about the Spirit which believers in him were to receive; for as yet there was no Spirit, because Jesus was not yet glorified.) (Jn 7:37–39)

Afterword

IN THE PAST COUPLE OF YEARS THERE HAS BEEN A POPULAR
TV program called *Extreme Makeover: Home Edition.* The team of de-
signers and builders takes a family and their home and radically
redesigns and updates the house. The team arrives, sends the oc-
cupants off for a week's vacation, and the demolition begins. The
bulldozers and wrecking balls arrive and within twenty-four hours
or less the house is gone. Sometimes they leave a part of the house—
rafters and studs—standing, but more often than not, only the
foundation remains. But before this day of destruction the team
does its homework: extensive research on the family who lives
there. The family is usually chosen because of physical need, the
services they provide to the surrounding community, and the state
of the home. They know how many people live in the house (number of bedrooms needed) and how many people come and go on a
regular basis (the need for kitchen, dining room, living room, family rooms, and utility rooms). Then they study the members of the
family individually: their interests, needs, ages, and plans for the
future. Only then do they demolish the existing house and begin
the task of rebuilding, adding extensive space, and crafting specific
rooms and outdoor spaces such as porches and the like.

It has been three years since I finished writing this book and so
much has happened both in the world and in the Church that it is
impossible to make a litany of what has transpired, in-house and between the structures and controlling members of the Church institution and groups outside. But in writing this book and during the
interim when it was prepared for publication, I have participated
in numerous groups, discussions, prayer and ministerial retreats. The

consensus among everyone I listened to and spoke with is unanimous: we need a new reality and it could be aptly called *Extreme Makeover: Church Edition*. The structures and experiences of the institution and those in control of the Church need to be reimagined, and many already have been reimagined, in spite of the directives not to speak of such things—ever. Now it is time for the wrecking ball, the bulldozers, and as the title of this book implies, hammers shattering rocks.

The hammer is the Word of God, the Scriptures, specifically the four gospels, the Book of Acts (the foundation of the house sometimes called the gospel of the Church), and books from the heritage of the Jewish people that we have appropriated as our own: the first five foundational books of the Bible, the Prophets, and the Psalms (the beams and studs of the existing structures). The decisions on what remains and what is taken down, stored, and/or converted to other uses is made by the Church, the Body of Christ, the people of God in dialogue with the existing leadership, using the Scriptures as blueprint and guide. A statement by Saint Jerome (347–420), a priest, translator of the Bible, and a Doctor of the Church, in his Letter 53 to Paulinus contained this about Holy Scripture:

> *"The words I have spoken to you are spirit and life."*
>
> *We read Holy Scripture: in my view, I think the Gospel is Jesus' body, Holy Scripture is his teaching. It's true that the text: "He who eats my flesh and drinks my blood" finds its most complete application in the mystery of the eucharist. But the true Body of Christ, the true Blood, is also contained in the word of Scripture and divine teaching. When we take part in the holy mysteries, we are concerned about it if a crumb should fall to the ground. When we hear the word of God, if we are thinking of something else while it enters our ears, what sort of responsibility will we not incur?*
>
> *Since the Lord's flesh is food indeed and his blood is real drink, to eat his flesh and drink his blood is our only good, not just in the eucharistic mystery but in the reading of Scripture too.*[1]

And the understanding and teaching of the Church over the centuries has consistently reminded us that the Body of Christ is first and foremost the people of God, the 1.2 billion people of the Church (less than 2 percent of whom are the leadership of the structure). Our mysteries are very Trinitarian. The Body of Christ is the people of God, the Eucharist, and the Scriptures. This is the foundation of the Church. This is where restructuring, rebuilding, adding on, and converting existing spaces begins: with the needs of the people, what goes on in the house—meals that are both worship and nourishment—initiation rites, and the missions of the Church. It is time to look at the immediate past history as well as the long-range history of the Church over the last nineteen hundred years in light of the Body of Christ and start converting, transforming, and transfiguring the people and the structures of the Church. In the May 2012 issue of *The Tablet,* a management consultant, Eddie Molloy, told of attending a week-long meeting where he was advising bishops on institutional change in the Church. This was how he ended his comments:

> About halfway through the week, one of the bishops put a fatherly arm around me and said: "You know that you can't pour new wine into old wine-skins." I asked him what he meant and he said: "You will never get change through us and our structures." What that says to me is that there is no point looking to the hierarchy or the Vatican as the wellspring of change; it is going to have to come from something outside of those structures.

The remainder of this afterword presents a number of principles or characteristics of how change is to be initiated and brought about in-house. They are all based in the Scriptures. They constitute attitudes, processes, how to come to consensus and decision-making, and to reaffirm the priorities of Jesus's kingdom, Jesus's communities, and Jesus's preaching and teaching found in the Good News to the poor. They are all rooted in these statements of Jesus during his last meal with his friends, found in John's gospel.

> "If you love me, you will keep my commandments. And I will ask the Father, and he will give you another Advocate, to be with you forever. This is the

Spirit of truth, whom the world cannot receive, because it neither sees him nor knows him. You know him, because he abides with you and he will be in you.

"I will not leave you orphaned; I am coming to you. In a little while the world will no longer see me, but you will see me; because I live, you also will live. On that day you will know that I am in my Father, and you in me, and I in you. They who have my commandments and keep them are those who love me; and those who love me will be loved by my Father, and I will love them and reveal myself to them." (Jn 14:15–21)

"I have said these things to you while I am still with you. But the Advocate, the Holy Spirit, whom the Father will send in my name, will teach you everything, and remind you of all that I have said to you." (Jn 14:25–26)

In the fourth Eucharistic Prayer we hear that the Spirit is the first gift given to those who believe: in baptism, confirmation, and the Eucharist. Each of us has a portion of that Spirit. The Spirit, along with the Father and the Son, abides in us, dwells in us, lives in us, and continues to teach us, reminding us of all that Jesus said and did, and encourages us, sending us out to be the presence of the Risen Lord in the world we live in today. In Jesus's words: "Very truly, I tell you, the one who believes in me will also do the works that I do and, in fact, will do greater works than these; because I am going to the Father" (Jn 14:12).

These are staggering words! They are words of power, of hope, and of continued presence among us. The Spirit continues to reveal the Truth of Jesus and the Trinity as the model of community in the Church in every generation. It is time to return to the foundation of what constitutes Church, our worship, our mission, our presence as the Risen Lord in the world, to be an invitation to all to be drawn into glorifying God and be a sign of hope in the midst of the struggle to be human. In the documents of the First Vatican Council of more than 150 years ago, five necessities, five supporting beams, were listed in the order of importance. They were specifically given for the structure of worship/liturgy, but they can serve for all of the Church's work, mission, and presence. They are, first, the people.

Second, the bread and wine. Third, the Word/Scriptures. Fourth, the care/collection taken up for the poor. And last, someone who gathers/calls the community to prayer. These form the rooms of the house, so to speak, and reveal what goes on inside the house.

The Church is first and always a gathering place/space for the Body of Christ, the people. Its life revolves around meals, the feast of friends, the Passover of freedom and hope, the Eucharist in the liturgical season of the Paschal Mystery and Sunday worship. It is the place of initiation drawing new members into the Body of Christ in the sacraments and renewing them in their dedication, commitment, and growth as individuals and as the Body of Christ in service of others. It is communities that gather around the Word of the Lord, in liturgy but also in small groups that study the gospels, especially for conversion of life, as believers and as those who are to be Good News in the world by their lives. It is the gathering of those who come to hear Good News—filled with encouragement, hope, conversion, and transfiguration in the presence of the Spirit of God revealing the will of God and God's kingdom in the lives and experiences of the people in history now. This is what Jesus did on earth, meeting in synagogues, temple precincts, out in the fields, and in people's homes, and when he was with the crowds, he was with them to encourage them, to touch them, to include them in the community, to heal them, to give them hope, forgive them, and feed them—bread and words that nourished them and gave them sustenance for their lives together.

And he cared first for the poor. The issues of food, water, shelter, medical care was ongoing and inclusive, and dealt with body, mind, and soul. Justice, reconciliation, and restitution held a privileged place for the poor and the outcast (seen as sinners) among his followers—the privileged place of revelation and peace that was born of justice and sharing. The gathering is always about being for and with others as the presence of the Risen Lord and what is needed for the majority and those in most dire need.

And lastly it is about the ones who organize, or call together, those who gather, the servants of the servants of God. Anyone who holds power in the community does so at the will of the community. They are chosen, blessed, and presented to the community by members of the community, not imposed by others from outside. In chapter 6 of Acts there arises a need in the community for the poor to be taken care of—specifically the widows and orphans. The Church in Jerusalem is growing and there are both Hellenistic (Greek) and Jewish widows and orphans, but because it is primarily a Jewish community, there is a complaint that the Jewish widows and orphans are receiving care and the Greek ones are being neglected in the daily distribution of food. And what follows is how the Spirit works in the community to appoint leaders for specific needs:

> And the twelve called together the whole community of the disciples and said, "It is not right that we should neglect the word of God in order to wait on tables. Therefore, friends, select from among yourselves seven men of good standing, full of the Spirit and of wisdom, whom we may appoint to this task, while we, for our part, will devote ourselves to prayer and to serving the word. What they said pleased the whole community, and they chose Stephen, a man full of faith and the Holy Spirit, together with Philip, Prochorus, Nicanor, Timon, Parmenas and Nicolas, a proselyte of Antioch. They had these men stand before the apostles, who prayed and laid their hands on them. (Acts 6:2–6)

The people choose those who will be called "deacons" and from their names all that are chosen are Greeks (new folk into the community), and we know from the early centuries of the Church that women were also chosen. There was no discrimination when it came to those believers who became servants of the community, those who cared for the poor in the name of the larger community or those who were the leaders of the local churches. The church serves as the gathering place for those who are called within it to respond on behalf of all as needed in daily life to meet the requirements of food, water, shelter, medicine, and the works of justice and mercy.

This is what the house is built and remodeled for—to accommodate those who are taken in, made to feel at home, and brought into the family. And just as the remodeling in a house begins with new wiring, heating, communication links, pipes, insulation, etc., the makeover of the Church needs to include these primary maintenance services. And old furniture, altars, clothing from generations hundreds of years past, and decorations of precious metals such as gold, silver, and platinum, need to be collected and sold either to museums or private collections (the money given to a fund for the poor) with selected pieces kept for use on special occasions as historical pieces to enhance memory. But they must be seen as "keepsakes" of another time and place so that the Spirit can be expressed in contemporary culture, in the art and life of people now, from all over the world.

THE PRINCIPLES FOR AN EXTREME MAKEOVER

1. *What the spirit reveals.* It has been said that there is nowhere where the Spirit is not and that the world and everything and everyone in it is the sacrament, the continuing revelation of the Spirit. Jesus says this and more in his closing words to his friends.

> "I still have many things to say to you, but you cannot bear them now. When the Spirit of truth comes, he will guide you into all the truth; for he will not speak on his own, but will speak whatever he hears, and he will declare to you the things that are to come. He will glorify me, because he will take what is mine and declare it to you. All that the Father has is mine. For this reason I said that he will take what is mine and declare it to you." (Jn 16:12–15)

These words of Jesus have rarely been mined and talked about, and many people believe that the time has come to hear and speak of these many things and that not only must we bear them now but we are in desperate need of them now! The Spirit suffuses everything and everyone. It is up to us, the people of God, to start listening, looking and speaking of what the Spirit is saying in the churches and among the people and the experiences of the world today. What follows is how the Spirit speaks in the Church and in the world today.

2. *Dialogue.* Our God is a community: the Trinity, three persons in open communication with one another, utterly transparent and faithful. One speaks, the other listens (obeys) and becomes flesh of the Word and the other is the breath, the life force and energy between them. There is nothing in the Church or the world that is, so to speak, "not on the table" or open to discussion. If there is no communication, no shared revelation, in the presence of the Spirit by believers, then there is no life and no possibility for communion.

3. *Diversity.* We have four gospels, but there need to be many more! We were told to go out into the whole world: "Go therefore and make disciples of all nations, baptizing them in the name of the Father, and the Son and of the Holy Spirit, and teaching them to obey everything that I have commanded you" (Mt 28:19–20). And in Acts we hear that "all of them were filled with the Holy Spirit and began to speak in other languages, as the Spirit gave them ability" (Acts 2:4). And "at this sound the crowd gathered and was bewildered, because each one heard them speaking in the native language of each" (Acts 2:6).

The vast richness of expression in language, prayer, images, stories, culture, and gesture, as well as in the art, music, and crafts of each people and nation, is a sure sign of the presence of the Spirit. The more uniformity and sameness there is, the less the Spirit can be heard or understood, and meaning shrinks. There are many ways to "stifle the Spirit," and the refusal to trust in multiple forms of expression is one of the deadliest. There is no one language or way of praying or book from any period of history that is meant to be used "only this way, by only these people, in only this language" to convey the creation of the Word.

4. *People Based, Especially the Poor.* The Spirit lives in people; the Kingdom and the will of God that is "life ever more abundant for

all" is found first in people, not primarily in books, canons, creeds, papal pronouncements, texts, and statements from other historical epochs of philosophy, theology, devotion, or catechisms. It is found first and foremost in the Good News to the poor and the people, the poor themselves. It is always a word of hope, of promise, of encouragement, of freedom and forgiveness, of reconciliation, of justice with mercy, of communion, and the compassion of our God.

The Spirit is not found in investigations, condemnations, judgments, and discouragement of groups or individuals by those who seek to posit what is wrong with others' words or ways of being, or disparagement of their very persons, especially by the in-house Church. There must always be the recognition of each person's dignity and faithfulness first, not a presumption of ignorance, lack of fidelity, error, or evil intention.

5. *The Spirit in Prophets.* In every generation and every group of people the Spirit is given in word and in groups and individuals who see with the eye of God (the gift of wisdom, knowledge, and understanding), and with courage and daring, what needs to be looked at now and changed so that there is a future for the people of God. As always, the majority of those already in positions of power do not want to hear or listen but would rather maintain the structures and traditions they favor because they are unable to see how destructive these ways of treating others can be to the health and welfare of the Body of Christ. If those in position of power can bend over backward to accommodate small groups and individuals who want to live in the past and not accept the teachings of the larger Church, such as the teachings of the pastoral council of Vatican II, then those who speak for the Spirit in the present for the future, the unknown mysteries of God still being revealed and told to us, must be even more honored, respected, and listened to—and obeyed.

The will of God is found in the majority of believers: the more than 98 percent of people struggling to live the Good News now, not necessarily in those who cling to the past and insist they alone (or first) have access to the mind of God and the will of the Spirit. The mystery of the Incarnation declares loudly that God came down to walk among humans, and Jesus told his followers that if they were to have authority among his people, then they must be the least, the servants of all, and not use their authority without responsibility or accountability to those they serve. Those chosen by the Spirit through the entire community must actually be servants, and they cannot continue to be chosen from an elite few who are not indicative at all of the people. They cannot be age- or gender-exclusive or confined to those ordained and already in the small pool of those who are allowed to be leaders. This too stifles and smothers the Spirit of God.

6. *The Mission of the Body of Christ.* The primary evangelization of the Church is not in words, classes, preaching, teaching, statements, etc., but is found in the lives of the people of God. We are the Good News, the invitation of God to others. The gifts of the Spirit are given for all followers of Jesus to use to draw others into the mystery and the compassion of Jesus's God, through the power of the Spirit. This is done through every manner of work, lifestyle, politics, economics, culture, technology, science, literature and arts, and communication through every group. These gifts are given at initiation: wisdom, knowledge, understanding, counsel, courage, piety (faithful devotion), and fear of the Lord. The Spirit is also given for this work—to everyone and to individuals and groups for the needs of the people in the Church and the world. In speaking of the Advocate (God's lawyer and character witness before God, for us as it were), Jesus says:

> "Nevertheless I tell you the truth: it is to your advantage that I go away, for if I do not go away, the Advocate will not come to you; but if I go, I will send him to you. And when he comes, he will prove the world wrong about sin, and righteousness, and judgment: about sin because they do not believe in me; about righteousness, because I am going to the Father and you will

see me no longer; about judgment, because the ruler of this world has been
condemned." (Jn 16:7—11)

This paragraph is dense with meaning—in short, the "world" includes the ruling or dominant systems of economics, nationalism,
politics, violence, even religions. The gift of the Spirit is given to
see the issues of evil, violence, injustice, destruction of any persons
and the earth, and to know righteousness, which is interchangeable
with the words *holiness* and *justice,* and to judge rightly about what
happens in the world and in the Church. The Spirit is given first
to the Body of Christ, all the people, and then to individuals such
as prophets, and then to individuals to act as witnesses to what is
truth, what is just and what is light and life, according to Jesus's
own Spirit, to the glory of God.

7. *Transparency, Forgiveness, Reconciliation, Restorative Justice, Commu-*
nion. This process of the Spirit is a daily expression and is meant
to be the daily and usual public and private way that the Church—
small churches, groups, and individuals—is drawn ever more deeply
into the conversion of life, forgiveness (given and received), and
undoing the harm done through restorative practices of justice and
atonement and is held accountable to others for its actions, words,
and inactions and their effects on the heart and life of the community, the Body of Christ. It is the daily breathing of the Church.
It begins at baptism, when we are drawn into the Body of Christ.
With the sacraments of initiation (confirmation and the Eucharist), all the members of the Body of Christ have the right to all
the other sacraments. And all the gifts of the Spirit are present in
all the communities of believers. So no one should be deprived of
the Eucharist, reconciliation, or any other sacrament because there
is no "ordained" minister. It is the right of the Body of Christ by
being the Body of Christ to do "liturgy" and give and receive the
Body of Christ.

These rights continue throughout one's life and affect all the
people of God in all circumstances. They apply as well to some of

the people receiving some of the sacraments: some the sacrament of holy orders, some the sacrament of marriage, which did not become a sacrament until the early eleventh and twelfth centuries, and even then there was much disagreement among those who were ordained (those married were never consulted). But now man-made canons and laws refuse more than half the people of God access to the Eucharist and the other sacraments because of their marital status, gender, sexual history, or the personal annoyance or preference of someone in authority with regard to a political or religious tenet that they decide is grounds for exclusion from the Body of Christ, on all levels. A quick read of any of the gospels reveals Jesus sharing the Eucharist with everyone—in the fields and on the hillsides, at banquets (even telling those who considered themselves worthy that they were not welcome at his table if they did not welcome those they thought were undeserving, as in Luke 15), and all those at his last feast of friends—all sinners, all who betrayed him.

Perhaps a last word: the Church exists primarily for the world, not for itself, and it is commanded to "love one another as I have loved you" and in so doing, worship God, with Jesus in the power of the Spirit as the Body of Christ here on earth today. And hopefully, what is ritualized in liturgy, word, and sacrament will be enfleshed in the lives and bodies of all the people of God, the Body of Christ. We were born and baptized to be light for all in the world and to delight our God who has made us. We are to be the Light, the Truth, and the Peace of the Risen Lord—a magnet that draws others in—and when we are not, it is time for the "hammer shattering rock" to be grasped and swung with all the force and energy to start an Extreme Makeover: Church Edition—on a universal structural and leadership level, on a diocesan and parish level, and in small communities dedicated to conversion of life through the Word of God and as individual believers always encouraged to become disciples in the Body of Christ.

A story is needed for hope, for encouragement, for the future and the amazing possibilities that our God expects and demands of us now, two thousand plus years after the life, death, and resurrection of Jesus, abiding still with us in the Spirit of the Living God we all belong to and are called to reveal to others. It is a story I have heard told in Nigeria and in Thailand but first on the northwest coast of the United States and Canada by the Native Peoples.

Once upon a time the earth and the sky were much closer together than they are now. If you stand outside now and look up, the sky seems miles away. But once it was close, so close that when people stood up straight, their heads and shoulders, sometimes half their bodies, were in the clouds or the mist or the rain. They were always wet, damp, soggy, and they often bent over to stay a bit dryer. They were stooped and went about their work in this position, sweeping, digging, building, farming, and reaping. Just standing erect got them soaked through. It was, of course, hardest on the slaves and those who did all the manual labor with broom, brush, hoe, shovel, and basket. The others could hide in their houses to try to keep the moisture at bay.

This went on for as long as anyone could remember, but one day one of the servants who was sweeping the courtyard of a great one's house was very tired of being bent over. She straightened up and the water ran down her hair into her face, soaking her dress. She was so frustrated and tired, she wanted to cry, or to scream—anything. And without thinking, she took her broom and swatted the sky, swinging at the air, the water, and dripping clouds all around her and above her. Of course nothing happened—or did it? She looked at the moist air around her—did it move? Even a bit? She whacked it again—and again and again, hitting out at the air around her. Amazed, she realized that it did move! Oh only a little, but it moved.

You see the sky has feelings, too, and it was put out, downright annoyed that this servant girl would hit it, whack at it like that, so it moved up a little. She went on whacking. The other servants thought she was crazy, but she told them: Watch, look at me and see what happens. In a few moments, they saw it, too—the sky was rising! They grabbed their mops, brooms, and rags and started whacking away. Soon they were exhausted and the sky had moved only a smidgen. They called to the others—the farmers and herders, the builders and gardeners, the laborers—and showed them what they had learned, so they all started with their shovels and hoes, rakes, and planks of wood, whacking away around them. Again, they were exhausted and it hadn't moved much.

But then the servant girl had a grand idea: we have to work together. Look, do it this way. Count. One, two, three, whack—all together. Get in a line. And they did. One, two, three, whack. One, two, three, whack, and the sky started to back away and move up and up. They climbed on stairs and then up on first floors, then onto roofs, and into the trees, calling out for all to join them, even the rich and the ones hiding in their houses. And then they moved up into the hills. In a line, in circles, and in small pockets of people they spread out across the land. One, two, three, whack. They danced all together! One, two, three, whack! They did it until they fell in heaps together, exhausted and spent. But the sky was higher, and with each day it moved away a bit more. They worked at it until it's the way you see it now—up there! Look! Look what they did together!

And just imagine. If they could raise the sky so that today we can all breathe freely and learn to fly and rise into the sky—if they could do that together, what can we do? It's time for us to make our move. Whether it's a bulldozer, a wrecking ball, a broom, a laptop, a pen, a shovel, whatever, it has to be the "hammer shattering rock," and it's time to grasp hold of one another's hands and together begin the Extreme Makeover: Church (and World) Edition. Let's go: one, two, three, whack. One, two, three, whack. And oh what the Spirit will do with us as a gift to those who come after us, down to the seventh generation. Amen.

Endnotes

INTRODUCTION
1. "Food for the Journey: Scripture Reading: Font of Spiritual Nourishment," *Living with Christ,* January 2006, pp. 2–3.

CHAPTER 1. THE GOSPEL: THE WORD OF GOD MADE FLESH DWELLING AMONG US
1. Jane Hirshfield, trans./ed., *Women in Praise of the Sacred* (New York: HarperCollins, 1995), p. 116, prayer 20.

CHAPTER 2. THE GOSPEL OF MARK THEN
1. Christine M. Bochen, ed., *The Courage for Truth: The Letters of Thomas Merton to Writers* (New York: Farrar, Straus and Giroux, 1993), pp. 57–58.

CHAPTER 3. THE GOSPEL OF MARK NOW
1. Ched Myers, "The Radical Nonviolent Witness of Jesus," *Friends Journal,* May 2009, pp. 8–15, 39.
2. Alan Jamieson, *Journeying in Faith* (London, England: SPCK, 2004), quoted in *The Tablet.*
3. Waler Wink, *The Human Being: Jesus and the Enigma of the Son of Man* (Minneapolis: Fortress Press, 2002).

CHAPTER 5. THE GOSPEL OF MATTHEW NOW
1. A version is found in "Seeds of God in Asian Soil" in *Once Upon a Time in Asia* (Maryknoll, NY: Orbis Books, 2006), pp. 149–50.
2. Peter C. Phan, "Kingdom of God: A Symbol for Asians," *Theology Digest* 47, no. 1 (Spring 2000), pp. 21–26.
3. The basis of the story is told in Rachel Naomi Remen, M.D., *My Grandfather's Blessings* (New York: Riverhead Books, 2000), pp. 277–78.

CHAPTER 7. THE GOSPEL OF LUKE NOW

1. "The Church's Mission in the Midst of the Country's Crisis," August 6, 1979, reprinted in *Catholic Worker*.
2. Richard Shaull, "Liberating Ourselves: Recovering the Gospel for North America," *The Other Side*, September/October 1989, pp. 42–46.
3. "Once There Was a Rich Man . . . ," *The Bible Today*, March 1988, pp. 98–103.

CHAPTER 8. THE GOSPEL OF JOHN THEN

1. Martin Buber, "Goblet of Grace," reprinted in *Parabola*, Summer 1998, pp. 81–84.

CHAPTER 9. THE GOSPEL OF JOHN NOW

1. John Coleman, *The Unexpected Teachings of Jesus: Encountering the Gospels All Over Again* (San Francisco: Jossey-Bass, 2002). Quoted in "Practicing Spirituality with Jesus, Day 33," April 2, 2004, spiritualityhealth.com.
2. From a transcript of the speech, selections of which were reprinted in *The Tablet* (n.d.).
3. Thich Nhat Hanh, "The World We Have," *Shambala Sun*, September 2008, pp. 48–52.
4. Quoted in Juan Williams, *Eyes on the Prize* (New York: Viking, 1987).

CHAPTER 10. THE OTHER GOSPELS TO BE WRITTEN NOW

1. "Oscar Arias Sánchez—Acceptance Speech," Nobelprize.org. Accessed June 14, 2012: http://www.nobelprize.org/nobel_prizes/ peace/laureates/1987/arias-acceptance.html.
2. "Oscar Arias Sánchez—Nobel Lecture," Nobelprize.org. Accessed June 14, 2012: http://www.nobelprize.org/nobel_prizes/peace/ laureates/1987/arias-lecture.html.
3. Tim O'Brien, "An Immoral Story" on *The Bruderhof Daily Dig*. Accessed July 24, 2004: http://www.bruderhof.com/articles/ ChristianSoldiers.htm.
4. Martin Luther King III, *Sojourners* "Quote of the Week," August 26, 2010 (source: *The Washington Post*).
5. Søren Kierkegaard, quoted in *Sojourners* "Verse and Voice," July 29, 2009.

6. Denise Levertov, "Beginners." Accessed June 16, 2012: www.
    panhala.net/Archive/Beginners.html.
7. William Sloane Coffin, *A Passion for the Possible: A Message to U. S.
    Churches* (Louisville: Westminster John Knox Press, 2004).
8. John Muir quote. Accessed June 16, 2012: www.sierraclub.org/
    john_muir_exhibit/writings/misquotes.aspx.
9. Thich Nhat Hanh in Danielle and Olivier Föllmi, *Awakenings:
    Asian Wisdom for Every Day* (January 30), (New York: Abrams,
    2007).
10. Ibid (August 9).
11. Albert Einstein, "The Merging of Spirit and Science." Accessed
    July 9, 2010: Gratefulness.org.
12. Margaret Meaders, "Flannery O'Connor: Literary Witch,"
    Colorado Quarterly 10, no. 4 (Spring 1962): 377.

AFTERWORD
1. Saint Jerome, quoted in *Daily Gospel*. Accessed April 24, 2010:
    http://dailygospel.org.

Bibliography

THE GOSPEL: THE WORD OF GOD AMONG US
General Background

Alfaro, Juan. *Getting to Know Jesus: What Do Matthew, Mark, Luke, and John Tell Us?* Liguori, MO: Liguori Press, 2000.

Bailey, Kenneth E. *Jesus Through Middle Eastern Eyes: Cultural Studies in the Gospels.* Downers Grove, IL: IVP Academic, 2008.

Balaguer, Vincente. *Understanding the Gospels.* New York: Sceptor Publishers, 2005.

The Bible Today: The Pontifical Biblical Commission vol. 48, no. 4 (July/August 2010), Collegeville, MN.

Brown, Raymond. *New Testament Essays.* New York: Doubleday Image Books, the Bruce Publishing Co., 1965.

Brueggemann, Walter. *The Word Militant: Preaching a Decentering Word.* Minneapolis: Fortress Press, 2007.

Brueggemann, Walter, William C. Placher, and Brian K. Blount. *Struggling with Scripture.* Louisville, KY: Westmister John Knox Press, 2002.

Dumm, Demetrius. *Praying the Scriptures.* Collegeville, MN: Liturgical Press, 2003.

Power, David N. *"The Word of the Lord": Liturgy's Use of Scripture.* Maryknoll, NY: Orbis Books, 2001.

Song, C. S. *The Believing Heart: An Invitation to Story Theology.* Minneapolis: Fortress Press, 1999.

Spohn, William C. *What Are They Saying About Scripture and Ethics?* Mahwah, NJ: Paulist Press, 1984.

Wansbrough, Henry. *The Use and Abuse of the Bible: A Brief History of Biblication Interpretation,* New York, NY: T&T Clark International, 2010.

Commentaries on Liturgical Texts for All the Gospels

Bergant, Dianne, with Richard Fragomeni. *Preaching the New Lectionary,*
    3 vol. Collegeville, MN: Liturgical Press, 2000.

Brown, Raymond, ed., and Ronald D. Witherup. *Christ in the Gospels of
    the Liturgical Year.* Collegeville, MN: Liturgical Press, 2008.

Donders, Joseph G. *With Hearts on Fire: Reflections on the Weekday
    Readings of the Liturgical Year.* Mystic, CT: Twenty-Third
    Publications, 1999.

Gutierrez, Gustavo. *Sharing the Word Through the Liturgical Year,* Maryknoll,
    NY: Orbis Books, 1997.

Hamm, Dennis. *Let the Scriptures Speak: Reflections on the Sunday Readings.*
    Collegeville, MN: Liturgical Press, 2000.

Harrington, Wilfrid J. *The Gracious Word: Commentaries on Sundays and
    Holy Days.* 3 vols. Dublin, Ireland: Dominican Publications, 1998,
    1999, 2000.

McBride, Denis. *Seasons of the Word: Reflections on the Sunday Readings with
    Full Gospel Texts.* London, England: Redemptorist Publications,
    1991.

McCarthy, Flor. *New Sunday and Holy Day Liturgies, Years A, B, and C.* New
    York: Dominican Publications, 1998, 1999, 2000.

McKenna, Megan. *Advent, Christmas and Epiphany Readings: Sunday and
    Daily for Years A, B, and C.* New York: New City Press, 2009.

———. *Lent: The Sunday and Daily Readings for Years A, B, and C.* Dublin,
    Ireland: Veritas Publications, 2008.

———. *And Morning Came: The Scriptures of the Resurrection.* Littlefield, MD:
    Rowland, 2006.

Pilch, John J. *The Cultural World of Jesus, Sunday by Sunday.* 3 vols.
    Collegeville, MN: Liturgical Press, 1995–1997.

Rahner, Karl, and Albert Raffelt, ed. *The Great Church Year: The
    Best of Karl Rahner's Homilies, Sermons and Meditations.* New York:
    Crossroads, 1987.

Rice, Marianne, and Laurie Brink. *In This Place: Reflections on the Land of
    the Gospels for the Liturgical Cycles.* Collegeville, MN: Liturgical Press,
    1998.

Shea, John. *The Spiritual Wisdom of the Gospels for Christian Preachers
    and Teachers.* 4 vols. Collegeville, MN: Liturgical Press, 2004–
    2006.

Stuhlmueller, Carroll. *Biblical Meditations for the Seasons.* 5 vols. Ramsey,
    NJ: Paulist Press, 1980.

A Taste of the Word of God: Commentaries on the Sunday and Daily Readings for Cycles 1 and 2, and A, B, and C. 2 vols. New York: New City Press, 2010.

Wallace, James A., Robert P. Waznak, and Guerric DeBona. *Lift Up Your Hearts: Homilies and Reflections for Cycles A, B, and C.* 3 vols. New York: Paulist Press, 2004–2007.

Online Resources

America Magazine. "The Good Word." www.americapress.org/theword. html.

Bread for the World. www.Bread.org.

Daily Gospel. DGO contact-am@dailygospel.org provides the readings for the day and a commentary, usually from early church teaching or contemporary documents/writers. http://dailygospel.org.

Dominican Friars Province of Saint Martin de Porres. "Homilias dominicales." Weekly hermeneutical study of the Sunday Lectionary in Spanish, also available as an e-mail service. www .opsouth.org/.

———. "Preachers Exchange." Weekly hermeneutical study of the Sunday Lectionary from Jude Siciliano, OP, also available as an e-mail service. www.opsouth.org/

Dominican Province of Saint Albert the Great, USA. "Preachers of the Word of God: Roman Catholic in the Dominican Tradition." www.preachers.org.

Dominican Sisters: Caldwell. "Reflections." www.caldwellop.org (article no longer available).

Dominican Sisters of Peace. "Preaching Charism." www.oppeace.org (article no longer available).

Feed Your Spirit: Weekly Seeds, United Church of Christ. www.ucc .org/feed-your-spirit/weekly-seeds.

Homilies by Bishop Thomas Gumbleton, Detroit. Available on the website of the *National Catholic Reporter.* http://ncronline.org.

Homilies by Thomas Rosica. CSB. Weekly at www.zenit.org.

Living With Christ: Your Daily Companion for Praying and Living the Eucharist. Also available in a monthly format in print. P.O. Box 293040, Dayton, Ohio 45429. www.LivingWithChrist.us.

National Conference of Catholic Bishops and United States Catholic Conference. "New American Bible and Lectionary for Mass." The USCC web page includes the complete text of the New American

Bible, as well as complete texts of the Roman Catholic Lectionary readings for each day of the current month. www.nccbuscc.org/nab/index.html.

National Institute of the Word of God. "The Good News Letter." Includes a preacher's page. www.wordofgodinstitute.org (site no longer exists).

Sanchez, Patricia Datchuck. "The Word: Scripted for Life." Available in the *National Catholic Reporter,* weekly (Kansas City, MO). http://ncronline.org/node/2928.

Shalom Place. "A Daily spiritual seed." A daily e-mail meditation on the daily lectionary at Shalom Place homepage. http://shalomplace.com.

Sisters of Saint Dominic: Blauvelt. "Scripture Reflection: Reflection on Sunday Lectionary. www.opblauvelt.org (article no longer available).

Sunday Reflections with Father Terry Tastard (England). This is the web page of *The Independent Catholic News of England.* www.indcatholicnews.com.

The Word Among Us. A daily approach to prayer and scripture, including daily mass readings and meditations. www.wau.org.

THE GOSPEL OF MARK

Achtemeir, Paul, Daniel Harrington, Robert Karris, George MacRae, Donald Senior. *Invitation to the Gospels.* Mahwah, NJ: Paulist Press, 2004.

Beck, Robert. *Nonviolent Story: Narrative Conflict Resolution in the Gospel of Mark.* Maryknoll, NY: Orbis Books, 1996.

Belo, Fernando. *A Materialist Reading of the Gospel of Mark.* Maryknoll, NY: Orbis Books, 1984.

Crotty, Robert, stories by Ernie Smith, Collins Dove. *Voices from the Edge: Mark's Gospel in Our World.* Victoria, Australia: HarperCollins, 1994.

Graham, Helen. *You Will Be Handed Over: The Persecution Prediction in Mark 13:9–13.* Quezon City and Manila, Philippines: Claretian Publications, 1987.

Hamerton-Kelly, Robert G. *The Gospel of the Sacred: Poetics of Violence in Mark.* Minneapolis: Fortress Press, 1994.

Harrington, Wilfrid J. *Mark: Realistic Theologian: The Jesus of Mark.* Dublin, Ireland: The Columba Press, 1966.

Hendrickx, Herman. *A Key to the Gospel of Mark.* Quezon City,
    Philippines: Claretian Publications, 1993.

———. *The Parables of Jesus: Studies in the Synoptic Gospels.* Makati,
    Philippines: St. Paul Publications, 1990.

———. *The Passion Narratives of the Synoptic Gospels.* Makati, Philippines: St.
    Paul Publications, 1989.

———. *The Resurrection Narratives of the Synoptic Gospels.* Makati,
    Philippines: St. Paul Publications, 1988.

Kelber, Werner. *The Kingdom in Mark: A New Place and a New Time.*
    Philadelphia: Fortress Press, 1974.

Kelber, Werner, ed. *The Passion in Mark: Studies on Mark 14–16.*
    Philadelphia: Fortress Press, 1976.

Kinukawa, Hisako. *Women and Jesus in Mark: A Japanese Feminist Perspective.*
    Maryknoll, NY: Orbis Books, 1994.

LaVerdiere, Eugene. *The Beginning of the Gospel: Introducing the Gospel
    According to Mark.* Vols. 1 and 2. Collegeville, MN: Liturgical Press,
    1999.

Martini, Carlo M. *The Spiritual Journey of the Apostles: Growth in the Gospel of
    Mark,* Boston: St. Paul Books and Media, 1991.

McBride, Denis. *The Gospel of Mark: A Reflective Commentary.* Dublin,
    Ireland: Dominican Publications, 1996.

McFadyen, Phillip. *Open Door on Mark.* London: Triangle, 1997.

McKenna, Megan. *On Your Mark.* Maryknoll, NY: Orbis Books, 2008.

Moloney, Francis J. *The Gospel of Mark: A Commentary.* Peabody, MA:
    Hendrickson Publishers, 2002.

Myers, Ched. *Binding the Strongman: A Political Reading of Mark's Story of
    Jesus.* Maryknoll, NY: Orbis Books, 1988.

———. *Who Will Roll Away the Stone? Discipleship Queries for First World
    Christians.* Maryknoll, NY: Orbis Books, 1994.

Myers, Ched, Marie Dennis, Joseph Nangle, Cynthia Moe-Lobeda,
    Stuart Taylor. *"Say to This Mountain": Mark's Story of Discipleship.*
    Maryknoll, NY: Orbis Books, 1996.

Newheart, Michael Willett. *"My Name Is Legion": The Story and the Soul
    of the Gerasene Demoniac.* Collegeville, MN: Liturgical Press, 2004.

Oden, Thomas, ed., and Christopher Hall. *Ancient Christian Commentary
    on Scripture, New Testament II, Mark.* Downers Grove, IL: Inter-
    Varsity Press, 1998.

O'Hanlon, Joseph. *Mark My Words.* Kildare, Ireland: St. Paul's, 1994.

Painter, John. *Mark's Gospel: Worlds in Conflict.* New York: Routledge,
    1997.

Pilch, John J. *The Cultural World of Jesus, Sunday by Sunday, Cycle B.*
    Collegeville, MN: Liturgical Press, 1996.

Reiser, William. *Jesus in Solidarity with His People: A Theologian Looks at
    Mark.* Collegeville, MN: Liturgical Press, 2000.

Rotelle, John, ed. *Meditations on the Sunday Gospels, Year B.* Hyde Park,
    NY: New City Press, 1996.

Sabin, Marie Noonan. *The Gospel According to Mark, New Collegeville Bible
    Commentary.* Collegeville, MN: Liturgical Press, 2006.

Senior, Donald. *The Passion of Jesus in the Gospel of Mark.* Collegeville,
    MN: Liturgical Press, 1984.

Trainor, Michael F. *The Quest for Home: The Household in Mark's
    Community.* Collegeville, MN: Liturgical Press, 2001.

Trocme, Andre. *Jesus and the Nonviolent Revolution.* Maryknoll, NY: Orbis
    Books, 2003.

Williams, Rowan. *Christ on Trial: How the Gospel Unsettles Our Judgment.*
    Grand Rapids: William B. Eerdmans Publishing, 2000.

More General Background/History

Carroll, James. *Constantine's Sword: The Church and the Jews. (A History).*
    New York: Houghton Mifflin Company, 2001.

Casey, Michael. *Fully Human, Fully Divine: An Interactive Christology.*
    Liguori, MO: Liguori Publications, 2004.

Crowe, Jerome. *From Jerusalem to Antioch: The Gospel Across Cultures.*
    Collegeville, MN: Liturgical Press, 1997.

Donnelly, Doris, ed., with James Dunn, Daniel Harrington, Elizabeth
    Johnson, John Meier and E. P. Sanders. *Jesus: A Colloquium in the
    Holy Land.* New York: Continuum, 2001.

Ehrman, Bart D. *Lost Scriptures: Books That Did Not Make It into the New
    Testament.* New York: Oxford University Press, 2003.

Freyne, Sean. *Texts, Contexts and Cultures: Essays on Biblical Topics.* Dublin,
    Ireland: Veritas Publications, 2002.

Needleman, Jacob. *Lost Christianity: A Journey of Rediscovery.* New York:
    Penguin (1980 Doubleday).

Neusner, Jacob. *Judaism in the Beginning of Christianity.* Philadelphia:
    Fortress Press, 1984.

———. *Judaism When Christianity Began: A Survey of Belief and Practice.*
    Louisville, KY: Westminister John Knox Press, 2002.

Taylor, Justin. *Where Did Christianity Come From?* Collegeville, MN:
    Liturgical Press, 2001.

Wylen, Stephen M. *The Jews in the Time of Jesus: An Introduction.* Mahwah, NJ: Paulist Press, 1996.

THE GOSPEL OF MATTHEW

Albright, W. F., and C. S. Mann. *The Anchor Bible Matthew.* New York: Doubleday, 1971.

Aune, David, ed. *The Gospel of Matthew in Current Study.* Grand Rapids: William B. Eerdmans Publishing, 2001.

Carter, Warren. *Matthew and Empire: Initial Explorations,* London, England: Trinity Press International, 2001.

———. *Matthew and the Margins: A Sociopolitical and Religious Reading.* New York: Orbis Books, 2000.

Crosby, Michael H. *House of Disciples: Church, Economics, and Justice in Matthew.* New York: Orbis Books, 1988.

———. *The Prayer That Jesus Taught Us.* Maryknoll, New York: Orbis Books, 2002.

———. *Spirituality of the Beatitudes: Matthew's Vision for the Church in an Unjust World.* Rev. ed. Maryknoll, New York: Orbis Books, 2005.

Harrington, Wilfrid J. *Matthew: Sage Theologian: The Jesus of Matthew.* Dublin, Ireland: Columba Press, 1998.

Hendrickx, Herman. *A Key to the Gospel of Matthew.* Quezon City, Philippines: Claretian Publications, 1992.

———. *The Household of God: The Communities Behind the New Testament Writings.* Quezon City, Philippines: Claretian Publications, 1992.

McKenna, Megan. *On Your Mark.* Maryknoll, New York: Orbis Books, 2009.

Perlewitz, Miriam, and Michael Glazier. *The Gospel of Matthew.* Collegeville, MN: Lit Press, 1977.

Senior, Donald, and Michael Glazier. *The Passion of Jesus in the Gospel of Matthew.* Collegeville, MN: Lit Press, 1985.

Simonetti, Manlio, ed. *Ancient Christian Commentary on Scripture, New Testament,* Ia, Matthew 1–13, and Ib, Matthew 14–28. Downers Grove, IL: InterVarsity Press, 2001.

Song. C. S. *Jesus and the Reign of God.* Minneapolis: Fortress Press, 1993.

ter Linden, Nico. *The Story Goes . . . Mark's Story and Matthew's Story.* London: SCM Press, 1999.

Wainwright, Elaine M. *Shall We Look for Another? A Feminist Rereading of the Matthean Jesus.* New York: Orbis Books, 1998.

Yeomans, William. *The Gospel of Matthew: A Spiritual Commentary.* Dublin, Ireland: Dominican Publications, 1993.

Preaching Sources for Matthew's Gospel

(Resources that were not included in chapter 1: general gospels and preaching.)

Eddy, Corbin. *Who Knows the Reach of God? Homilies and Reflections for Year A.* Ottawa, Canada: Novalis, 2001.

Karaban, Roslyn A., and Deni Mack, eds. *Extraordinary Preaching: Twenty Homilies by Roman Catholic Women.* San Jose, CA: Resource Publications Inc., 1996.

McArdle, Jack. *And That's the Gospel Truth: Reflections on the Sunday Gospels, Year A.* Dublin, Ireland: Columba Press, 2001.

McBride, Alfred, and O. Praem. *Year of the Lord, Cycle A.* Dubuque, IA: William C. Brown Company, 1983.

Rotelle, John, ed. *Meditations on the Sunday Gospels, Year A.* New York: New City Press, 1995.

Tisdale, Leonora Tubbs, ed. *The Abingdon Women's Preaching Annual, Series 2, Year A.* Nashville, TN: Abingdon Press, 2001.

THE GOSPEL OF LUKE

Bailey, Kenneth E. *Poet and Peasant: A Literary-Cultural Approach to the Parables in Luke.* Grand Rapids: William Eerdmans Publishing, 1976.

———. *Through Peasant Eyes: More Lucan Parables.* Grand Rapids: William Eerdmans Publishing, 1980.

Cassidy, Richard, and Philip J. Scharper, eds. *Political Issues in Luke-Acts.* Maryknoll, NY: Orbis Books, 1983.

Dale, Ronald W. *Windows on Luke: An Anthology to Amplify the Gospel Readings for Year C of the Lectionary.* Suffolk, UK: Kevin Mayhew Ltd., 2000.

Graham, Helen. *There Shall Be No Poor Among You: Essay in Lukan Theology.* Quezon City, Philippines: JMC Press, 1978.

Hamm, Dennis. *The Beatitudes in Context: What Luke and Matthew Meant* (Zacchaeus Studies: New Testament). Wilmington, DE: Michael Glazier, 1990.

Harris, Maria. *Proclaim Jubilee: A Spirituality for the Twenty-first Century,* Louisville, KY: Westminster John Knox Press, 1996.

Hendrickx, Herman. *The Sermon on the Mount: Studies in the Synoptic Gospels*. London: Geoffrey Chapman, 1984.

———. *The Third Gospel for the Third World*. Vols. 1–8. Collegeville, MN: Liturgical Press, 1996–2004.

LaVerdiere, Eugene. *The Annunciation to Mary: A Story of Faith, Luke 1:26–38*. Chicago: Liturgical Training Publications, 2004.

———. *Dining in the Kingdom of God: The Eucharist in the Gospel of Luke*. Chicago: Liturgical Training Publications, 2003.

———. *Luke: New Testament Message #5*. Collegeville, MN: Liturgical Press, 1980.

McBride, Denis. *The Gospel of Luke, A Reflective Commentary*. Dublin, Ireland: Dominican Publications, 1991.

McKenna, Megan. *Advent, Christmas, and Epiphany: Stories and Reflections on the Sunday and Daily Readings*. 2 vols. New York: New City Press, 2008.

———. *Luke: The Book of Blessings and Woes*. New York: New City Press, 2009.

———. *Mary: Shadow of Grace*. New York: New City Press, 2007.

———. *Parables: Arrows of God*. Maryknoll, NY: Orbis Books, 1994.

O'Flynn, Silvester. *The Good News of Luke's Year*. Dublin, Ireland: Columba Press, 2000.

Paoli, Arturo. *Meditations on Saint Luke*. Maryknoll, NY: Orbis Books, 1977.

Patella, Michael F. *The Gospel According to Luke*. Vol. 3.(New Collegeville Bible Commentary.) Collegeville, MN: Liturgical Press, 2005.

Pobee, John S. *Who Are the Poor? The Beatitudes as a Call to Community*. Geneva: WCC Publications, 1987.

Senior, Donald. *The Passion of Jesus in the Gospel of Luke*. Collegeville, MN: Michael Glazier, Liturgical Press, 1990.

Sobrino, Jon. *No Salvation Outside the Poor: Prophetic-Utopian Essays*. Maryknoll, NY: Orbis Books, 2008.

Yong, Amos. *Hospitality and the Other: Pentecost, Christian Practices, and the Neighbor*. Maryknoll, NY: Orbis Books, 2008.

Preaching the Gospel of Luke

Alves, Ruben A. *The Poet, the Warrior, the Prophet*. Philadelphia: Trinity Press International, 1990.

Brueggemann, Walter. *Cadences of Home: Preaching Among Exiles*. Louisville, KY: Westerminster John Knox Press, 1997.

——. *The Threat of Life: Sermons on Pain, Power, and Weakness.* Charles
    Campbell, ed. Minneapolis: Fortress Press, 1996.
Burghardt, Walter J. *Speak the Word with Boldness: Homilies for Risen
    Christian Christians.* Mahwah, NJ: Paulist Press, 1994.

THE GOSPEL OF JOHN

Brown, Raymond. *The Community of the Beloved Disciple: The Life, Loves, and
    Hates of the Individual Church in New Testament Times.* Mahwah, NJ:
    Paulist Press, 1979.
——. *The Gospel According to John I–XII.* 2 vols. Bible Series. Garden
    City, NY: Doubleday, 1966.
——. *An Introduction to the Gospel of John.* New York: Doubleday,
    2003.
——. *A Retreat with John the Evangelist: That You May Have Life.* Cincinnati:
    St. Anthony Press, 1998.
Cassidy, Richard J. *John's Gospel in New Perspective.* Maryknoll, NY: Orbis
    Books. 1992.
Collins, Raymond. *These Things Have Been Written: Studies on the Fourth
    Gospel.* Grand Rapids: Peeters Press, Louvain/Eerdmans, 1990.
Coloe, Mary L. *God Dwells with Us: Temple Symbolism in the Fourth
    Gospel.* Collegeville, MN: Michael Glazier, Liturgical Press,
    2001.
Comblin, José. *Sent from the Father: Meditations on the Fourth Gospel.*
    Maryknoll, NY: Orbis Books, 1974.
Crosby, Michael H. *"Do You Love Me?" Jesus Questions the Church.*
    Maryknoll, NY: Orbis Books, 2000.
Donahue, John R., ed. *Life in Abundance: Studies of John's Gospel in Tribute
    to Raymond E. Brown.* Collegeville, MN: Liturgical Press, 2005.
Ellis, Peter F. *The Genius of John: A Composition-Critical Commentary of the
    Fourth Gospel.* Collegeville, MN: Liturgical Press, 1984.
Fehribach, Adeline. *The Women in the Life of the Bridegroom: A Feminist
    Historical-Literary Analysis of the Female Characters in the Fourth Gospel.*
    Collegeville, MN: Liturgical Press, 1998.
Howard-Brook, Wes. *Becoming Children of God: John's Gospel and Radical
    Discipleship.* Maryknoll, NY: Orbis Books, 1994.
——. Wes. *John's Gospel and the Renewal of the Church.* Maryknoll, NY:
    Orbis Books, 1997.
King, Nicholas, trans. *The New Testament John.* Study Guide Series.
    Suffolk, UK: Kevin Mayhew, 2006.

Kostenberger, Andrew J. *The Missions of Jesus and the Disciples: According to the Fourth Gospel.* Grand Rapids: William Eerdmans Publishing, 1998.

Lewis, Scott M. *The Gospel According to John and the Johannine Letters.* Collegeville, MN: New Collegeville Bible Commentary, 2005.

Ling, Timothy J. M., *The Judean Poor and the Fourth Gospel.* New York: Cambridge University Press, 2006.

Maline, Bruce J., and Richard L. Rohrbaugh. *Social-Science Commentary on the Gospel of John.* Minneapolis: Fortress Press, 1998.

Marsh, Charles. *The Beloved Community: How Faith Shapes Social Justice, from the Civil Rights Movement to Today.* New York: Basic Books, Perseus Book Group, 2005.

Minear, Paul S. *John: The Martyr's Gospel.* New York: The Pilgrim Press, 1984.

Newheart, Michael Willett. *Word and Soul: A Psychological, Literary, and Cultural Reading of the Fourth Gospel.* Collegeville, MN: Michael Glazier, Liturgical Press, 2001.

Schneiders, Sandra M. *Written That You May Believe: Encountering Jesus in the Fourth Gospel.* New York: Crossroads Publishing, 1999.

Schreiter, Robert J. *In Water and Blood: A Spirituality of Solidarity and Hope.* Maryknoll, NY: Orbis Books, 2008.

Sister Vandana. *Waters of Fire.* Bangalore, India: Asian Trading Corporation, 1989.

Vanier, Jean. *Befriending the Stranger.* Ontario, Canada: Novalis, 2005.
———. *Drawn into the Mystery of Jesus Through the Gospel of St. John.* Mahwah, NJ: Paulist Press, 2004.

Yoder, John Howard. *The Politics of Jesus: Vicit Agnus Noster.* Grand Rapids: William B. Eerdmans Publishing, 2002.

THE OTHER GOSPELS

The Gospel of Peace

Cobban, Helena. *The Moral Architecture of World Peace: Nobel Laureates Discuss Our Global Future.* Charlottesville, VA: University Press of Virginia, 2000.

Dalai Lama with Jean-Claude Carrière. *Violence and Compassion: Dialogues on Life Today.* New York: Image, Doubleday, 1994.

Fahey, Joseph J. *War and the Christian Conscience: Where Do You Stand?,* Maryknoll, NY: Orbis Books, 2005.

Fahey, Joseph, ed., and Richard Armstrong. *A Peace Reader: Essential Readings on War, Justice, Non-Violence and World Order*. Mahwah, NJ: Paulist Press, 1992.

Gandhi, Mahatma, *The Words of Gandhi: Selected*. New York: Newmarket Press, 2000.

Gandhi, Mohandas, *Mohandas Gandhi: Essential Writings*. Modern Spiritual Masters Series. Maryknoll, NY: Orbis Books, 2002.

Hauerwas, Stanley, and Jean Vanier. *Living Gently in a Violent World: The Prophetic Witness of Weakness*. Downers Grove, IL: IVP Books, 2008.

Ikeda, Daisaku. *For the Sake of Peace: Seven Paths to Global Harmony: A Buddhist Perspective*. Santa Monica: Middleway Press, 2001.

Schreiter, Robert J., R. Scott Appleby, and Gerard F. Powers, eds. *Peacebuilding: Catholic Theology, Ethics, and Praxis*. Maryknoll, NY: Orbis Books, 2010.

Yoder, John Howard. *Nonviolence: A Brief History: The Warsaw Lectures*. Waco: Baylor University Press, 2010.

The Gospel of the Poor

Coffin, William Sloane. *The Heart Is a Little to the Left: Essays on Public Morality*. Hanover, NH: Darmouth College, University Press of New England, 1999.

Collins, Chuck, and Mary Wright. *The Moral Measure of the Economy*. Maryknoll, NY: Orbis Books, 2007.

De La Torre, Miguel A. *Doing Christian Ethics from the Margins*. Maryknoll, NY: Orbis Books, 2007.

Gutierrez, Gustavo. *The Power of the Poor in History*. Maryknoll, NY: Orbis Books, 1983.

Kinsler, Ross, and Gloria Kinsler, eds. *God's Economy: Biblical Studies from Latin America*. Maryknoll, NY: Orbis Books, 2005.

Longenecker, Bruce W., and Kelly D. Liebengood, eds. *Engaging Economics: New Testament Scenarios and Early Christian Reception*. Grand Rapids: William B. Eerdmans Publishing, 2009.

Metz, Johannes B. *Poverty of Spirit*. Mahwah, NJ: Paulist Press, 1968.

Metz, Johannes Baptist, and Jürgen Moltmann. *Faith and the Future: Essays on Theology, Solidarity, and Modernity*. Maryknoll, NY: Orbis Books, 1995.

Mitchell, Donald W., and James Wiseman, eds. *Transforming Suffering: Reflections on Finding Peace in Troubled Times*. NY: Doubleday, 2003.

Novogratz, Jacqueline. *The Blue Sweater: Bridging the Gap Between Rich and Poor in an Interconnected World*. NY: Rodale Books, Macmillan, 2009.

Rose, Or N., Jo Ellen Green Kaiser, Margie Klein, eds. *Righteous Indignation: A Jewish Call for Justice*. Woodstock, VT: Jewish Lights Publishing, 2008.

Snyder, Larry. *Think and Act Anew: How Poverty in America Affects Us All and What We Can Do About It*. Maryknoll, NY: Orbis Books, 2010.

Van Til, Kent A. *Less Than Two Dollars a Day: A Christian View of World Poverty and the Free Market*. Grand Rapids: William B. Eerdmans Publishing Company, 2007.

Williams, Terry Tempest. *The Open Spaces of Democracy*. Barrington, MA: The Orion Society, 2004.

Also helpful are any of the *No-Nonsense Guides* of the past ten years: to water, by Maggie Black; to globalization, by Wayne Ellwood; to world food, by Wayne Roberts; or to world poverty, by Jeremy Seabrook. They are published by New International Press in Toronto, Canada.

The Gospel of the World-Earth

(This bibliography looks at both the earth and the concept of the world.)

Caldicott, Helen. *If You Love This Planet: A Plan to Save the Earth*. New York: W. W. Norton & Co., 2008.

Davis, Ellen F. *Scripture, Culture, and Agriculture: An Agrarian Reading of the Bible*. New York: Cambridge University Press, 2009.

Echlin, Edward P. *Climate and Christ: A Prophetic Alternative*. Dublin, Ireland: The Columba Press, 2010.

Edwards, Denis, ed. *Earth Revealing—Earth Healing: Ecology and Christian Theology*. Collegeville, MN: Michael Glazier, Liturgical Press, 2001.

Gingerich, Ray, ed. *Transforming the Powers: Peace, Justice, and the Domination System*. Minneapolis: Fortress Press, 2006.

Keogh, Martin, ed. *Hope Beneath Our Feet: Restoring Our Place in the Natural World, An Anthology*. Berkeley: North Atlantic Books, 2010.

McDonagh, Sean. *The Death of Life: The Horror of Extinction*. Dublin, Ireland: Columba Press, 2004.

McFague, Sallie. *A New Climate for Theology: God, the World, and Global Warming*. Minneapolis: Fortress Press, 2008.

Moore, Kathleen Dean, and Michael P. Nelson, eds. *Moral Ground: Ethical Action for a Planet in Peril*. San Antonio: Trinity University Press, 2010.

Northcott, Michael. *Cuttle Fish, Clones and Cluster Bombs: Preaching, Politics, and Ecology*. London, England: Darton, Longman and Todd, 2010.

Wink, Walter. *Naming the Powers: The Language of Power in the New Testament*. Vol. 1. Philadelphia: Fortress Press, 1984.

———. *Unmasking the Powers: The Invisible Forces That Determine Human Existence*. Vol. 2. Philadelphia: Fortress Press, 1986.

———. *When the Powers Fall: Reconciliation in the Healing of Nations*. Minneapolis: Fortress Press, 1997.

These last three books look at the difference between the concept of "the world" and the reality of the world/earth as we look at it today—the powers of the world as the dominant sources of destruction and the reality of the world—"that God so loved" (John 3).

The Gospel of Science and Religion

Barnes, Michael Horace. *Understanding Religion and Science: Introducing the Debate*. New York: Continuum International Publishing, 2010.

Brown, William P. *The Seven Pillars of Creation: The Bible, Science, and the Ecology of Wonder*. New York: Oxford University Press, 2010.

Harris, Sam. *The Moral Landscape: How Science Can Determine Human Values*. New York: Free Press, 2010.

Haught, John F. *Christianity and Science: Toward a Theology of Nature*. Maryknoll, NY: Orbis Books, 2007.

Ravetz, Jerome. *The No-Nonsense Guide to Science*. London: New International Press, 2005.

Suzuki, David. *The David Suzuki Reader: A Lifetime of Ideas from a Leading Activist and Thinker*. Vancouver, BC, Canada: Greystone Books, 2003.

Tippett, Krista. *Einstein's God: Conversations About Science and the Human Spirit*. New York: Penguin Books, 2010.

Wouk, Hermon. *The Language God Speaks: On Science and Religion*. New York: Little, Brown and Company, 2010.

The Gospel of Art

(These suggestions reflect primarily the arts of poetry, short stories, essays, and photography, but this category includes dance, music, film, pottery, fabric design, flower arrangement, architecture, choreography, mime, painting, visual and tactile art, etc.)

Akpan, Uwem. *Say You're One of Them.* New York: Little Brown and Company, 2008 (stories).

Deane, John F. *The Works of Love: Incarnation, Ecology, and Poetry.* Dublin, Ireland: Columba Press, 2010.

Feldman, Christian. *Silence: How to Find Inner Peace in a Busy World.* Berkeley: Rodmell Press, 2003 (photographs and reflections).

Felstiner, John. *Can Poetry Save the Earth?: A Field Guide to Nature Poems.* New Haven: Yale University Press, 2009.

Hirshfield, Jane. *Nine Gates: Entering the Mind of Poetry.* New York: HarperCollins, 2007.

Moyers, Bill. *The Language of Life: A Festival of Poets.* New York: Doubleday, 1995.

O'Driscoll, Dennis. *Stepping Stones: Interviews with Seamus Heaney.* New York: Farrar, Straus and Giroux, 2008.

Rosenberg, Marshall B. *Nonviolent Communication: A Language of Life.* Encinitas, CA: Puddle Dancer Press, 2003.

Sewell, Marilyn, ed. *Cries of the Spirit: More Than 300 Poems in Celebration of Women's Spirituality.* Boston: Beacon Press, 1991.

Solnit, Rebecca. *As Eve Said to the Serpent: On Landscape, Gender, and Art.* Athens, GA: The University of Georgia Press, 2001.

Ullman, Robert, and Judyth Reichenberd-Ullman, eds. *Mystics, Masters, Saints, and Sages: Stories of Englightenment.* Berkeley: Conart Press, 2001.

Walker, Scott, ed. *Buying Time: An Anthology Celebrating 20 Years of the Literature Program of the National Endowment for the Arts.* St. Paul, MN: Gray Wolf Press, 1985.

The Gospel of Church Transformation

Alison, James. *Broken Hearts and New Creations: Intimations of a Great Reversal.* New York: Continuum, 2010.

Basset, Lytta, Eric Fassin, and Timothy Radcliffe. *Christians and Sexuality in the Time of AIDS.* New York: Continuum, 2007.

Boff, Leonard. *Ecclesiogenesis: The Base Communities Reinvent the Church.* Maryknoll, NY: Orbis Books, 1986.

Brown, Raymond E. *The Churches the Apostles Left Behind.* Mahwah, NJ: Paulist Press, 1984.

Capon, Robert Farrar. *The Astonished Heart: Reclaiming the Good News from the Lost-and-Found of Church History.* Grand Rapids: William B. Eerdmans Publishing Co., 1996.

Casaldaliga, Pedro, and Jose-Maria Vigil (with Ernesto Cardenal and Gustavo Gutierrez). *Political Holiness: A Spirituality of Liberation.* Maryknoll, NY: Orbis Books, 1994.

Clark, Matthew H. *Forward in Hope: Saying AMEN to Lay Ecclesial Ministry.* Notre Dame, IN: Ave Maria Press, 2009.

Coleman, John A., and William F. Ryan, eds. *Globalization and Catholic Social Thought: Present Crisis, Future Hope.* Maryknoll, NY: Orbis Books, 2005.

Comblin, Jose. *People of God,* Maryknoll, NY: Orbis Books, 2004.

Crosby, Michael H. *The Paradox of Power: From Control to Compassion.* New York: Crossroads, 2008.

Curran, Charles. *The Social Mission of the U.S. Catholic Church: A Theological Perspective.* Washington, DC: Georgetown University Press, 2011.

Dennis, Marie. *Diversity of Vocations.* Maryknoll, NY: Orbis Books, 2008.

An Ethical Compass: Coming of Age in the 21st Century: The Ethics Prize Essays of the Elie Wiesel Foundation for Humanity. New Haven: Yale University Press, 2010.

Fagan, Sean. *Does Morality Change?* Collegeville, MN: Michael Glazier, Liturgical Press, 1997.

Gaillardetz, Richard R. *By What Authority: A Primer on Scripture, the Magisterium, and the Sense of the Faithful.* Collegeville, MN: Liturgical Press, 2003.

———. *Ecclesiology for a Global Church: A People Called and Sent.* Maryknoll, NY: Orbis Books, 2010.

Gallagher, Michael Paul. *Clashing Symbols: An Introduction to Faith and Culture.* London: Darton, Longman and Todd, 1997.

Harrington, Daniel, and James Keenan. *Jesus and Virtue Ethics: Building Bridges Between New Testament Studies and Moral Theology.* Lanham, MD: Sheed and Ward, 2002.

Hinze, Bradford E., ed. *The Spirit in the Church and the World.* Annual vol. 49. Maryknoll, NY: Orbis Books, 2003.

Kim, Kirsteen. *The Holy Spirit in the World: A Global Conversation.* Maryknoll, NY: Orbis Books, 2007.

Kung, Hans, ed. *Yes to a Global Ethic: Voices from Religion and Politics.* New York: Continuum, 1996.

Linden, Ian. *Global Catholicism: Diversity and Change Since Vatican II.* New York: Columbia University Press, 2009.

Orsy, Ladislas M. *Probing the Spirit: A Theological Evaluation of Communal Discernment.* Denville, NJ: Dimension Books, 1976.

Rowthorn, Anne. *The Liberation of the Laity.* Eugene, OR: Wipf and Stock Publishers, 2000.

Salzman, Todd A., and Michael G. Lawler. *The Sexual Person: Toward a Renewed Catholic Anthropology.* Washington, DC: Georgetown University Press, 2008.

Schori, Katharine Jefferts. *A Wing and a Prayer: A Message of Faith and Hope.* Harrisburg, NY: Morehouse Publishing, 2007.

Tamez, Elsa. *Struggles for Power in Early Christianity.* Maryknoll, NY: Orbis Books, 2007.

The Gospel of Interreligious Dialogue

His Holiness the Dalai Lama. *Toward a True Kinship of Faiths: How the World's Religions Can Come Together.* New York: Doubleday Religion, 2010.

Johnston, William. *"Arise, My Love . . .": Mysticism for a New Era.* Maryknoll, NY: Orbis Books, 2000.

Panikkar, Raimon. *The Experience of God: Icons of the Mystery.* Minneapolis: Fortress Press, 2006.

Smith, Huston. *The World's Religions.* San Francisco: Harper, 1958.

Teasdale, Wayne, and Martha Howard, eds. *Awakening the Spirit: Inspiring the Soul: 30 Stories of Interspiritual Discovery in the Community of Faiths.* Woodstock, VT: Skylight Paths Publishing, 2004.

AFTERWORD

Britz, Andrew Murray, and Dennis Gruending, ed. *Truth to Power: The Journalism of a Benedictine Monk.* Muenster, Saskatchewan: St. Peter's Press, 2011.

Crosby, Michael H. *Repair My House: Becoming a "Kingdom" Catholic.* Maryknoll, NY: Orbis Books, 2012.

Curran, Charles E. *Loyal Dissent: Memoir of a Catholic Theologian.* Washington, DC: Georgetown University Press, 2006.

———. *The Social Mission of the U.S. Catholic Church: A Theological Perspective.* Washington, DC: Georgetown University Press, 2011.

Delio, Ilia. *Christ in Evolution.* Maryknoll, NY: Orbis Books, 2008.

———. *The Emergent Christ: Exploring the Meaning of Catholic in an Evolutionary Universe.* Maryknoll, NY: Orbis Books, 2011.

Gaillardetz, Richard R. *Teaching with Authority: A Theology of the*

Magisterium in the Church. Collegeville, MN: Liturgical Press, 1997.

Gaillardetz, Richard R., and Catherine E. Clifford. *Keys to the Council: Unlocking the Teaching of Vatican II.* Collegeville, MN: Liturgical Press, 2012.

Kung, Hans, and John Bowden, trans. *The Catholic Church: A Short History.* New York: Modern Library, 2003.

Lewis, Chris, ed. *Letters to a Future Church: Words of Encouragement and Prophet Appeals.* Downers Grove, IL: InterVarsity Press, 2012.

O'Mahony, T. P. *Why the Catholic Church Needs Vatican II.* Dublin, Ireland: Columba Press, 2010.

Robinson, Geoffrey. *Confronting Power and Sex in the Catholic Church: Reclaiming the Spirit of Jesus.* Collegeville, MN: Liturgical Press, 2008.

Salzman, Todd A., and Michael G. Lawler. *The Sexual Person: Toward a Renewed Catholic Anthropology.* Washington, DC: Georgetown University Press, 2008.

NOTE: Any book by these authors will be helpful. This list is a jumping off place; many others could be added to it.

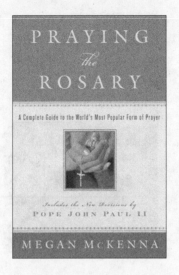

PRAYING THE ROSARY

Contemplating Catholicism's Most Popular Form of Devotion

Much more than a how-to manual, this book explains the fundamentals and theological understanding of praying the rosary. McKenna sheds light on the mysteries, including the newest "luminous mysteries," and reveals the relevance of the rosary to a new generation.

272 pages / ISBN: 978-0-385-51082-0 / U.S.: $16.95
(Canada: $25.95)

Also available in ebook format
272 pages / ISBN: 978-0-307-42379-5 / U.S.: $11.99
(Canada: $13.99)

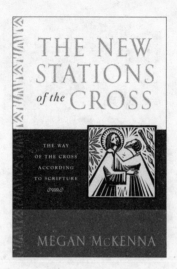

THE NEW STATIONS OF THE CROSS

Returning Tradition to Scripture

After four hundred years of upholding the same stations of the cross at Good Friday mass, Pope John Paul II revised several stations, citing that a return to scripture was healthy and necessary for the Church. Now, Megan McKenna seeks to explain the true meaning behind each station and the gospel's account of Christ's execution.

144 pages / ISBN: 978-0-385-50815-5 / U.S.: $15.00
(Canada: $17.50)

Also available in ebook format
144 pages / ISBN: 978-0-307-42401-3 / U.S.: $12.99
(Canada: $13.99)